UNPLUGGING

THE

PATRIARCHY

A Mystical Journey
into the Heart of a New Age

Lucia René

Crown Chakra
PUBLISHING

First edition: December 2009

Printed in the United States
Content editing by Hilary Hart and Michael Schwab
Copyediting by Deanna Brady
Cover design by David Drummond, Salamander Hill Design
Interior design and graphic art by Launie Parry, Red Letter Creative
Pen and ink drawings by Patti Blair, One Heart Artworks

Library of Congress Cataloging-in-Publication Data

   René, Lucia.
    Unplugging the patriarchy : a mystical journey into
   the heart of a new age / Lucia René. -- 1st ed.
    p. cm.
   LCCN 2009928294
   ISBN-13: 978-0-9823776-2-8
   ISBN-10: 0-9823776-2-2

   1. Male domination (Social structure)--Fiction.
   2. Women--Fiction. 3. Shamans--Fiction. 4. Mind and body
   --Fiction. 5. New Age fiction. I. Title.

   PS3618.E5748U57 2009   813'.6
      QBI09-600075

Crown Chakra Publishing
Williamsburg, VA
info@CrownChakraPublishing.com

ACKNOWLEDGEMENTS

*Special thanks to Hilary Hart, Michael Schwab,
and Deanna Brady for their editing,
all of my test readers and proofreaders for their invaluable feedback,
and Mary MacNab of Delphic Wave
for her advice and support.*

For Rama

CONTENTS

PREFACE

Unplugging the Patriarchy is part truth, part fiction—what might be described in literary terms as a fictionalized memoir.

My accounts of spiritual teachings, for instance, which have been woven throughout the book, can be classified as nonfiction. They are drawn from journals I kept in the 1980s, during my apprenticeship to an enlightened master who taught the art of advanced mysticism. In addition, it is true that I collaborated with other women—all of whose names have been changed here—to investigate the formative energies of the male-dominated patriarchal system that has oppressed females for more than five thousand years.

As for the psychic perceptions and mystical experiences that drive the story...those are more difficult to classify, as they are impossible to verify with the left brain. Psychic perception cannot be verified objectively because it is the art of seeing things that lie beyond the physical plane. The seer transcends the three normal methods of perception—loosely defined as *sensing* (with the physical body's five senses), *analyzing* (with the mental body's electrical activity), and *feeling* (with the emotional body's chemical reactions)—and enters a realm where she or he simply *knows* things. It is a fourth method of perception, a shorthand for apprehending something's true nature.

All of us are psychic at birth. Living in an age that worships *reason*, however—one in which we are constantly programmed to deny or, at best, belittle this precious gift—very few of us retain our psychic abilities beyond childhood. Most of us, if we are so inclined, must relearn this skill, an undertaking that has engaged me for more than a quarter century.

Mysticism, at least for the purposes of this story, is the art of power. Because the word *power* has come to be associated with its *abuse*, one might, in order to avoid any negative connotation, define it as the art of energy, or the mechanics of how energy works in our world. It is an art that involves perfect form and movement—movement into alternate dimensions.

Before meeting my teacher, I, like most people, assumed that the third dimension—our physical environment that we commonly refer to as the "real world"—was the sum total of reality. Then my teacher's mystical training catapulted me into alternate dimensions—planes of awareness that intersect and overlap the third dimension—and shattered my former concept of reality forever.

Both psychic perception and mysticism deal with alternate dimensions. Psychic perception consists of *discerning* things in alternate dimensions. Mysticism involves *entering into* them.

Seen in this light, mysticism is a high art that has been practiced in the mystery schools of Atlantis and ancient Egypt, remembered by adepts as they have incarnated in one lifetime after another, and handed down from teacher to student in halls of esoteric knowledge far from the beaten path. As such, my own training in mysticism with my teacher began in the Atlantean cycle, took a left turn in ancient Egypt, and was completed in America in the 1990s.

In the pages that follow, psychic perception, mysticism, and alternate dimensions are further defined, along with related concepts. Seasoned travelers on a spiritual path are welcome to skip over these passages. Other sections of the book explain ways in which various components of the New World Order—the banking system, the World Trade Organization, the Council on Foreign Relations, and the Bilderbergers, to name a few—limit consciousness. Readers well educated in these matters may wish to bypass such descriptions.

Finally, one additional term begs defining: the *solar feminine*, a style of femininity that my spiritual teacher cultivated in his female students. The solar feminine embodies *yang* energy, strength, passion, creativity, and action—qualities that have not been appreciated in females since the Matrilineal Era of some 6,000 years ago. The solar feminine is quite different from the lunar feminine, whose *yin* energy is gentle, receptive, and nurturing...the only type of femininity that has been acceptable throughout the Patriarchal Age.

Quite recently, this solar feminine energy has taken root on the planet in a profound way and has begun to manifest more and more in the physical world. The Divine Feminine, in all of her lunar/solar glory, has taken the reins on Planet Earth. This shift has resulted from the tireless efforts of innumerable light-workers around the world who have prayed and meditated in order to assist Earth as she transitions out of the Patriarchal Age into the new Aquarian Age of post-2012.

The comprehensive story of how this accomplishment came to be is like an intricate tapestry woven of countless threads. *Unplugging the Patriarchy* is but one thread, one tale, one journey of service and spiritual growth.

Lucia René, March 2009

"We're at the end of a cycle. All of you have known this since childhood. The Hindus call it the Kali Yuga, the dark age. At the end of a cycle, Shiva, the Hindu lord of death, dances. At the end of a cycle, certain energetic configurations go away and others come into being."

- The Teacher

PART ONE

SPIRITUAL

MARCHING

ORDERS

1

TAKING ON THE PATRIARCHY

I knew I had an appointment. I just didn't know with whom. I was, however, certain of the place and time. My intuition had been clear: *Be in New Mexico on the solstice.*

It was June of 2002. I had just returned home to Los Alamos, and my suitcases still stood at attention in the foyer, demanding to be unpacked. A storm was brewing, and the somber house—neglected during my three-month absence—was filled with the clanking sound of unruly wind chimes.

Ignoring the luggage, I walked to the patio door and opened it. A warm blast of air careened past me, unsettling the dust on the terra cotta tile floor.

Ominous dark clouds churned in the skies as the wind whipped the branches of the pines back and forth. As I made my way to the fence above the red-rock mesa, the thought came to me clearly: *Something important is going to happen.*

I suddenly felt compelled to go to a place of power called the Valle Grande, in the Jemez Mountains above Los Alamos. Locals call this area the Caldera, which means *cauldron* in Spanish—in this case a cauldron of ancient volcanoes. Surrounded on all sides by peaks and ridges, the land there resembles a gigantic, grassy bowl. Most visitors comment on its size, snap pictures of the grazing elk, then return to their cars in pursuit of more exciting destinations, but for those who can peer beyond the third dimension—our physical environment that we call the "real world"—the Caldera is a place of magic.

A shiver of anticipation rose up my spine. I spun around, strode inside, and phoned Anders, a young Scandinavian friend who lived nearby.

"How would you like to go to the Caldera and meditate?" I ventured.

Anders loved nothing better than meditation. His shaved head and disciplined demeanor were suggestive of past lives in Zen monasteries. In this life, he had recently sacrificed the job security of his military career in Norway, moved to Santa Fe, learned to meditate, and enrolled in the University of New Mexico at Los Alamos. We had met a year earlier at a meditation gathering and had bonded instantly. He had been keeping an eye on the house while I was away.

"Right now?" he replied in his engaging Norwegian accent.

"Well, yes. The solstice is only a few hours away. I thought we might do a sunset meditation."

I had regaled Anders with tales of the Caldera's magical qualities, but he had never been there. "On my way," he said, and I heard the click as he hung up.

By the time he arrived and we began driving to the Caldera, the wind had eased up a little. Leaving the Los Alamos mesas far behind, I navigated the hairpin turns of the mountain, and we ascended through groves of pine to almost eight thousand feet, where we saw the Caldera stretching out to our right.

Previously part of a private ranch, the land had only recently been sold to the government and was not yet open to the public. We risked a fine if we trespassed, so we decided that our safest option was the hiking trail farther west that wound along the Caldera's edge.

I stopped the car in a small parking area near a wooden gate that marked the entrance to the trail, and we began our hike. Anders, wearing army fatigues and sturdy canvas boots, took the lead and practically sprinted up the mountain. His physical frame was slender, but every part of it was muscular, the result of rugged training with the Hærens Jegerkommando—the Norwegian Army Special Forces Command. Occasionally he paused, turned, and shot me an encouraging smile.

The climb doesn't faze him, I thought as I stopped to catch my breath. *But after all, he's in his early thirties. God, I wish I had that much energy!* At the summit overlooking the Caldera, we took shelter from the wind in a small grove of pines. I diligently cleared the rocks next to a boulder, spread my outdoor meditation blanket, and struggled to find a comfortable sitting position. Anders dropped down onto the dirt some distance away, closed his eyes, and was immediately absorbed in meditation.

Life seems so easy for him! Why is it so difficult for me...?

Tears welled up in my eyes, and I took a deep breath to calm myself. I hadn't realized I was feeling so emotional. Looking for solace I turned toward the Caldera, now bathed in the light of the setting sun. It was vast, silent, and completely devoid of emotion, which helped me feel more balanced.

Before beginning to meditate, I reached out to Spirit with a prayer. As the summer and winter solstices are the two most powerful days of the year, I hoped I would have a better chance than usual of getting an answer.

"I'm really in need of some guidance down here," I murmured softly.

I hesitated, sorting through the events of the past few months and groping for the words to describe my feelings. My father had just passed away in March. When I'd returned from his funeral and gone back to work, I was unexpectedly fired—and all that was within one week! It was like having the rug yanked out from under me. Then my father's affairs needed to be settled. That had taken three months— three stressful, exhausting months. Now I'd returned to New Mexico, a place where I would never have moved had my former company not transferred me here...and for what, I didn't know.

"Spirit, every single support structure in my life is gone. I feel completely alone. My mother is gone, my father is gone. I'm an only child. I'm single, I have no children, and I have no long-term friends in this area...."

Feeling helpless, I stopped and took another deep breath. "I have no idea where to go from here." I continued slowly, closing my eyes. "If you have some guidance for me, I would be grateful."

I held my breath, listening.

Spirit was silent.

Immersion in Patriarchal Energy

Later I asked Anders to drive us back down the mountain. Climbing into the passenger seat, I pulled down the mirrored visor and ran my fingers through my shoulder-length, sandy-blond hair, then turned my head slightly and wondered who had decided that graying temples looked dignified.

I scrutinized my reflection more closely. Tired hazel eyes peered back at me, with dark circles underneath. I had lost fifteen pounds while struggling to liquidate my father's estate, and my face now looked gaunt.

Women in their early fifties aren't expected to look like they're twenty, I reassured myself. *And besides, why should I care how I look?*

Snapping the visor back in place, I stole a glance at Anders—in his prime and smiling to himself. Perhaps he was imagining being the proud owner of a Mercedes. Sighing, I reclined the passenger seat and gazed sightlessly out the side window as dusk blanketed the mountain.

This was not the first prayer of mine that had gone unanswered. Over the years I had entreated Spirit countless times for guidance; always asking to be shown how I could discover, align with, and prepare for my life's work, something I felt certain had to do with being of service to the planet and all her peoples.

I had prayed in the desert and prostrated myself on the tops of mountains. I had clocked thousands of hours meditating and ruined my knees sitting in the lotus position. I had poured over ancient texts and studied ardently with spiritual teachers, learning arcane methods for working with the subtle energies beyond the third dimension.

For the past month, I had been feeling a nagging sense of urgency, as though some distant bugle was playing reveille, urging me to line up, stand at attention, and receive my orders. Surely, after all these long years of preparation, the time was at hand. It had to be! I had actually expected to get those orders two years earlier, after an experience I'd had in South Africa.

Before traveling there, I'd learned that South Africa was colonized by the Dutch and English who had taken control of the land and the country's wealth, dominated the indigenous black population, and implemented strict racial segregation policies that became known as *apartheid*. Once in Capetown, I made it a point to tour the colonial fort built by the Dutch upon their arrival in South Africa.

As our tour group entered the central courtyard, the guide gestured toward the white, three-story buildings surrounding us.

"They built the fort in the shape of a pentagram," he explained, "and construction proceeded in a counterclockwise direction. Nobody knows why they did that."

I had a guess. I recalled that the five-sided pentagram is sometimes associated with the practice of lower mysticism—what some call the dark arts—and the counterclockwise direction could have indicated that the designers were pulling an inter-dimensional force down into the fort. A clockwise direction radiates energy outward; a counterclockwise direction drills down.

Did they summon some malevolent force, then anchor it into the Earth? I wondered. *Could it have been done with the intent to subjugate South Africa?*

It was a mystical puzzle…and I was fascinated. I left the tour and walked to the center of the courtyard. The security guards glared at me, but I ignored them. I sat on the bare ground, closed my eyes, allowed my awareness to drop down into the underlying feeling, and merged with its vibration.

Almost immediately my body began to feel strange. I hadn't felt it before because I had been standing on the paving-stone sidewalk, a walkway that was inundated with the thoughts and impressions of thousands of tourists. I had been feeling the tourists, not the fort. Now a wave of nausea rose from my stomach into my throat.

My stomach was fine before!

It happened a second time, and I fought the urge to leave.

Unexpectedly my emotions spiraled out of control. Anger arose. Depression set in. A haywire mix of negative feelings engulfed me. I scrambled to my feet, twitched like a dog shaking dirt off of its coat, and made a beeline for the nearest exit.

During my next two morning meditations in my hotel room, I attempted to investigate the energy I had felt in the fort, but each time I approached it a wall of nausea blocked me. I knew that sudden nausea sometimes indicates negative mystical energy. Repeatedly I tried to push beyond it and then, finding it too uncomfortable, backed off...but something inside of me refused to give up.

I sensed that I was tapping into the unbalanced energy of apartheid and that it was really a microcosm of the unbalanced energy that animated the power structures of our male-dominated, fear-based Patriarchy. I was determined to merge with it to find out.

This was something that had haunted me for the past twenty years. Why was the world so horribly out of balance? What was the underlying cause of all of the poverty, injustice, and violence...the starvation, rape, and endless war?

If I investigated any one of these cultural phenomena on a spiritual level—if I grabbed hold of it and followed the line of energy attached to it back to its source—I always found the same root issue: the imbalance between the masculine and feminine energies on the planet, an imbalance born of five thousand years of female oppression by men. It expressed itself through male conditioning that assumed superiority and sanctioned dominance, female conditioning that imposed second-class citizenship and counseled passive compliance, religious teachings that degraded women as chattel, and misogynistic attitudes that permeated all our social systems.

Over the years my investigation had made me first angry, then depressed, and finally determined. There had to be a way to reconcile masculine and feminine energies. There had to be a way to shift the balance and bring sanity to the world!

In my meditations in South Africa, I suspected that if I could merge my awareness with the energy of apartheid, I would be able to merge with the essence of Patriarchy and comprehend, on a much deeper level, this imbalance that had obsessed me for so long. Maybe then I could see some way to help rectify the imbalance. Maybe helping to correct the imbalance was the way I was supposed to be of service to humanity.

During the third attempt in my hotel room, clenching my hands in my lap and exerting all my will, I succeeded in pushing my awareness through the wall of nausea. I crossed an invisible threshold, merged with apartheid, and found myself at the core of the patriarchal regime.

I was seized by a ruthless intent to control, an unscrupulous need to dominate, and intense hatred of the feminine. I *became* the Patriarchy and felt it in every cell of my body. It was difficult to know how long I stayed there—perhaps only four or five seconds—but within that timeless moment I experienced the mindset completely.

As my awareness returned to my physical body, I doubled over in pain. Every cell was on fire. Tears streamed down my face. My mind, stupefied with horror, had stopped functioning.

Taking deep breaths, I gradually managed to sit up. Slowly the burning sensation subsided, and as it did I sensed some emotion rising to the surface. Initially the feeling was so overwhelming that I failed to identify it. Then it registered. I was infuriated. I was a woman sitting in a hotel room, in the midst of a patriarchal system that had beaten women into submission for the past five thousand years, and I was filled with rage.

Without thinking, I raised a lamentation to Spirit: *If there is anything I can do to change this, let it be known that I volunteer!*

There was silence as I watched my projected thought travel into the cosmos. Then suddenly, unexpectedly, I heard a voice cry out:

"Prepare to do battle!"

Time stopped. Space changed. I felt confused. All around me a hundred invisible doors flew open. A hundred dimensions stretched out through space. A hundred beings snapped to attention. The sound terrified me. It was the sound of a hundred soldiers on a military parade ground, slapping their rifles to their chests in one synchronized gesture.

BAM!

The noise resounded throughout the universe.

My God! What have I done?

No matter how many deep breaths I took for the rest of the day, I could not stop my body from shaking.

It was obvious that Spirit had accepted my offer that day in South Africa, so why was I now returning from the Caldera empty-handed? What had *"Prepare to do battle!"* meant, if not that my services to combat the Patriarchy had been accepted?

I had known for more than two years that I was due to receive an assignment. I'd been feeling a sense of urgency and had rushed home for some sort of an appointment. Had I been wrong to assume that it had something to do with finally being of service? Who was this appointment *with*? My *hairdresser*?

My Assignment

The solstice occurred at 6:24 the following morning. At around 8:00, I sat to meditate.

I didn't feel much like meditating. I had gone numb after the trip to the Caldera. It was easier to feel numb than to deal with Spirit's apparent rejection. Underneath the numbness, however, I was seething. I had no job, no income, no family and—not from lack of effort on my part—no spiritual guidance from the divine realms. My life had been shattered into pieces that were now blowing in the winds of the summer solstice.

But I always meditated. I had meditated every morning for more than thirty years.

Closing my eyes, I settled myself in my chair and, after a few moments, managed to still my mind. Immediately I began to hear words being spoken telepathically—the sound of many voices speaking in unison, each word articulated slowly and clearly. My anger evaporated, and I held perfectly still.

"For the next six months," I was told, *"between the summer solstice and the winter solstice, research what is happening in the world. Read about politics, economics, and global affairs. Look behind the scenes to*

learn what is happening on a mystical level. Figure out the underlying mystical structure. Once you have identified the structure, your job will be to disassemble it. You have been trained for many lifetimes to accomplish this. You know how to take things apart. Your body has been wired for the task."

I sat frozen, unable to respond. *Disassemble the Patriarchy?* It was an outrageous proposal. No human could disassemble the entire Patriarchy. It was colossal!

"*You are not the only person working on this problem,*" the voices continued. "*There are many. Some of them will collaborate with you.*"

Fear rushed through my body. I thought, *I realize that I asked to be of service, but this is insane!* Maybe I was imagining it. I had to be rational. *But how can I be imagining it? The instructions are so clearly stated. The presence in the room is undeniable.*

A minute passed. Despite my best efforts to formulate a response, I could not. The only sound was that of my heart colliding with my breastbone as it tried to function normally.

Finally, cautiously, I projected a thought back to the ensemble— the only thing I could think to reply: *This is going to take a lot of time. I shouldn't look for a job? I should just do this research?*

The response was definitive.

"*Yes.*"

Then silence.

After a long pause, they spoke again, more softly this time.

"*Don't you see that all of this has been set up for you? Your father has died. You have some money from him. You don't have to work for the time being. Devote all your energy to this project. It's important...very important.*"

The Voices Behind the Assignment

For the rest of the day, I struggled to put things into perspective. I went back in time—a very long way back in time—to a shadowy memory that predates all my incarnations on Earth.

In this memory, I could see myself standing in a long line. There were about seventy of us, members of an ancient lineage—a lineage of enlightenment, a lineage of warriors. We had volunteered to join an expedition, travel to the planet Earth, and use our expertise to facilitate an experiment in consciousness. In return we would be gifted with a giant leap in evolution.

We faced a table where five beings were seated. The male figure in the center spoke.

"This is a difficult assignment. When you incarnate on the planet Earth, you will lose all memory of who you are—not just once, but repeatedly as you journey from lifetime to lifetime. Many of you will lose your way. Many will fall by the wayside. In the end, everyone comes home….but you must be prepared for the possibility that, while you are there, you will not remember who you are."

To my left, at the end of our long line, was a great warrior soul. He stood perfectly erect, stock still, gazing straight ahead. He was to be the commander of our army, our spiritual teacher. At that moment I was not aware that time and time again, during our incarnations on the Earth, he would find me, brush off the dust of forgetfulness, and remind me who I was. The personal evolution I experienced, the spiritual lessons I learned, the psychic abilities I developed, would be the direct result of his unfaltering commitment to the expedition and to the evolution of consciousness.

In our most recent lifetime, he recruited his army of spiritual warriors during the late seventies and early eighties. Although some had been born in far-flung corners of the world this time, we all converged in California, influenced by an intuition, a dream, or perhaps a psychic reading. There we found ourselves in the midst of a familiar soul group with whom we had often incarnated.

After the honeymoon feeling of reunion had worn off, we awoke one morning to discover that a tremendous amount of serious work lay ahead of us. Our teacher had a mission, with limited time to accomplish it. He was bent on training his warrior students in preparation for a golden age that was due to commence at the end of 2012…and he was a perfectionist. To become his apprentice was to submit to spiritual boot camp. For me, that boot camp lasted seventeen years.

Then, in the spring of 1998, he informed us that our training was complete and his mission, accomplished. Shortly thereafter, he passed away.

When he left us so suddenly, I was utterly shocked. My teacher had been everything to me, my spiritual apprenticeship consuming every waking moment. It seemed that the grief I felt would never subside.

After a year I emerged from mourning and began reaching deep within my soul to figure out what to do with the rest of my life. My teacher had successfully trained an army of spiritual warriors, but what were we supposed to do now? He had given no hints. Although he had spoken occasionally about the Kali Yuga—the ending of the current time cycle, according to Hindu scriptures, and the beginning of a new golden age—he had never discussed the role we would play.

Something he had said came back to me after he left us: "You think that I'm important because I'm the one who sits up on the stage. I'm just the guy who came here to network all of you. You're the ones who are going to be on the front lines in this lifetime."

But the front lines of what?

I also recalled him speaking on occasion about his spiritual lineage, a group of beings that works in unison for the well-being of humanity. "The Lineage," he explained, "is really one being, but it divides itself into countless forms as if it were multiple beings. Think of it as a network of enlightenment. We send our beings out, and they incarnate in a world—some physically, some not physically. We travel through time and space, roaming the universes, the galaxies, the inter-dimensional planes. Our job is to keep the dimensional planes open, to guard the secret power places that exist between the dimensions. We are warriors of Light, warriors of power, warriors who do battle with the forces that obstruct enlightenment."

Without the physical presence of my teacher, I felt at a loss for guidance, so I began to search the invisible realms. Since he was my teacher, I must be part of this Lineage, as he had described it. Surely my teacher and his Lineage would provide guidance from another dimension…but how could I make a connection?

It finally happened two years after my teacher's death, when several of his students gathered in the desert at a retreat to ask the Lineage for direction. As we sat in a circle in the sand, I could suddenly feel the Lineage assembling, joining our circle: a large group of magnificently beautiful and powerful beings, both male and female, whose presence caused the circle to radiate with an otherworldly light. They were so noble, so ancient, and yet so humble. Something inside me collapsed. All my petty worries about my life suddenly seemed small and insignificant. I felt truly honored, and had there not been other people present, I would have prostrated myself in the sand.

Now, on the evening of the summer solstice in 2002, things began coming into focus. I knew that the long line I had stood in before coming to Earth had been populated by members of my lineage. In South Africa it had been my teacher's voice that had said, *"Prepare to do battle!"* and disincarnate members of the Lineage who had snapped to attention. In my meditation earlier this morning, it had been those of my lineage who had spoken to me.

I had been given my spiritual marching orders. I was being sent to the front lines.

2

STUDYING PATRIARCHAL POWER

Borders Bookstore and the Internet soon became my best friends. Gradually I assembled a library of books. Some came as recommendations; others nearly jumped off of the bookstore shelves, demanding my attention.

For thirty years I had been part of the country's workforce, never bothering to question the ethical structure of the corporate world where I slaved or the banking system in which I deposited my paycheck. For thirty years I had devoted myself to spiritual studies, rarely reading a newspaper, never questioning public policy. Now I questioned everything. Drinking in new knowledge, my initial fear and doubt subsided and I became positively intoxicated.

I educated myself about the major power-wielding organizations of the world. Intrigued by a theory that thirteen wealthy families rule the globe, I skimmed the biographies of the Rothschild and Rockefeller lines. Encountering speculation that certain secret societies have passed down power and knowledge through history to the present time, I studied information about Cecil Rhode's Round Table and the Illuminati. I tapped alternative news sources on the Web and on shortwave radio. I ordered audio tapes of speeches given by Noam Chomsky, professor of linguistics at MIT and world-renowned political dissident, then listened to them over and over in my car when I did errands.

It suddenly didn't seem to matter so much that I had no job or family. At that point, I would hardly have had time for them anyway.

The Power to Rewrite History

As my research began, I stumbled onto the Carnegie Endowment Fund for International Peace, founded by Andrew Carnegie, a wealthy US industrialist and a leading internationalist of his day. I had attended Carnegie-Mellon University, also founded by Carnegie, and had always pictured him as the generous benefactor of my alma mater, a kindly father figure. My research revealed a radically different image.

The Carnegie Endowment Fund, a private, nonprofit organization, was founded in 1910. Its stated mission was to advance cooperation between nations and promote active international engagement by the United States.[1]

In 1954, the United States Congress launched the US Congressional Committee to Investigate Tax Exempt Foundations. One of the foundations that came under scrutiny was the Carnegie Endowment Fund. Studying the Carnegie minute books, the committee learned that its board had in-depth discussions on how to alter life in America and move the national psyche toward collectivism.[2] In politics, collectivism emphasizes the rights and responsibilities of various groups or classes. It proposes collective strategies for improving the conditions of disadvantaged groups and classes and, although it does not necessarily deny individual rights, it considers group rights primary.[3] All totalitarian governments, including those espousing Nazism, fascism, and socialism, are based on the model of collectivism.[4]

What the committee learned staggered them. The Carnegie minute books stated that in order to get Americans to give up their traditional principles—the rights of individuals, as framed in the Declaration of Independence and the Constitution—in exchange for those of collectivism, these elite funders must take control of the educational system. They indicated it was most important to control the teaching of history.[5] They teamed up with the Rockefeller, Guggenheim, and Ford Foundations. They eventually assembled a group of favored historians—men who were willing to view history, write textbooks, and teach the subject from the perspective that collectivism was the most positive future for the world.

In later years Norman Dodd, who headed the congressional committee, summarized its findings. I read his words with growing trepidation.

> "This group of twenty historians eventually formed the nucleus of the American Historical Association. Then toward the end of the 1920's the Endowment grants to the American Historical Association $400,000 [over $4 million in today's dollars] for a study of history in a manner that points to what this country can look forward to in the future. That culminates in a seven-volume study, the last volume of which is a summary of the contents of the other six. And the essence of the last volume is, the future of this country belongs to collectivism...."[6]

So these nonprofit foundations implemented a scheme to steer the freedom-loving citizens of the United States toward a more fascistic state by controlling education! I closed my book and stared blankly ahead. My stomach churned. I had heard the proverb *The victors always rewrite history,* but reading proof that even America's history had been rewritten made me feel sick.

This constituted a conspiracy, a sweeping propaganda effort that had affected three generations. It meant that the textbooks I had been given in school presented a version of history that was suspect. It meant that these foundations—Carnegie, Rockefeller, Guggenheim, Ford, organizations I had grown up with as a child, that I had been taught were working for the welfare of humankind— had been masking the personal agendas of men hungry for power. It meant that I needed to wipe clean the blackboard of my mind and completely reeducate myself. I feared it also meant that the research on which I was embarking would change my life forever.

The Man in the South Pacific

A week after receiving my spiritual assignment, I had a vision. One morning as I washed breakfast dishes and placed them in the drying rack, a psychic window suddenly opened, and unexpected images played on the screen of my mind. I found myself standing on the open veranda of a house in the South Pacific, looking into one of its rooms. A soft, warm breeze wrapped the smell of tropical flowers around me as it wafted into the house. I stood spellbound, hardly breathing, spying on someone else's private life.

A tall, well-built man in his fifties sat in a rich brown leather chair at a highly polished, antique French desk. He wore an extremely expensive-looking, custom-tailored business suit. His features were classic—those of a beautiful Greek statue—but not too beautiful… simply handsome. This was someone whom the years had treated well, someone whose lack of worry lines indicated that he had always been handed everything on a silver platter.

He appeared to be going about his normal business, leafing through some reports. He would read for a while, then get up and walk around, pondering their content.

The room through which he walked was furnished with exquisite taste. No expense had been spared. There were original paintings by the masters, oriental rugs, rare antiques, and potted orchids. Everything was refined and impeccably maintained. I sensed that if one of his business associates flew to the South Pacific to meet with him in this home—of which few ever had the privilege—and if there were even the slightest disagreement or trace of negative energy, he would have all the furniture removed and the entire room redecorated. He felt that only if his environment was completely pristine would he have the clarity to conduct business.

I somehow knew that he had two male secretaries who generated high-level daily reports on politics, business, and the financial markets. They were well aware of their employer's mind and his goals—at least as much as he cared to share with them. He also had a family—a young wife and a couple of children, perhaps—but they were all elsewhere. Everyone in the house respected the man's desire for absolute quiet.

I sensed that he was a highly advanced soul, someone with psychic and mystical abilities. I tuned in to his awareness field and felt a very particular vibration. It was technical. There was a calculated precision about him. He was interested in the mechanics of things, the mechanics of how energy worked. He absorbed his executive reports, then scanned the invisible realms to see how he could affect global events. He was pondering, in a precise but effortless way, how he could invest a hundred million dollars in a business venture on one side of the globe and bring an underdeveloped country to its knees on the other. Money was no object—he controlled billions—and he wielded tremendous power.

When the vision ended, I walked out onto my patio. Oblivious to my surroundings, I was still focused on the man in the South Pacific, not understanding why I had been given this vision or what he had to do with my research. There was something familiar about him. I consciously stopped my thoughts and allowed my awareness field to merge with his. Where had I known that feeling before?

Suddenly all the energy drained out of my body. Egypt—I had known him in ancient Egypt.

A Ring of Power

In a past life in ancient Egypt, long before the time of the pharaohs, I had been trained in a mystery school where my teacher had served as high priest. His female students there had formed a ring of power.

A ring of power is a mystical configuration. The trained mystics who compose the ring, or circle, are networked energetically in another dimension, and the whole is exponentially greater than the sum of their parts is. The power they can potentially wield through their common intent is enormous.

So strong was the bond in our Egyptian ring that we hadn't needed verbal communication. When we took on a project, we executed it with one unified mind, in silence, each woman sensing what needed to be done.

When we had gathered again as my teacher's students in this lifetime, the ring had been as strong as the day it was formed. We weren't necessarily aware of our connection; we didn't seek out each other's company; yet, in some other dimension, we were still networked. It was only when my teacher pointed it out that we became consciously aware of our ring of power.

Had the man in the South Pacific been part of a ring of power in Egypt? As I focused on him, I could feel that he was connected to other men of like mind. If these men had formed a ring of power in Egypt, they would still be networked energetically in this lifetime. If they wanted to control the world, they wouldn't necessarily need to meet to discuss their common goal; they wouldn't even need to be aware of it with their conscious minds.

How could I find their ring of power?

"Money is power in this age," my teacher had told his students on numerous occasions. "If you want to find the power, follow the money." Intuitively I knew that this was exactly what I needed to do. If I followed the flow of money through the Patriarchy, I could find the pockets where it all ended up.

Money

I hadn't had a course in economics since high school, and as I began studying, I was overwhelmed by the complexity of the subject. As I gained a deeper understanding of paper money, however, a mind-boggling fact emerged: It wasn't real! Paper money was actually something with little or no intrinsic value, something that had been manipulated for personal gain over the centuries by master magicians.

In the late Middle Ages in Europe, people graduated from bartering goods and services to using coins as a medium of exchange. Gold was particularly popular. It was limited in supply and, thus, always desirable, but heavy sacks of gold coins were burdensome and were a temptation to thieves. Goldsmiths began advertising their services to store gold coins for safekeeping. They issued promissory notes to the owners of the gold—the first paper money. The holders of the notes could claim the gold at any time and gradually people accepted the idea that paper money had a value equal to gold.[7]

Eventually the goldsmiths determined that it was unlikely all of their customers would demand their gold coins at the same time, so they fabricated additional paper money and made it available as loans. This excess paper became known as *fractional money*—paper money with precious metals backing a fraction, but not all, of its stated value.[8]

With the passage of time, fractional money degenerated into *fiat money*—government-issued paper money with *no* precious metal backing. With the creation of fiat money, the magic show began. The first major use of fiat money occurred in Colonial America. With the invention of the printing press, the Colonies went into the business of manufacturing fiat currency and grossly expanded the money supply. Dollars became nearly worthless. By the late 1750s, Connecticut had inflated the price of the dollar by 800%, Rhode Island by 2,300%. Colonial periods of inflation sparked political unrest and were followed by periods of deflation that triggered economic depression.[9]

By 1882, states no longer managed their own money supply, and the US government had introduced *gold certificates*. Any person holding this paper money could redeem it at any time for the corresponding amount of gold coin, a troy ounce of gold being worth around $20. This system of fractional money, while not perfect, stabilized US currency, but only for fifty years, when—in an extravagant display of monetary policy manipulation—the gold certificate met its demise.

In 1933, in the wake of the Great Depression and with the onset of World War II, Americans were in a state of panic. Banks were failing every day as people clamored to withdraw their money. Surviving banks called in old loans and refused to make new ones. Businesses failed. Workers lost their jobs and stopped spending. People were afraid that the government would resort to printing fiat money to meet the massive withdrawal requests. Those who held gold certificates rushed to banks to redeem them for gold.

In order to avoid complete chaos, Franklin Delano Roosevelt, who had just been inaugurated as president, took an unprecedented step. He declared a national emergency, closed the nation's banks, and assumed complete control over the banking system, something that had never been done in the history of America. He decreed that this four day "banking holiday" was to prevent the hoarding and export of gold, so as to stop the drain on the nation's gold supply. His action was completely devoid of legal justification. Nowhere in the Constitution is any branch of government, let alone the Chief Executive, given the power to close privately owned banking institutions.

In the days that followed, Roosevelt railroaded legislation through Congress and issued three Executive Orders: One forbade banks from paying out gold; another increased the value of a troy ounce of gold from $20.67 to $35.00, thereby devaluing the dollar; and yet another ordered the confiscation of all gold held by US citizens.[10] People were forced to accept dollars in exchange for their privately held gold—gold that was then placed under the control of the Commander-in-Chief and shipped to the Federal Reserve.[11] Owning gold without a government-approved license became punishable by fine, imprisonment, or both; and it was more than forty years before that law was reversed and it again became legal for Americans to own gold.

Then in 1944, as World War II was drawing to a close, delegates from forty-four Allied nations gathered in Bretton Woods, New Hampshire, to rebuild the international economic system.[12] The outcome was the Bretton Woods Agreement, which had the effect of elevating the US dollar, still valued at 1/35th of an ounce of gold, to the preeminent global reserve currency, replacing the British pound. The world readily embraced the dollar because America had vast quantities of physical gold in storage and an abundance of political and military muscle. Once again, the money-printing presses started to roll.[13]

In the late 1960s, the French and others demanded that America fulfill its promise to pay one ounce of gold for each $35. This siphoned off much of the U.S. gold reserve. By 1971, gold backing for the dollar had dropped from 55% to 22%, and President Richard Nixon put an end to gold leaving the country by closing the "gold window." His action precipitated the present-day *floating currency* system. It completely severed the dollar's connection to gold and linked it to the foreign exchange market. By refusing to pay out any of the remaining 280 million ounces of gold in reserve, Nixon, in essence, confessed to the insolvency of the United States.[14]

Shortly thereafter, the US cut a deal with OPEC to price worldwide oil transactions exclusively in dollars. This agreement essentially backed the dollar with oil. From that point forward, any country that switched from the dollar to the euro for their oil transactions—such as Saddam Hussein's Iraq did in November, 2002—threatened the preeminence of the United States. With an oil-backed dollar, the government gave its blessing for the money-printing presses to go into full swing.[15] I marked the page and placed my book on my desk, shaking my head in disbelief. Money was only *paper*! The value of the US dollar was dependent on nothing but a written agreement with OPEC. Since that agreement was made, fiat money had proliferated and every American felt the repercussion of that on a daily basis through the ever-inflating value of the dollar.

But inflation spawns a second outcome, as well, one that is purposely hidden from public view through sleight of hand: Inflation makes a few individuals supremely wealthy. So who were these magicians? My research led me from money to bankers—specifically international bankers.

Bankers

I learned that the first bankers were goldsmiths. In the Middle Ages, as people deposited gold for safe-keeping, received paper notes in exchange, and rarely demanded all their gold back at one time, the goldsmiths realized they could create additional paper money to make available as loans—loans on which they charged interest. Suddenly, in addition to the fees the goldsmiths charged for storing gold, they reaped a profit from lending.

These men intrigued me. What kind of man was the village goldsmith? How did he feel as he sat at a crude wooden desk working by candlelight, contriving his fraudulent money? Did he feel guilty? The next day, when he pawned it off on the merchant down the street and outlined the interest payments, did the risk of exposure make his heart pound? He could have been dishonored, financially ruined, ostracized by his community, even stoned to death by an angry mob; but he persisted, wagering that not everyone would demand gold at the same time.

If I had been a goldsmith, would I have been able to stomach it? *No!* It made me wince. I was the product of five thousand years of female conditioning. Throughout the history of the Patriarchy, women were seldom allowed to handle money, much less make a profit from enterprise. In this lifetime I had been conditioned since birth to accept the inherent value and scarcity of money: "Money needs to be saved"; "There will never be enough"; "I will be destitute without it." Of course I couldn't imagine sitting at the goldsmith's desk. These first bankers were men—intelligent, inventive men who, in spite of their fear, perpetrated a monetary fraud. Not only did they get away with it, they developed a taste for it—a taste for money and power—and as their appetites increased, they became rich.

I also learned that today's banks work in a similar way to the early goldsmith banks, except there is no gold backing. The goldsmith's practice of loaning the greater portion of the wealth while retaining only a small fraction of gold backing for emergencies was known as fractional banking. Present-day banks operate under what is known as the *fractional reserve system.*

Banks get their money from depositors, people who deposit cash into bank accounts. But bankers lend out more than just the cash in their vaults. The fractional reserve system sanctions them to keep only a fraction of their total deposits in the bank. In the United States, that fraction ranges from zero to 10%, depending upon the total amount of a bank's deposits. This means that US banks hold on reserve less than 10% of the country's money. Put another way, it means that more than 90% of the money supply is nonexistent, nothing more than electronic numbers on general ledgers throughout the American banking system. Banks appear solvent, but their solvency is actually rooted in the expectation that no more than 10% of their depositors will demand their money at any given time.[16]

For lending fictitious money, bankers profit by charging interest on it. In addition, if the loan recipient defaults, the banker seizes real, not fictitious, wealth in the form of a house, an automobile, or whatever has been offered as collateral. To make matters worse, the system perpetuates itself with each loan. Upon receipt of loan money, the borrower spends it, as planned; then the subsequent recipient deposits it in a bank, and bankers begin their 90% reserve lending policy all over again![17] My forehead wrinkled. Ninety percent of money was not even paper! The US banking system gave bankers a *legal license* to foist an illusion on the American public and, in order to keep people in the dark, they had created a bewildering maze of procedures. Invariably my long hours of sifting through complex material would lead to underlying concepts that were quite simple. Thankfully, my perseverance paid off. As my research on banking drew to an end, and I moved from the subject of domestic bankers to international bankers, I knew I was hot on the trail of the master magicians.

I discovered that the most powerful bankers—international investment bankers—prefer lending money to governments rather than to individuals or businesses.[18] A government borrows vast sums, so the interest profit is substantially larger. Individuals and businesses supply collateral to obtain a loan, but what can a government offer to ensure repayment? It can promise to levy more taxes if it gets in a tight spot, but this is typically unpopular with its citizens.[19]

The international banker has two guarantees at his disposal. The first is the understanding that, in return for a loan, the government will grant him influence in national policy. The second is that if the government displeases the banker, the government can expect to be taken to war, as the banker simply finances the government's enemy.[20]

War is a lucrative option. Nothing more rapidly generates government borrowing. The international banker profits by financing both sides. Then, when the war is over, he profits by making loans to rebuild both war-torn infrastructures.[21]

The most renowned international bankers are the Rothschilds. Mayer Amschel Rothschild, who launched the family into the banking business during the nineteenth century, said, "Let me control a people's currency and I care not who makes their laws."[22] He and his five sons, who headed Rothschild offices in major European cities, collected vast amounts of wealth.

Economics Professor Stuart Crane wrote this about them:

"If you will look back at every war in Europe during the nineteenth century, you will see that they always ended with the establishment of a 'balance of power.' With every reshuffling there was a balance of power in a new grouping around the House of Rothschild in England, France, or Austria. They grouped nations so that if any king got out of line, a war would break out and the war would be decided by which way the financing went. Researching the debt positions of the warring nations will usually indicate who was to be punished."[23]

The international banking game makes such bankers supremely wealthy. Through the use of war, the bankers amass both profit and increased influence over the country's national policy. With this influence they can then demand monopolies within that country, such as control of natural resources and transportation. Of course the most lucrative monopoly is the country's banking system, its central bank.[24]

I closed my book, walked to the window, and crossed my arms over my chest. *What kind of man is an international banker? What kind of man holds the fate of countries in the palm of his hand like spare change? Does he feel the pain of an ordinary man or woman struggling to feed children with inflated currency? Does he feel the grief of an indigenous tribe when their homeland is destroyed to make way for a new economic policy?* I feared the answer was no.

My heart opened to the despair of the Earth's people—people enslaved by a system of money—and one, hot tear trickled slowly down my cheek.

3

A SUPPORT NETWORK EMERGES

During the last week of June, I left the rugged mesas of Los Alamos and drove to the brown adobe heart of Santa Fe to stock up on organic food at the Whole Foods Market. At the front of the building, I reached out to take a shopping cart, and so did the woman beside me. I smiled at her politely, then froze. I couldn't believe my eyes! It was my long-lost friend Alexandria.

"My God!" she exclaimed, her large brown eyes sparkling as she enclosed me in a warm but rather formal embrace.

"Alexandria…," I stammered, returning her hug.

When she was in her twenties, Alexandria had been a ballet dancer. After a stint with the New York City Ballet, she had worked her way up to soloist with the Joffrey. I had always admired this accomplishment. It took considerable physical discipline and personal power to succeed in the world of dance. Now in her mid-fifties, she still looked the part and carried herself with regal grace. She wore a flattering white jersey top and form-fitting designer jeans that accentuated her slender legs. Her short, perfectly cut and styled brown hair revealed not a trace of gray, and her French manicure was flawless. She might have just left a dance rehearsal and been on her way down Broadway to meet Balanchine for lunch.

I flushed with embarrassment over my worn jogging suit with the broken zipper and regretted not wearing makeup. Then I pushed the feelings aside. I knew Alexandria wouldn't care. She had been my spiritual sister for twenty years, my truest friend, one of those rare individuals who sticks by you through anything. We had both cut our spiritual teeth on Transcendental Meditation in the seventies and had then had become students of my teacher, but after his passing, his students had drifted apart, and I had lost touch with her.

"You look fabulous!" I told her.

"So do you!" she replied with genuine love in her voice.

I looked deep into her eyes, drinking in the sweetness of our friendship for a moment.

"What are you doing here in Santa Fe?" I finally asked.

"I live here. After our teacher left the body, I moved here to work more closely with Celeste. Do you remember her?

I nodded. "Of course."

"She's mentoring me in her techniques for clearing the personal ego, and we're working together to launch a project to support AIDS orphans and marginalized communities in South Africa. We've also been doing quite a bit of meditative work for the planet." She paused. "In fact," she continued, with a hint of intrigue in her voice, "Celeste and some of her students are meeting on Sunday at my house for a meditation. We'll be looking at the world situation to see if there is anything we can do to help. Do you want to come? I'm sure Celeste would love to see you."

My eyes widened. "You have no idea just how much I would like that!"

I spent the week continuing my studies, but all the while I couldn't help anticipating the Sunday meeting with Alexandria and Celeste.

I had met Celeste in the early eighties when she had studied with my teacher for a few years. She had been brought up by a nanny in a well-to-do South African family replete with servants and had the most enchanting English accent. She was also a wonderful painter. The thing that most impressed me was her kindness. She was genuinely concerned about other people.

I had reconnected with Celeste in 2000 when I attended one of her meditation events. I had been astounded. My peer from the old days had built up a spiritual organization with hundreds of students! I was also awed by her spiritual progress—she seemed to live in a state of complete equanimity. Maternal and nurturing, she fielded questions from her students with great patience.

Her selflessness had made me painfully aware of how self-absorbed I had been all my life, but I loved the deep sense of peace I experienced with her and the way my mind, normally scurrying from one thought to the next, lapsed easily into silence. When we meditated I saw the most delicate gold light radiating from her. I had been so inspired that I'd signed up for her month-long spiritual sojourn to South Africa, the journey that had culminated in my life-changing immersion in patriarchal energy.

Celeste's intent for the trip had been to investigate the remnants of the apartheid system. I was fascinated. As we traveled, she and her students uncovered imbalances in the collective consciousness, the repository of thought forms that produced mass agreements, then did energetic work. They joined forces with benevolent beings in higher dimensions—ascended masters, bodhisattvas, angels—and offered to facilitate the reconciliation of the imbalance.

Because I had acquired psychic and mystical skills while studying with my teacher, I could follow what was going on, and each piece of their energetic work afforded me the opportunity to learn. Little did I know at the time that this schooling would prove invaluable in the not-so-distant future.

Fellow Mystics

The following Sunday afternoon, I entered Alexandria's adobe house, nestled in the high desert, and marveled at the interior décor. Diffuse light filtered through windows set in eighteen-inch-thick walls, illuminating a room decorated completely in white and beige, with pastel accents in the form of floral arrangements, candle groupings, and silk throw pillows. It could have been a set designed for a performance of Swan Lake.

I smiled and bowed slightly to Celeste, who sat on a white couch at the end of the room. She wore a flowing white caftan ornamented with a simple crystal necklace. Her thick, shoulder-length, dark brown hair framed the warmth of her smile, and her green eyes held me in a steady gaze. When Celeste and I had known each other in the early eighties, she could have passed as a fashion model. Now in her late fifties, she was heavier, but just as beautiful as ever.

Celeste gave me a broad smile. "It's nice to see you! Alexandria told me you might be coming." She gestured for me to take a seat. "I'm delighted you'll be joining us."

Twenty people, mostly women, filled the room. As we waited for everyone to get settled, I watched Celeste. Working tirelessly, she had dedicated her life to her students and the welfare of the planet. A wave of gratitude enveloped me.

The session began, and I listened intently, trying to understand what the group was discussing. It seemed they had been talking about September 11th for some time, and Celeste believed it had been a turning point for the world. Everyone seemed to know something I didn't.

I raised my hand slightly to signal Celeste. "Can you brief me on your intuitions about 9/11?"

A slight scowl crossed her features as she smoothed her caftan, then folded her hands in her lap. "The moment I saw it on television," she began quietly, "my spiritual guides told me it was an inside job. I was horrified. I wondered who would do such a thing, and why, and I've been pondering that question ever since. I spend every available moment trying to educate myself, through both reading and meditation.

"Since 9/11 the US government has passed one restrictive new law after another, and the people are simply letting them do it. People are afraid, and it's no mistake that they're afraid. The purpose of 9/11 was to make them afraid. Remember, I grew up in South Africa under apartheid. From the time I was a little girl, I knew what it felt like to be afraid, to live in a country controlled by a powerful, elite group of men.

"Most of you grew up in America. You didn't have that experience. For me, a deep knowledge of political control through fear is ingrained in my being. The collective consciousness of the US is now filled with fear. It feels just like South Africa did in the 1950s. Someone is vying for control. People who are educated about what's going on in the world point the finger at the US government, but it's bigger than that. My study and meditation have been focused on who is behind the government, who truly runs things on the planet."

My vision of the man in the South Pacific and the international bankers flashed through my mind. "Do you have an inkling of who it might be?" I asked.

She sighed. "I'm not certain, but at times I've sensed the presence of some male souls who lived in ancient Egypt."

My heart skipped a beat.

She continued. "I first encountered these men on a group trip I led to Egypt. We read about them in the Egyptian museum in Cairo. Do you recall who they were, Alexandria?"

"Absolutely," Alexandria answered from her cushion by the French doors. "They were the priests of Amon Ra, and they influenced the politics of many Egyptian dynasties. When we read about them at the museum, our psychic perception was that they had practiced lower mysticism, remember?"

Celeste nodded. "Yes, that's it. And another thing I have identified is that there is someone—I don't know exactly who—pushing a wall of distorted energy at people, trying to confuse everyone. It seems like they want to create a wall of distortion so no one can perceive what they are really doing." She looked at me again. "It's easy to feel. It's like a veil that is right up against your awareness field. If you close your eyes and move your awareness back slightly, you can see it."

My teacher had taught his students the art of psychic perception, how to use the third-eye chakra, or energy center, in the middle of the forehead. By focusing on the third eye and suspending thought, one can learn to peer into realities beyond the physical world. It was an art at which Celeste excelled.

I followed her instructions. She was right. I could sense it.

After the meeting I drove back up the mountain to Los Alamos, feeling elated. The afternoon was more than I could have hoped for. Celeste had recommended books. Alexandria had prescribed listening to *Democracy Now* and other alternative radio programs. There was even a group in Santa Fe focusing on the type of work I had been given.

So many women meditating for spiritual change! Would the reunion with Alexandria and Celeste lead to some sort of collaboration? My heart was full of hope. With a group of us working together, I felt certain I could grapple with the bankers and the man in the South Pacific.

Once I was back in my office, though, amid an expanding library of books, the slow and tedious research seemed unending. I wasn't collaborating with Alexandria and Celeste yet; I was awash in information, completely on my own.

Fellow Samurai

Anders had enrolled fulltime at the University of New Mexico in Los Alamos for the fall 2002 term and had leased an apartment on campus in advance, to begin September 1st. He planned to travel home to Norway in August, so I offered him my spare bedroom for the month of July.

I had booked a vacation in August, as well. I planned to go to Scotland to attend the internationally acclaimed Edinburgh Festival. A week of fringe theatre, dance, and Scottish bagpipe music would be a perfect antidote to my studies. I suggested Anders use the money he was saving on rent to rendezvous with me in Edinburgh. He liked the idea, and we began looking forward to the trip.

On the evening of July 4th, Anders paused at my open office door and found me staring out the window. The book on my desk lay untouched.

"What's the matter?" he asked.

"It's nothing," I stammered without turning around.

He knew I was lying. Walking over to my office chair, he knelt at my feet. "Can I help?"

I was embarrassed. "It's really nothing. I'm just feeling overwhelmed by all of this studying."

He reached up and stroked my arm.

It felt nice to be comforted. I let down my guard a little. "There is so much to learn," I continued, "and I feel pressured that I've only been given six months. And these men—whoever they are—are so powerful, so well organized…." I tried to hold back the emotion but it rose into my throat, blocking the words, and I let out a sob.

Encircling me in his arms, Anders laid his head on my lap and held me. Gradually I calmed down.

Taking my face in his hands, he brushed away the tears and kissed my cheek. We looked at each other without speaking.

I smiled. "Thank you," I whispered, then slid onto the floor beside him. I wrapped my arms around him and laid my head on his shoulder. As we held each other, he stroked my back and the embrace deepened. For more than a year we had ignored the attraction we felt for one another. Now that attraction swelled into desire.

After a few moments, I pulled back. "Anders," I said, shaking my head, "I'm so much older than you."

He nodded. "I know that. That doesn't matter to me."

I looked into his eyes for a long time. Then I let my fingers trace the lines of his face. As our lovemaking unfolded, the sweetness of coming together for the first time settled into an age-old familiarity.

We had been partners in many past lives. I could feel one lifetime keenly. As samurai, we had committed ourselves not so much to each other, but to right action. Our marriage, steeped in pristine etiquette, had been purely for spiritual evolution. Anders had journeyed to distant lands, wielding his samurai sword for the cause of justice. I had remained in our home, constantly monitoring his consciousness. I could feel when he entered battle. I could feel when his attention wavered even for an instant. I would intervene, using the strength of my mind, to bring him back into balance. Then, when the opponent's sword fell, it missed.

"You have a karmic debt from that lifetime," I told him as we lay in bed, holding each other. "In this life, I'm the one on the front lines. I'm the one who will need help. The debt doesn't have to be repaid, of course. If we don't have a relationship, Spirit will provide another way. But my intuition tells me that this is why we've come together."

Anders kissed me, and I had no difficulty relinquishing the

past. He smiled and pointed at the window. Outside, Fourth of July fireworks rained down over the mesa.

My Teacher

While the prospect of collaboration with fellow mystics and reinforcement from a former samurai partner bolstered my confidence about the task I had been assigned, I felt that my greatest support would come from my teacher, who I knew didn't need to be with me in the flesh to guide me. In this lifetime we had met in 1981, but his influence on my life had actually begun two years earlier than that.

In 1979, my teacher completed his PhD in English literature at Stonybrook College in New York, moved to San Diego, and began giving lectures on self-discovery. At that time I lived in New York City, ignorant that my teacher from past lives had been only miles away on Long Island. I was engrossed in my budding career. In 1973, after receiving a Bachelor of Fine Arts degree in drama from Carnegie-Mellon, I had headed straight for the New York stage, intent on becoming a famous actress, and I'd made a fair start, landing leading parts in New York and regional theatre; but in the spring of 1979 I began hearing a voice during meditation, instructing me to "go to Los Angeles." It happened every time I sat and closed my eyes.

I thought that Los Angeles could only mean the film industry, which held no allure. I'd felt destined to become a great actress of the *stage*, so I ignored the voice. Much to my dismay, my life began falling apart. My auditions resulted in no job offers. My career crumbled. My theatrical agent dropped me. I became more and more despondent. Everything had been going so well. What had happened?

Finally, after a year of desperation, I went to see a psychic. As he was preparing to lay out his tarot cards, he turned, stared at me intently, and said, "I'm getting L.A. Have you ever thought about moving to L.A.?"

"Well, yes," I replied meekly, "about a year ago."

"Go!" he scolded me, brandishing a tarot card in my face. "I see that you're going to meet a teacher there. He will completely change your life. Just pack up and go!"

Within three weeks I was living in Santa Monica, on the west side of Los Angeles.

Years later I pieced together all the facts from statements my teacher had made. He had moved to California at the exact time I began hearing the voice. Once in San Diego, he used his laser-sharp psychic vision to locate his students around the globe, then began communicating with us through meditation and dreams. His technique was simple. By making our lives fall apart, he could then use our desperation to coax each of us to California. We would think we were seeking a better life. In reality we were seeking him, our teacher.

I finally met my teacher in physical form in the spring of 1981. A friend phoned one day to say he wanted to check out a spiritual teacher who reportedly had mystical powers.

This could be the one, I thought.

We arrived early and jostled to get seats in the second row of the L.A. Convention Center's vast auditorium. A tall American man walked onstage, sat down, and began talking. He was extremely knowledgeable and extremely funny, and I liked him right away.

When we started to meditate, he suggested that we keep our eyes open. *Absurd! An open eye meditation?* But as I sat there, mentally complaining, he looked at me.

This was the final device he employed to find his students from past lives.

When I met his gaze, I left this world. It was as though the light from his eyes formed a golden tunnel, and I was pulled through to the end. Suddenly there was no time and no space. The room didn't exist. Nothing existed. I was poised on the edge of nothingness. It was the most beautiful experience I had ever had, and I longed to have it over and over again. It felt like coming home, like finally coming home after being away for a long, long time.

At that moment I didn't understand that I had indeed come home, that he had been my teacher before, and that I had just reconnected with my spiritual family. All I knew was that I had spent my entire life searching for something, and now I had found it.

Alexandria and Celeste had also been summoned by an inner call. We had all forsaken our former lives and moved to Los Angeles. Alexandria had given up her ballet career in New York, Celeste had divorced her husband in South Africa, and I had exchanged the New York stage for temporary secretarial work. We became his students, and we became friends.

During those days in the early eighties, we watched with interest as our teacher assembled his students. Word slowly spread throughout the California spiritual community that something unusual was happening. "I saw this teacher who turns the room gold while he lectures," one spiritual seeker said to the other. "You should check it out."

And they did—by the thousands. While the workshops at UC San Diego were small and mostly attended by students, his events in Los Angeles resembled rock concerts. The line to buy a $5 admission ticket at the L.A. Convention Center stretched down the street and wrapped around the block. The large, ornate church in San Francisco was standing room only, with people spilling out onto the portico.

During each of his lectures, he would ask people to report their experiences. "You became invisible," someone would say. "You levitated." "You turned into a Buddhist monk"; "...an Egyptian priest"; "...a Hindu figure with many arms."

Almost everyone reported seeing golden light, a fine gold mist that circuited through his body and flowed out into the room. As he meditated, stillness would descend on the audience, and the golden light would become more apparent. As the evening progressed, the light intensified. The walls of the room seemed to dissolve. The light streamed past people in the front rows, dissolving the solid shapes of their bodies.

During each lecture, my own body dissolved, as did my mind. It felt like melting into a blissful void. I had no psychic abilities when I met my teacher, but that wasn't necessary. Merely sitting in the force field of his energy was an admission ticket to another world, one where miracles happened.

When the lectures ended, the audience sat for a long time,

unwilling or unable to move. When they finally stood up, they walked as though they doubted the floor would be there to support them. Some bumped into walls, everyone smiled, and baby boomers familiar with psychedelic drugs thought they'd found the cheapest high since the 1960s.

Everyone liked my teacher, but he was an enigma. He didn't fit anyone's description of a spiritual leader. He was a tall, rather gangly Caucasian male whose primary focus was the enlightenment of women. He had an alarming shock of curly, brown hair. He might arrive at a lecture wearing slacks with a shirt and tie, or a black leather jacket, or even jogging shorts. He meditated listening to contemporary electronic music. His reading assignments included books by J. R. R. Tolkien and Stephen King, in addition to classic spiritual texts. His movie recommendations ranged from The Last Temptation of Christ to Terminator II. He swore, he was a standup comedian, and every woman in the audience wanted to jump into bed with him.

I never jumped into bed with my teacher, but he was still the love of my life.

The Chakras

In each of his public lectures, my teacher spoke about meditation, the cornerstone of his teaching. He defined meditation as the art of stopping all thoughts and all thought-impressions in the mind—the complete cessation of thought. "Thought defines you," he instructed us. "When you stop all thought, you stop your idea of who you are. When you stop thought, you dissolve into Spirit."

During meditation, we focused on a *chakra*, or energy center, within the subtle physical body. He explained to us how chakras work:

"The subtle physical body lies just on the other side of the physical body. It is composed of millions of luminous strands of light, woven together, and there are a number of different junctions where the strands of light intersect. These are called chakras. There are seven major chakras, or intersections, in the subtle body. There's a line called the *sushumna*—an astral tube, or *nadi*—that runs from the base of the spine to the top of the head." He gestured to illustrate his point. "There are seven junctions, or train stations, along the sushumna—places where the train stops, if you will. These chakras are access points, gateways to other worlds.

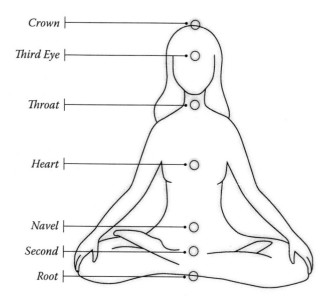

"The chakra at the base of the spine is the center of *kundalini*, raw power. The Hindus believe that the kundalini, or spiritual energy, resembles a snake coiled around this root chakra. When the kundalini rises, the snake uncoils and passes up through the various energy centers.

"The chakra around the spleen is the chakra that endows life force. Sexual energy flows through this second chakra, as does creative energy.

"The navel chakra is located a couple of inches below the physical navel." He straightened his torso and moved his hand to his navel, then slightly below it. "If you place your hand below the physical navel, you can feel where it is. This chakra can be used to develop will power, the *chi* harnessed in martial arts. It's the chakra of mysticism. It can be used for the transference of power and in the production of the mystical body, a nonphysical body capable of navigating other dimensions. The mystical body leaves and, after it does its work, reenters through the navel chakra.

"The chakra in the center of the chest," he said, moving his hand up and pointing to it, "is the heart chakra. Say 'me' silently to yourself, and point to your chest. This is the central chakra. There are three above and three below. It is the center of balance in the psyche. It's also the chakra of psychic love, oneness, and beauty. It leads to the psychic planes, the higher astral world.

"The throat chakra is connected with higher creativity and spiritual vision. It is the center of creative expression and speaking the truth.

"The chakra at the forehead, the third eye or *ajna* chakra—located between and slightly above the eyebrows—is the chakra of timelessness. When you meditate on this chakra, you will find that it's very easy to go into a timeless state of being. It's also the chakra of the *siddhas*. Many of the siddhas, or mystical powers, are connected with the third eye—for example, seeing into both the past and the future. It also has to do with discrimination, discerning that which is real from that which is unreal. The physical eyes show us things in the physical world. The sixth chakra is the eye with which we can see beyond the physical.

"These six chakras are all connected via the sushumna, but the top chakra, the crown center, is not connected. It's separate. It's the thousand-petaled lotus of light, the chakra of the supra-conscious awareness—*sat chit ananda*, or existence, consciousness, bliss. It only becomes active when a person is very advanced in meditation.

"Initially, when you sit to meditate, you are not really meditating. You are practicing concentration. Using the classic definition, meditation begins when you are able to stop all thought in the mind. So until then, we practice. We learn to focus the mind on a single object. Focus for a third of your meditation on the navel chakra, then move up to the heart, and finally to the third eye. Each time the mind wanders, when you become aware that you are having thoughts, return to your point of concentration. Return to the chakra.

"With practice you will learn to pass through the gateway of the chakra into dimensions of light. Beyond these dimensions of light lies the ocean of *nirvana*. The result of true meditation is the stateless state of *nirvikalpa samadhi* or nirvana, when the individual self is absorbed into the Universal Self."

4

FIELD TRIP FOR LESSONS ABOUT POWER

During July and the first part of August of 2002, I buried myself in my books, only taking breaks to organize my trip to Scotland. Repeatedly in my research, I found myself stumbling across references to a group called the Bilderbergers. A BBC columnist had called them "perhaps the most powerful organization in the world."[25] I had never even heard of them before; now they seemed to crop up everywhere I looked.

Like an animal bristling the fur along its neck, I would instinctively go into red alert when I read the name. My interest only intensified when I learned the group had held one of its secretive meetings at a five-star resort in Turnberry, Scotland. Suddenly my impending vacation assumed a whole new dimension.

I learned that the group had been formed in 1954 by Prince Bernhard of the Netherlands, together with Joseph Retinger, Polish political advisor, and Paul Van Zeeland, Prime Minister of Belgium. It became known as the Bilderbergers because the first meeting took place at the Bilderberg Hotel in Oosterbeek, in the Netherlands. Each year since then, the royalty of Europe has met with elite invitees from across Europe and North America—international financiers, central bankers, prominent political leaders, defense experts, top-ranking businessmen, trend-setting educators, and mass media press barons—in a conference of the world's richest and most powerful.[26]

Prince Bernhard was a German royal who, through alliance in marriage with Princess Juliana of the Netherlands, became Prince

Bernhard of the Netherlands. Later, when she ascended the throne, he became the Queen's Consort, HRH The Prince of the Netherlands. During World War II, he worked for IG Farben, a large chemical company based in Frankfort that provided the Nazis with poison gas and other supplies. Though he was apparently not anti-Semitic, critics say he was a Nazi party member.[27] This part of his past has been a subject of debate, and the official Web site of the Dutch royal family politely skirts the issue.

After the war, he became his adopted country's Inspector General and later founded and led the World Wildlife Fund, but he was also involved in a number of subsequent scandals, both national and personal, which reportedly caused great strain on his marriage. In 1980, because of financial misconduct by the Prince, Queen Juliana abdicated in favor of her daughter, Beatrix, but both Juliana and Bernhard remained active in the Bilderberg group, along with Queen Beatrix.

Each year, usually around the spring equinox, the Bilderbergers convene at a five-star resort, typically in Europe but occasionally in the US or Canada. More than a hundred attendees are invited by the Bilderberg steering committee. The annual lists include world leaders and others with great influence. Donald Rumsfeld (Secretary of Defense under Presidents Gerald Ford and George W. Bush) has been an active Bilderberger, as has Paul Wolfowitz (Deputy Secretary of Defense under President George W. Bush and President of the World Bank). Other public figures from the US who have attended include Richard Perle (Assistant Secretary of Defense 1981-1987), Henry Kissinger (Secretary of State 1973-1977), Zbigniew Brzezinski (National Security Advisor to five presidents), President Bill Clinton, and David Rockefeller (an original US founding member, life member, and member of the steering committee).[28]

The annual Bilderberg guest list is available to the public, as is the agenda. What is discussed at the meetings, however, is cloaked in mystery. Attendees take a vow of confidentiality. The Bilderbergers claim that this concealment allows attendees to speak freely without fear of being misinterpreted by the press.[29] Although attendees include powerful heads of media corporations, editors-in-chief, and highly influential journalists, the working news media are prohibited from covering the meetings. They are, in fact, generally barred from the grounds. The hotels are heavily guarded, often by the military of the country hosting the event.[30]

The group stated originally that their purpose was to create a political tie between Europe and the United States in opposition to the USSR and the threat of communism.[31] Some political and financial scholars, however, believe that "the fate of the world is largely decided by Bilderberg."[32] A columnist for the conservative Financial Times stated this:

> "It is [its] close identification with the megaton-weights of the international business community that has encouraged the growth of the idea that Bilderbergism is the arm of a movement whose main aim is to create 'a world fit for multinationals to live in'—which may indeed even see itself as spear-heading the establishment of World Government…."[33]

Were the Bilderbergers the behind-the-scenes group that Celeste had sensed? Did the man in the South Pacific attend their meetings?

I could hardly wait for my trip to Scotland. What I had assumed was a vacation now appeared to be a field trip to investigate the corridors of power.

The Power of Mother Earth

Edinburgh enjoys the reputation of being one of Europe's most beautiful cities. Its main thoroughfare, Princess Street, features shops along one side and, across a dramatic ravine, the towering splendor of Edinburgh castle on the other.

During the month of August, the city erupts in activity as it hosts the world's largest art festival. Anders and I enjoyed theatre, marveled at Japanese drummers, and were moved to tears by the national anthems of marching bands from across the world at the Military Tattoo. At the end of our week-long vacation, I was sad to watch Anders depart for the States to begin school, yet I also couldn't help feeling that magic lay just around the corner.

Before traveling to Turnberry on my Bilderberg sleuthing mission, I drove to the western coast of Scotland and took the ferry to Mull, a large, unspoiled island of craggy coastlines and surprisingly few people. On a previous trip to Scotland, I had fallen in love with its tranquility and its natural beauty—moors, waterfalls, forests, beaches—and I felt pulled to return.

The day after I arrived, I drove at sunrise to Calgary Bay on the island's northwest coast. I parked my car, walked on the white sand beach still bubbling from the receding tide, and amused myself with picking up shells. It was too early for sunbathers; I had the beach to myself. After half an hour I stopped. My inner being was perfectly still. There were no thoughts in my mind. As I basked in the experience, I suddenly felt my teacher's presence.

"I have drawn you here to show you this," he told me telepathically. *"This..."* He paused for me to assess my surroundings. *"This is who you are."*

The energy was tremendously clear, the air vibrant with otherworldly light, the waves lapping the sand, the sunlight glistening on the deep turquoise water. Everything was in harmony. Nothing was lacking. Nothing needed to be added. Everything rested in Divine Presence—including me. My mind was still. My heart was open. I was completely at peace, yet it was more than peace; I was one with everything around me. There was no difference between my own awareness and my surroundings. I *was* the beach in all its perfection.

"In your day-to-day life," he resumed, *"your mind is filled with thoughts. Emotions course through your body. But these thoughts and emotions are not who you are. You are this, the perfection of existence, Spirit itself. You forget because you live in the Kali Yuga, a time of violence and destruction. You forget because there are billions of people on the planet. Everyone is psychic. Everyone is awash with the thoughts and emotions of six billion people. All of that has nothing to do with you. This is who you are. Trust yourself. Trust this."*

I scanned the ocean and the beach, my eyes finally coming to rest on the woodlands in the distance. A feeling of sadness washed through me. *I miss the Earth,* I confessed to my teacher on the inner planes. *Not so many years ago, when the energy of the world was less convoluted, you could take a walk in nature and feel the Earth, but now it's almost impossible. Moments like this are so rare.* I sat down on the sand, crossed my legs, and drank in the beauty.

"*You have lived many lifetimes on this planet,*" he said, "*and you have come to love her deeply.*"

My awareness expanded and gradually descended into the Earth itself. Her body was my body; her oceans were my oceans. I could feel her trees rooted in my flesh. I merged with the spirit of Mother Earth, feeling all her strength, her depth, her vast presence.

I ask you for your power, I said spontaneously to the Earth. *I ask for all of the qualities your magnificent female form holds. I must take apart the Patriarchy, and I beseech your help. Please, for the sake of the human race, help me with this task.*

The beach was perfectly still, save for the salty breeze that caressed my face and the solitary cry of a gull overhead.

In order to do this task, I said, now directing my telepathic thought toward my teacher, *I'm going to need the power of the Earth. Is that right?*

"*That's right,*" he answered. "*It's good that you've asked. Ask and you shall receive.*"

Spiritual Teachings on Psychic Development

Throughout the eighties, my teacher had taught a variety of subjects, including psychic perception. He believed that everyone is born with psychic ability but that, in an age of reason, people are conditioned from childhood to disregard psychic input.

"Being psychic," he explained one evening to a group of students, "has to do with having the ability to perceive beyond the physical. It's the study of perception, how to become perception itself eventually. As we develop our psychic perception, we become more aware of ourselves and those around us, of different planes of consciousness, different beings, different energies.

"Two chakras are involved in psychic perception: the heart and the third eye. The heart is associated with feeling and intuition. The third eye allows for clairvoyance, clairaudience, seeing into the future and the past, knowing what's going on," his eyes widened, "in other people's bedrooms!" Everyone laughed. "...without having to be there and go through the experience yourself." He now joined us in our laughter.

He explained that everyone can typically use three methods of perception: sensing (with the physical body, by way of the five senses), analyzing (with the mental body), and feeling (with the emotional body). Psychic perception is a fourth method of perception. "With psychic perception we can simply *know* things. We can know what something looks like without having to look at it physically. We can know what something feels like without having to go through an emotional process. Psychic perception is shorthand. It's a faster method of apprehending something's true nature."

His first instruction was simply to *believe*, to move beyond the rational concept that the psychic doesn't exist. When I first met my teacher, I had no psychic abilities. I wanted to believe, but I couldn't *see* anything.

"Don't be misled by the term 'seeing,'" he instructed us. "Sometimes psychic perception is visual, but sometimes it is a feeling, a knowing."

This advice helped. I struggled to unhook from my physical vision. It was easier if I concentrated on feeling.

My teacher would often ask us to look at something—either in the physical or in another dimension—and report our psychic perception. I felt like a fish out of water. If I was lucky, I could identify a feeling while other students described visuals in enormous detail. It was infuriating.

I badgered my teacher. "Why am I unable to see?"

"Too much baggage," he explained. "You need to lighten up."

I shook my head in frustration.

"What blocks the development of psychic perception," he explained patiently, "is your attachment to your thoughts, ideas, beliefs, emotions—liking some while avoiding others—and your senses. You have a description of the world. You see life in a certain way. We are conditioned to see life in a certain way. But that's not really the way life is. Life is a flux. It's fluid. We simply *order* it in a particular way. You focus your attention on certain things and ignore others. If you want to become psychic, you need to learn to let go."

Sometimes, as I listened to people describe their seeings, I recognized I had felt or even seen the same thing. Hearing them voice their experiences brought my cloudy perception into sharper focus. It was like studying a foreign language. I slowly assimilated a psychic vocabulary, learning to associate feelings with visuals and ultimately to interpret them.

"If you really want to learn to be psychic," my teacher told us, "spend time with someone who is. It's not your intellect that learns this skill; it's your awareness field. By associating with someone who is psychic, your body of awareness learns from their body of awareness."

The best person to learn from, of course, was my teacher, who was phenomenally developed psychically. He could read us like a book, describing details about our lives that even we didn't know. He would kick off lectures by giving a psychic readout of what was happening in the world. I was continually astounded. My hazy understandings about world affairs would become crystal clear as he reported the "energetic news."

My teacher advocated using a meditation technique to develop psychic perception. He called it gazing. It was an open-eye meditation in which we stilled our thoughts and gazed at an object. We were to hold our attention on the object steadily without using a particularly intense focus. Because the gazer takes on the energy of the object on which she gazes, he suggested objects in nature—a stone, a candle flame, the center of a flower—rather than those that were human-made. The trick was not to anticipate anything. Expecting something to happen was a sure way to remain locked in the three-dimensional, physical world. By remaining neutral and keeping the intellect at bay, the awareness field, which was far more intelligent than the mind, had a chance to take over and capture knowledge about the object.

I began making steady progress by practicing. After a few minutes of gazing, I would see the object begin to shift and change. I was phasing in and out of different dimensions, seeing what the object looked like in alternate realities. A red rose, for example, was only solid in the physical. In an alternate dimension, I perceived it as a radiant, otherworldly red hue. In yet another dimension I saw the rose break into individual particles of consciousness, each surrounded by an ethereal red light.

"What does it mean," I asked my teacher, "when the rose breaks into particles of consciousness?"

"It doesn't *mean* anything. Stop trying to understand it with your mind. Seeing has nothing to do with the mind. It's a completely different method of apprehending things. After some time, when your skill is more developed, you'll be able to decode what you see and bring it down through the conscious mind, but when you are engaged in the act of seeing, don't try to figure it out. Just see."

It had been twenty years since my teacher explained his gazing technique, and since that time I had clocked thousands of hours gazing. Now, in Scotland, my practice was about to pay off.

The Transformational Power of Love

Leaving behind the beautiful, nature-filled Isle of Mull, I returned to the Scottish mainland and drove south down the coast, past Glasgow. Busy highways narrowed to country roads that wound through Scottish villages. Long-horned Scottish cattle stared at me across stone walls. Weather-worn farmers tipped their woolen caps as I passed.

Then fifteen miles outside of Turnberry, the place where the Bilderbergers had met just four years earlier, I hit a wall of dark, heavy energy. It was almost palpable, and I suddenly felt intense fear. I reached out on the inner planes to my teacher.

"*I'm right beside you,*" he told me telepathically. "*Just listen to everything I tell you while you're here.*"

I slowed the car and focused on the road. Five miles from the hotel, I began to feel nauseated. Taking some deep breaths, I labored on. As I crested the hill overlooking Turnberry, I caught my breath and pulled the car to the side of the road. Emerald moors sloped down toward the sea. Beyond the craggy coastline was an island, a gigantic rock. It felt extraordinarily powerful but had a dark, sinister cloud of energy around it.

What in God's name is that? I wondered.

A half an hour later, standing at the window of my modest eighty-dollar-a-night hotel, I stared at the luxurious five-hundred-dollar-a-night Turnberry Hotel, ensconced on the Scottish coastline opposite the rock island. The hotel's long, white façade and red-tiled roof found a perfect complement in the red-hued sand traps of the golf course below and the cumulus clouds overhead. My eyes drifted beyond it to the churning sea. I wanted to inspect the hotel but was put off by that island. Its distorted energy made me tremble. I turned inward to my teacher for advice.

I'm thinking about going to the Turnberry for dinner tonight. What do you think?

"I just hope you brought something to wear."

An hour later, sporting a handmade silk jacket over a classic black shift, I parked my economy rental car next to a Rolls Royce and, bolstering my confidence, entered the Turnberry's marble lobby. An attractive young woman at the front desk looked up and smiled. I approached and inquired if she could help me with a dinner reservation.

When she had completed a phone call to the dining room on my behalf, I asked, "Have you worked at the hotel for some time?"

"Yes," she replied, "for a number of years."

"You wouldn't happen to know if the Bilderberg Conference was held here in 1998, would you?"

"Oh, yes," she answered quickly. "I actually worked during the conference. Not all of our employees did—they brought in their own staff. But I'm a manager, and a few of the high level staff stayed on during the conference."

I nodded. "That must have been *very* interesting for you."

"Indeed," she replied, her eyes brightening significantly. "I've never seen so many dignitaries. They instructed the staff not to look into anyone's eyes and only to speak when spoken to…" She lifted her eyebrows and lowered her voice, "…but sometimes I would glance at people as they walked through the lobby. I'd think to myself, 'I can't believe it! That's the Queen of England!' I'd only seen her on the telly." She smiled broadly. "It was such an honor."

"I can imagine." I patted her arm. "Thank you. You've been very helpful."

I sauntered through the lobby, stopping to admire the enormous vases of fresh flowers, and discovered the bar, a large, airy room with high ceilings and enormous windows overlooking the sea. Victorian tables and chairs were arranged on Oriental rugs, each grouping positioned at a discreet distance from the next.

After I selected a table and seated myself, the waiter approached— not a moment too early or too late—bowed slightly, and took my order. Just as my glass of wine arrived, a lone piper in full highland regalia appeared outside the windows. Facing the ocean far below, he played Scottish ballads to the sunset for the pleasure of the hotel guests. The strains of the bagpipe were enchanting, and for a few minutes I forgot the purpose of my visit. As he finished, however, I began to sense the energy of the Bilderbergers.

"What do you feel here?" I heard my teacher ask.

I paused, closing my eyes so I could concentrate. *The vibration of the group's energy is refined.*

"But what is its movement?" he questioned.

I couldn't perceive what he was referring to.

After a pause he asked, *"See how it moves like a snake?"*

I sank more deeply into the Bilderberg energy and suddenly identified what he was pointing out.

It moves back and forth. It undulates!

"Right," he agreed. *"The refined energy is neither here nor there. You are picking up on the fact that these are wealthy people who live gracious lifestyles. Exuding a sense of refinement simply helps them convince people that their ideas are benevolent. How could a highly cultured queen possibly be involved in something like world control?"* He paused to allow me to feel what he was saying, then continued. *"But*

remember the movement. It makes them hard to track."
I knew that by this my teacher was referring to one of his mystical lessons: A moving target is harder to hit. When someone's activities are routine, they can be anticipated and the person easily stalked. While this principle applies to activities in the physical world, in this case he was referring to activities on the mystical planes. A mystic who is crafty purposely breaks up routines, throws up smokescreens, or uses camouflage. He was telling me that the Bilderbergers were pros, that they purposely moved the energy of their organization in such a way that it made them difficult to track on the mystical planes.

At the appointed time, I left the bar, migrated to the other end of the hotel, and entered the expansive dining room, the sound of my footsteps echoing on its highly polished wood floor. It seemed I was unfashionably early; it was deserted. The maitre d'hôtel seated me at a corner table with a white linen tablecloth. The china, silver, and crystal were perfectly positioned. Heavy red velvet swags hung above windows that revealed another breathtaking view of the ocean. I glanced out the window and marveled that I was sitting at the table nearest the rock island.

"Can you tell me about the island?" I asked the maitre d'.

"It's a bird sanctuary now," he said politely. "No one lives on it anymore, but there was once a monastery long ago."

So, I thought to myself when he left, *that means it is a power place.* The Christians often built monasteries and churches on places of power that had formerly been used by ancient European religions based on the worship of the Mother Goddess.

After a superb dinner, I ordered tea. I wasn't particularly interested in drinking it; I just wanted an excuse to linger a bit longer. It was twilight, a time of day when it is easier to shift one's awareness into other dimensions.

I moved my chair slightly so that I had a clear view of the island. Using my teacher's gazing technique, I stilled my mind, allowing my eyes and my attention to rest on the island. After my thoughts settled down, my awareness began to drift in and out of various dimensions. Then I had a psychic perception. It was as though a block of information opened in my mind, and I suddenly knew why the energy of the island felt so heavy. The Bilderbergers had *used* it.

How curious! What exactly did they do? I wondered.

As I held my awareness unflinchingly on the island, an entire series of psychic perceptions played out in my third eye.

I saw the hotel bar and somehow knew that it was 1998, immediately after the Bilderberg Conference. There were three men in business suits seated at the same cocktail table I had used earlier. All the other conference participants, after debating world affairs, had gone home. The huge hotel was silent. A few dirty glasses sat on the bar. The staff had not yet cleaned the room; evidently they had been sent away.

The three men talked quietly together, assessing where the Bilderberg group had stood on various issues. One of them gazed out the window, just as I had done. I sensed that he had flown to Scotland only that day. He had not attended the conference but, rather, relied on the other two men to give him their impressions of what had transpired.

He was the important one. He was a mystic; he wielded the power.

Together the three men formulated a plan based on what had happened at the conference, but he was only giving half of his attention to the conversation. The other half was focused on something outside the window. I gazed exclusively at him and merged with his awareness field. As decisions were made, he wove them, like a spider, into a mystical web, a complex matrix of intersecting energies. Then he spun a single energetic line—a mystical thread that came out of the bottom of the web—and anchored it onto the island of rock!

My teacher spoke to me inwardly: "*Stop your thoughts and feel the island. Don't resist it.*"

I wanted to know how they planned to use the web of energies but surrendered my psychic perceptions in order to follow his suggestion. Waves of nausea passed through my body. I continued to gaze at the island; then I suddenly understood that it was in bondage, that the man had enslaved it. He had forced the island, against its will, to anchor his web.

Can we undo this? I asked my teacher. *Why can't we undo what he did?*

"*We can,*" he replied. "*Meditate on it.*"

Taking a deep breath, I straightened myself in my chair and focused on the island. All at once I could sense my mystical lineage assembled above me in another dimension. My crown chakra opened. Then, from somewhere far away—from a place that felt like it might be the center of the universe—energy descended, passed through the Lineage, entered my being, and pooled in my heart.

A wave of intense heart energy, more intense than I had ever experienced, emanated from the center of my chest and streamed out to the island. Again it happened…and again. For ten minutes, waves of heart energy bathed the massive rock as the dimensions shifted in the dying embers of twilight.

When the meditation was over, a feeling emerged from the island and traveled across the distance to me. "*Thank you,*" it seemed to express.

I was stunned. The island now radiated the most beautiful feminine energy: heart-centered and receptive, yet stately and strong. Speechless, I bowed to her.

As I sat back in my chair, my teacher concluded softly, "*Love is the most powerful force in the universe. Always remember this.*"

The following morning he suggested that I splurge and take a lesson at the world-class Turnberry golf course. I laughed. Learning to play golf was the furthest thing from my mind, but in an odd way I found the idea appealing. It provided an antidote to the previous evening.

"*Beginnings are important,*" he told me, as he had done so many times before. "*If you're going to learn golf, a five-star Scottish golfing resort is the place to do it.*"

In the high-tech classroom, the instructor videotaped and replayed my beginning swings as I hit balls down an immaculate green toward the sea, where an ecstatic island gleamed in the sun.

Spiritual Teachings on Power

I had many questions after Turnberry: How did the Bilderbergers fit into the big picture? Were they connected with international banking? What role did the man in the South Pacific play? I didn't know the answers, but I did know that the steering members of the Bilderberg organization were obsessed with power. I knew because I had gleaned a deep understanding of power during the time I'd spent with my teacher.

He had trained his students in mysticism, and mysticism is the study of power. Today, the word *power* has a negative connotation, but that is because we associate it with abuse of power. Power is neither good nor bad; it is simply energy. It might be said that mysticism is the study of energy and the way it works in the world.

"I've had many incarnations where I've practiced mysticism," my teacher told his students, "particularly in ancient Egypt and Atlantis. But mysticism in those days was a high art. Today mysticism is your local fortune teller. This is not mysticism. These are people who are dabbling with forces they don't necessarily understand. Mysticism is a beautiful art, much like ballet. It involves perfect form and movement. You have to be able to move perfectly through the mystical realms... and many things will tempt you. If you can still give in to temptation, then you will give in; but if you realize that the only thing that matters is Light and that your true essence is Light, then you are free to play in the mystical realms." He paused to collect his thoughts.

I sat in the first row of the Ebel theatre in Los Angeles, along with three-hundred of my teacher's students. It was 1983. I was steeped in gold light, hanging on every word, ecstatic that he was about to lecture on the spiritual topic that intrigued me most.

"The study of mysticism," he continued, "is different than the study of psychic perception. Psychic perception is not so much the study of power, although there are certainly some powers that develop as a result of that study. Psychic perception is the ability to *perceive* things that are in alternate planes of attention. Mysticism is the ability to *enter into* alternate planes. Entering into alternate planes requires power.

"Everything has power. There is power within you. In the study of mysticism you learn to increase your personal power by eradicating your ego and purifying your being. You learn to gain power and avoid the loss of power. You learn the art of reordering yourself—not of reordering yourself consciously, because the mind can't possibly order the depth of your being, but of opening yourself to the winds of Spirit and allowing Spirit to reorder you. This reordering happens in the mystical planes.

"There are all sorts of different planes of awareness that intersect and overlap each other. Most people look at the physical world and think that's all there is. But there are an infinite number of planes. Think of them as different frequencies of being. For example, there are different frequencies that a radio can pick up. The mystical frequency is one frequency—a plane of mysterious power, effect without cause. The mystical plane is neither good nor bad, neither emotional nor unemotional. It's a plane of pure intensity, a plane of power.

"We all have various bodies: the physical body, the subtle physical body, the psychic body, the mystical body, the mental body, the emotional body, the ego, the life force, and the *giva*, or soul, that eternal spark which is the ultimate perceiver. The mystical body is a field of attention, your extended awareness, a wind tunnel that connects the different realities.

"You can use your mystical body to travel through the mystical plane. You can send the mystical body anywhere—to any place in this world, to any plane of existence, to any universe. Using the mystical body, you can do things like gather knowledge, communicate, transmit power, start things happening, prevent things from happening, and all without leaving your room. The mind doesn't even have to be aware of the mystical body. The mind is very limited. It may only have glimpses of what the mystical body is doing.

"In mysticism we work with that which is unseen. In some forms of spirituality, we are dealing with the seen. We can see cause and effect. In the yoga of love, for example, we can see the expression of love or compassion. The yoga of mysticism is different. We are dealing with power that is unseen, power that is not directed in an obvious manner.

"If you're going to practice mysticism, you've got to be detached. You've got to bring your emotions under control. That's not to say that there is anything wrong with emotions. That's not to say that a mystic doesn't feel compassion or that her heart is not open. What I'm suggesting is that a mystic must act from a place of detachment. In the mystical realms, there are no emotions. There is only power and various uses of power. And if your heart is pure, you will use power only for the greater good of all and never to advance yourself. If you are impure, then you will use the power in impure ways…and anyone who uses power in impure ways will suffer tremendously.

"The mystical planes are tricky. They're filled with different beings. It's a world of warriors, survival of the fittest…at least, in a way. Some beings in the mystical world help people in their spiritual evolution, but there are also negative forces that can destroy people. The mystical reality is like a wild jungle. To go into the jungle, you have to be a warrior, fearless and smart.

"I teach the art of higher mysticism, but there is also lower mysticism—what some people refer to as occultism or black magic. When you practice lower mysticism, you are opening a door that leads into the lower mystical realm. Its vibration is very different than the higher mystical realm. Once you open that door, it doesn't necessarily close. So as you explore things in that realm, things in that realm explore you. You have to understand that the mystical body can be used in ways that are not very progressive. A lower mystic is someone who has learned to manipulate energies, someone who uses power badly. They may try to injure someone, to gain power over them, to steal their power or even kill them."

My teacher scanned the room for a long moment. As I, a naïve aspiring mystic, waited for him to continue, I recoiled from his description of a lower mystic. *That doesn't apply to me,* I thought. *I would never use power badly.*

"I realize that some of this shocks you." My teacher smiled. "You really need to get beyond your moral conditioning. If you travel the path of mysticism, you need to understand power in all of its aspects: gaining power, losing power, storing power, reclaiming power from past lives, transferring power, and, finally—the most difficult—abusing power. At some stage along the way, the student of mysticism becomes obsessed with power and ends up having the experience of abusing it. But that experience is a necessary phase of the study if you want to evolve into a mature practitioner of mysticism, someone with the ability to wield power in a balanced way for benevolent purposes."

In the years that followed, as I became acquainted with the dark side of my being, I became considerably humbled and my teacher's words made perfect sense. Little by little, I saw that anytime I used power to fulfill a desire or defend my ego against a perceived threat I was using power badly.

My teacher leaned forward in his chair. "Always remember this: Balance is the key to mysticism. Mysticism is a pathway to higher consciousness through power, but with balance—the careful balance of power, light, and love. It's very important to love this world and its people."

My trip to Scotland was a field trip into the world of power, a real-time illustration of my teacher's mystical teachings. The Bilderberg mystic had used power in Turnberry. He had used it in an impure way. By enslaving the island and forcing it to anchor the Bilderberg web of ideas, he was manipulating energies, advancing his own agenda, trying to gain control over others. He was obsessed with power.

I understood. As my teacher had predicted, at one stage of my schooling I had indeed become obsessed with power. I also remembered past lives where I had been obsessed with power. These experiences had been filled with pain. My obsession had blinded me to the sweetness of life. Now I felt sorry for the Bilderberg mystic, who I knew must be suffering.

I too had used power in Turnberry. I had used my mystical body to travel into the mystical planes, gather information, and undo the work of the Bilderberg mystic. I had used power, but a power unlike anything I had ever experienced before: enormous but extremely quiet.

Love, my teacher had reminded me, is the greatest power in the universe and the self-serving agenda of the world's richest and most powerful group had been undone quite effortlessly in Scotland by the careful balance of power, light, and love.

5

THE DARK FORCES VERSUS THE LIGHT

After my return from Scotland, I spent the remainder of August and all of September curled up on my couch with one book after another, building on the knowledge I had already acquired about the control of education, the manipulation of history, the smoke-and-mirrors nature of money, the self-serving games of the bankers, and the secretive agenda of the Bilderberg group.

I had been directed to take apart the underlying mystical structure of the Patriarchy. What was that structure? I had no idea, but I knew I could find out if I continued to educate myself about the world's most powerful organizations, run by the global elite.

Although religion wields tremendous power in the world, and the military demonstrates powerful physical force, I didn't feel drawn to investigate either of them. I sensed that a deeper understanding of the role of religion would come later in the project, and my reading about government would also cover the military as its right arm.

At this stage of my research, I felt pulled to understand the incestuous relationship between corporations, government, and elite organizations such as the Council on Foreign Relations. Growing up in the United States, I had been taught that government was "of the people, by the people, for the people."[34] Gradually I was becoming aware that my country had strayed a long way from the original vision of its founding fathers.

The Forces of Darkness

The ancestor of the modern-day corporation can be traced back to ancient Rome, where *corpora* performed public duties and, later, municipal administration.[35] They had been created to act as public servants but are no longer. Corporations have evolved into associations of private businesspeople that form the dominant institutions in society. They provide and control the majority of products and services upon which we depend—including essential public services such as water, electricity, and healthcare—and the jobs. They shape our view of the world through advertising, public relations, and mass media. Even public schools, universities, and churches have become vulnerable to commercialization by relying on corporations for funding.

A corporation is a legal entity with all of the legal rights of a human being: it pays taxes, can own property, can go into debt, and can make use of the legal system to protect itself.[36] Noam Chomsky describes corporations as "immortal persons, persons of immense power...major private tyrannies which are unaccountable".[37] Some corporations are huge. Fifty-one of the hundred largest economies in the world are corporations. In the recent past, the sales of General Motors and Ford have been greater than the GDP of sub-Saharan Africa.[38]

I began to scan one author's list of the twenty-five most powerful companies: American Express, AT&T, British Petroleum, Citicorp, Coca-Cola, Daimler-Benz, DuPont, Exxon, General Electric...[39] I smiled. I knew what they had in common.

Years before, my teacher had exhibited a can of Coca-Cola during his lecture. "Why do you think I drink Coke instead of Pepsi?" he asked.

I wracked my brain. I had no idea. Apparently no one else in the audience did either. No one volunteered an answer.

"Because Coke is a mystical company," he said, shaking his head, as if it were the most obvious thing in the world. "Close your eyes for a moment. Meditate on both companies. Scan them. Look at Coke on the inner planes then look at Pepsi. Can you see the difference?

Coke feels very precise, clearly delineated, tightly woven. That's the hallmark of a company run by mystics."

Once my teacher had pointed it out, I could psychically perceive the configuration of the two companies.

He toasted us with his Coke, took a sip, placed it on the table beside him, and leaned forward. "Every really successful businessperson, in some lifetime, has had mystical training," he explained. "They may not call themselves mystics. They may not be consciously aware of their training. But somewhere along the way they have studied power and know intuitively how to apply it in this lifetime."

I closed my book. Were the mystics behind powerful corporations running the show? Had they taken over a government that used to represent people? I chose another book from the stack on my coffee table and continued to read.

I learned that corporations bankroll politicians and political parties. The vast majority of Americans don't contribute to political campaigns at a federal level. Business contributes millions and, in return, gets influence and legislation.[40] Corporations wield so much influence today that they can simply make up the rules as they go along. They use sophisticated tax dodges to keep their money offshore, they find tax loopholes, and governments look the other way because they know that if these big corporations don't get what they want, they will simply pack up and move to a more hospitable country. Using tax dollars, government's job has become to provide the infrastructure that business needs and to help corporations demolish any remaining trade barriers in the forward march of globalization.[41]

Globalization has been fashioned in recent years by multinational companies, corporations that have facilities and other assets in two or more countries.[42] Initially, in the absence of global rules, multinationals had no trouble dominating underdeveloped economies without having to answer to their citizens. For example, no one told Nike they couldn't run a sweatshop outside the US. As globalization spread and opposition arose, however, multinationals turned to governments for help, especially that of the United States. Bowing to the power of multinationals, governments legislated various trade deals and other accords to keep the opposition in check.[43]

With the advent of the World Trade Organization (WTO) in 1995, this ad hoc system of trade deals became formalized.[44] The WTO claims that its purpose is to help trade flow as freely as possible, provided there are no undesirable side effects—which is important for economic development and well-being—while allowing governments to meet social and environmental objectives.[45] Critics state just the opposite, that the WTO made it more difficult for a nation to set policy to protect its people—ensuring the safety of food, pharmaceuticals, and motor vehicles—and its environment—ensuring the proper use of land, water, minerals, and other resources. They go on to paint a dismal picture of reduced standards of living in underdeveloped countries, reduced standards of living in the US, increased unemployment worldwide, increased political chaos, increased environmental degradation, and a growing global sense of despair.[46]

When I moved to Los Angeles, I began working in the corporate world, initially as a secretary but eventually in the field of computers, a career my teacher recommended to his students. During those years, as one small cog within a giant machine, I had focused on the papers coming across my desk and had been blind to the bigger picture. Now the image of multinationals steamrolling the planet, concerned only about profit, made me feel sick to my stomach.

When speaking of globalization, Margaret Thatcher, former Prime Minister of Britain, had coined the acronym TINA: There Is No Alternative. Was that true? How long could Mother Earth and her peoples survive being brutalized by multinationals?

It was clear that government wasn't going to stop them. Politicians like campaign contributions. Most politicians have no problem dishing out influence and legislation in response, and politicians know that the corporate world will welcome them with open arms when their terms of office are complete. There is a revolving door between Capitol Hill and the world of business. Was it reasonable to hope that US politicians with corporate ties would draft policy to rein in the corporate world?

Who *does* draft US policy? My question led me to the door of the Council on Foreign Relations (CFR), a quasi-governmental organization formed in 1921. This was not just a door, but actually another revolving door, this time between Capitol Hill and the CFR in New York City. Again, membership in this group is strictly by invitation and includes only the most influential leaders in finance, commerce, communications, and academia.[47] What is discussed there? The CFR bylaws state that members who reveal details of meetings may be asked to leave.[48] Another secret society?

For the past forty years, members of this little-known organization have filled 10% of the high government offices in both Democrat and Republican administrations. Under President Bill Clinton, the entire cabinet was composed of CFR members, except for the Secretary of Defense.[49] The CFR recommends government policy, foreign policy in particular. It then instructs various think tanks to develop arguments which will support the new policy and discredit any opposition.[50]

Admiral Chester Ward, former Judge Advocate General of the US Navy, was invited into the CFR, remained in the organization for twenty years, then became one of its sharpest critics. He had formed the impression that CFR members want to undermine the sovereignty of the United States, bring about a global government, and gain control of the world banking monopoly.[51]

The CFR in New York has a sister organization, the Royal Institute for International Affairs in London, about which comparatively little has been written. These two entities, together with the European-led Bilderberg group, were formed during the days of what was known as *atlanticism* when the most powerful nations flanked the Atlantic Ocean. Japan had not yet earned its place in the club. *Trilateralism* came into being in 1973 with the formation of the Trilateral Commission, which opened offices in New York, Paris, and Tokyo.[52] Another elite organization, it was unaccountable to any government. Many believe it provided the next significant stepping stone to the formation of a world government, a political body that would make, interpret, and enforce international law requiring individual nations to pool or surrender their sovereignty.

Former US senator Barry Goldwater wrote:

> "The Trilateral Commission is intended to be the vehicle for multinational consolidation of the commercial and banking interests, by seizing control of the political government of the United States. The Trilateral Commission represents a skillful, coordinated effort to seize control and consolidate the four centers of power—political, monetary, intellectual and ecclesiastical. What the Trilateral Commission intends is to create a world-wide economic power, superior to the political governments of the nation-states involved. As managers and creators of the system, they will rule the future."[53]

David Rockefeller and Zbigniew Brzezinski founded the Trilateral Commission. At that time Rockefeller was chairman of the Chase Manhattan Bank, a director of many major multinational corporations and endowment funds, and a member of both the CFR and the Bilderbergers. Brzezinski had been a Bilderberger, a professor at Columbia University, the author of several books that served as policy guidelines for the CFR, and an open proponent of a world government. He acted as the Trilateral Commission's executive director for three years until he was appointed by President Jimmy Carter as Assistant to the President for National Security Affairs.[54] He had been criticized for encouraging the Soviet invasion of Afghanistan by supporting the radical Islamist, anti-Soviet forces that later formed the foundation for the Taliban and Al Qaeda. Brzezinski predicted:

> "...the gradual appearance of a more controlled society. Such a society would be dominated by an elite, unrestrained by traditional values. Soon it will be possible to assert almost continuous surveillance over every citizen, and maintain up-to-date complete files containing even the most personal information about the citizen. These files will be subject to instantaneous retrieval by the authorities."[55]

This made me very nervous. Brzezinski's *prediction* of a more controlled society had been written in 1970. Now, in 2002, it *existed*. The Patriot Act, passed on the heels of 9/11, had drastically expanded the US government's power over its own citizens. The government could now invade people's privacy, imprison them without due process, and punish dissenting voices. It had purchased billions of personal data records on Americans from information technology firms such as ChoicePoint and LexisNexis. These detailed records, once used for consumer profiling, had become the basis of a national intelligence infrastructure.[56] The government had a detailed record on each of us!

I looked up from my book, closed my eyes, and tried to calm my quivering body. We did not have a government of the people. We had a government of corporations, by corporations, and for corporations. We had a government whose policy was written by secretive, unaccountable organizations. We had a government of the global elite.

The global elite. Who *were* they? It was frustrating. The more I learned, the more evident it became that dark forces were controlling the planet, but I couldn't see the big picture. I stood up and started to pace. Some of them, like the man in the South Pacific, used lower mysticism and knew exactly what they were doing. Some, as my teacher had said, must have studied mysticism in past lives but were unaware of their skills in this one. Others were not mystics at all but merely worked for those who were. All were caught up in an ocean of obsession and a tidal wave of power that destroyed everything in its path. Were they willing to sacrifice the entire planet to gain power?

That's the way it felt when I focused on the man in the South Pacific. He and his cronies were absolutely determined, no matter the cost, to bring the world to its knees and rule as its masters, and they had assembled the organizations to do it: the Trilateral Commission, the Council on Foreign Relations, the Royal Institute for International Affairs, the think tanks, the nonprofit foundations, the central banking system, the World Trade Organization, the Bilderbergers...

Where had I been? Completely in the dark? Had I been totally oblivious while they were growing more and more organized, getting closer and closer to their goal of One World Government, this ultimate consolidation of patriarchal power, this endgame of oppression and control?

My divine guidance struck my mind like lightening. *"Disassemble it!"* the Lineage had told me. Were they mad? I was a nobody—one frail woman against behemoths bent on world control. I was completely unprepared.

"Why me?" I shouted angrily to the Lineage. "Surely you could... surely...!"

I threw my book on the coffee table and stomped out of the house.

As the crisp autumn air hit my face, it settled my nerves and cleared my head. I turned inward to my teacher.

If I am really supposed to do this assignment, give me the strength to pit myself against the dark forces of the global elite.

The Forces of Light

When I was desperate, I always turned to my teacher for help, and he never failed me. His presence was instantaneous. It didn't matter that he had left the body. In my experience, any enlightened being—including the world's great teachers, sages, and saints, incarnate or disincarnate—was ready, willing, and able to help those who sought guidance. I suppose I called on him because he had been my teacher in this and other lives. He was an enlightened being, one of the forces of light—the antithesis, in my mind, of the global elite.

Years before, I had read a book that measured and categorized levels of human consciousness.[57] Its author calibrated the level at which consciousness takes a giant leap forward—where love colors all activities, creativity comes into full expression, and altruism becomes the motivating factor. By his calculations, only four percent of the world's population exhibited this level of consciousness, but to counterbalance entire populations at lower levels, very few at this level were required. As these rare individuals ascended even further, they moved into enlightened states, and their affect on society was even more profound. They often became inspirational leaders who created new paradigms, visionaries focused on uplifting society as a whole.

My teacher was one of these. As his student for seventeen years, I had observed firsthand the powerful influence of an enlightened being. Under his tutelage, my personal transformation had been extraordinary as I had grown from a secretary drifting from job to job into a well-paid computer consultant, from someone with a muddled view of the world into a seer with clear psychic perception, from an inexperienced seeker groping for spiritual knowledge into a seasoned spiritual warrior.

My teacher had helped me change my life, and I observed him doing the same for all of his students. It was the difference between night and day. I watched him transform the consciousness of complete strangers at public lectures or even in restaurants when he meditated on them and filled their being with light. I heard people report how he had healed their cancer or brought them back from the brink of death, leaving disbelieving doctors at a loss for words. I listened to my teacher recount how he had used his mystical powers to affect world affairs: getting a political candidate elected, bolstering an economy, even helping to bring down the Berlin wall.

His enlightenment process began in 1979, at the age of twenty-nine, and ranged over many years. "You don't just wake up one morning and ZAP! you're enlightened," he told us. "It's an ongoing process. Every day brings another change."

He explained that as a person's enlightenment unfolds, the light of the supra-conscious shines through them more and more because there are fewer and fewer egoic structures to block it. "The highest octave of *kundalini* is the golden light, which occurs in the supra-conscious. The golden light *is* the supra-conscious. Exposure to it creates profound spiritual transformation." When my teacher entered into *nirvikalpa samadhi*, it was easy to see this light on the subtle physical plane. It was like a refined golden mist.

By the time I met him in the early eighties, still in his initial stages of enlightenment, my teacher often meditated on two female beings in the Hindu tradition, two aspects of the Divine Feminine: Lakshmi, the goddess of beauty, prosperity, and abundance, and Kali, the goddess of destruction and transmutation. The energy of the two couldn't have been more different—the gentle, caring, nurturing of the one and the passionate, fiery, ego trampling of the other—but, remarkably, they always led him to the same place: nirvikalpa samadhi.

He would begin talking about one of them—a small child filled with awe of his beloved—and suddenly, mid-sentence, he would close his eyes, melt into the Divine Feminine energy, and be gone. Nirvana would wash over him like a wave of perfect silence, enveloping him and everyone in the room. We often sat like this and meditated for hours, but it never seemed like hours. It seemed I could have sat there forever, bathed in the golden light of this most remarkable teacher as he modeled supreme ecstatic consciousness, beyond masculine and feminine, beyond space and time.

As the years passed, he explained that he was "cycling," or going higher in his enlightenment. He became more powerful, more multidimensional. He was increasingly detached from the third-dimensional world of humans. This was most obvious when I approached him to ask questions. His eyes looked like no eyes I had ever seen. Gazing into them, I had the feeling that his being was spread across the universe. How could he walk around? How could he function in the world? "Enlightenment," my teacher once said, "is when you have one foot in this world and one foot in nirvana, and you don't know which foot is which." Looking at his eyes, I could sense that that was indeed his experience.

Each time he cycled higher in his enlightenment, the golden light changed. Gradually it shifted from a subtle gold mist to a clear golden radiance.

He remembered many past incarnations where he had been enlightened. "Admittedly, I've been interested in enlightenment for some time. It began when I was a samurai—a long time ago in another cycle of time. I used to kill people for a living. Sometimes, as they died, I would study them closely and wonder where they were going. That's how I became interested in spirituality. I had a very good teacher in that lifetime, a teacher of the dark arts, but I left him and began to pursue enlightenment. Lifetime after lifetime I meditated and sought enlightenment until finally I woke up."

He looked down at his hands resting on his knees. "I'm telling you about each stage of my enlightenment process in this lifetime." He lifted his head and gazed at us. "I'm not a special person. I'm not different from you. Each stage I have gone through, you'll go through, and once the final stages begin, when you really start to remember who you are, there's nothing you can do about it."

As he recalled a past life in which he had been enlightened, he would resurrect the teaching style he had used in that life, including Hinduism, Zen, Tibetan Buddhism, and numerous other yogas, paths that lead to union with the Universal Self. My teacher taught four yogas: *bhakti* (the path of love), *jyanna* (the path of discrimination), *karma* (the path of selfless-giving), and mysticism (the path of power).

By 1982, my teacher had changed his home base from San Diego to Los Angeles and had more than three thousand students. He shared his knowledge not only with those who had been his students in past lives but with a large, diverse group of other spiritual seekers.

Celeste had not studied with my teacher in past lives but spent a number of years as his student in this one. She seemed to be interested in acquiring mystical knowledge, then she departed to study other things. As her own enlightenment process unfolded, an entirely unique body of teachings came through her; but observing her recently at Alexandria's house, I could detect my teacher's influence. Alexandria and I, on the other hand, could recall many past lives in which we had known my teacher, and we remained his students for the duration of his teaching career.

In 1984, my teacher walked nonchalantly into the lecture hall, took his seat in front of his large student population, and announced, without ceremony, that he was moving to Boston.

There was dead silence.

"A particular energy is rolling in over the Pacific Ocean," he explained calmly. "It will hit Los Angeles in '85. You can already feel it. It's a sort of reddish-brown, lower mystical energy, and it's going to get worse. Practicing self-discovery will become increasingly difficult. The energy on the planet will get heavier and heavier until sometime around 2003 or 2004. At that point humanity will make a decision: Is it going to blow itself up or is it going to stick around? If the decision is to stick around, then the heaviness will gradually start to taper off going out to 2012."

He paused and scanned his audience. "We're at the end of a cycle. All of you have known this since childhood. The Hindus call it the Kali Yuga, the dark age. At the end of a cycle, Shiva, the Hindu lord of death, dances. At the end of a cycle, certain changes occur. The Earth has always had upheavals and will continue to do so. That's no big deal. Earthquakes come, earthquakes go. But at the end of a cycle, certain energetic configurations go away, and others come into being."

He paused again, allowing us to absorb the magnitude of what he was saying. He leaned forward. "I have a mission," he said quietly. "I've come to accomplish certain tasks." A faint smile played across his face. "Anyone who wants to move to Boston with me can stay ahead of the lower mystical energy and buy themselves another year of so of clear sailing before this energy engulfs the whole continent."

It was a turning point in my teacher's organization. Many people didn't want to leave California. Some had families and careers there. For others, it was simply too radical. I sold the oak antiques I had shipped from New York and used the money to fund my cross-country drive. If my teacher was going to Boston, I didn't want to be anywhere else.

With the move to Boston, the study gradually became more demanding, and additional students left. Some people slipped out the door seeking a more leisurely spiritual pace. Others stormed off after being personally confronted with my teacher's brutal honesty. During the next fourteen years, he moved the group about once a year—to San Francisco, Washington, DC, Palo Alto, New York City, Seattle, Chicago—as the numbers dwindled to a core group of seventy students who continued to work with him closely. He said the moves were part of our training, a way to increase our personal power because in every city we had to hit the ground running.

As we continued to move, my teacher continued to cycle in his enlightenment, and the golden light that flowed through him grew steadily more intense. What began as a refined gold mist and transformed into a clear golden radiance progressed, in the end, to a molten gold—golden light so thick and solid that it almost burned your eyes to look at it. The supra-conscious state that he had drifted in and out of in the early eighties had, by the late nineties, obliterated any remaining attachment he had to the human world. He had become even more powerful, more multidimensional. Those who dared meditate with my teacher near the end of his life were defenseless against the onslaught of molten gold. It annihilated all thought, including the idea that enlightenment was "sugar and spice and all things nice," as it catapulted one mercilessly into the universal Void of perfect no-mind.

6

FIELD TRIP FOR SPIRITUAL LESSONS

"Come to the East Coast with me," I told Anders at the end of October. I had decided to shelve my books for a week in order to take psychic readings of some of the places I had studied.

"I can't." He wrinkled his forehead. "I've got midterms."

"I thought you were keen to learn more about my teacher."

His face brightened. "I am."

"It's one thing to read books he wrote years ago," I said, feeling impatient with him, "but on these field trips, he's teaching me in real time. He guided me through the steps to take in Scotland. He gave me tips about power and how to use it. I went head to head with the Bilderbergers and faced them down. Surely as an ex-soldier, that's interesting to you."

Anders studied me for a moment. "It is, but I've got to stay here for exams," he said ponderously, as though he were thinking of something else.

"Well, it's too bad you can't go. Who knows what will happen in DC? I've got a lot more knowledge at this point, certainly more than when I went to Scotland. It'll be a fascinating trip. Sleuthing the world of the global elite! Detective extraordinaire!" I finished with a bow.

Anders looked puzzled. "I was listening to a tape your teacher made the other day," he began cautiously. "It was called 'Purity and Humility.'"

I nodded.

"He said that humility was the most important spiritual quality—

that without humility, all spiritual growth stops."

I nodded again, not understanding where he was taking the conversation. "Right. That's what he said."

"Are you all packed?" he asked.

"Yes," I replied. "Packed and ready to go."

He took my hand and kissed it. "Maybe, if you packed a little humility, you'd have a better trip."

Reconciling Self-importance and Worthlessness, Arrogance and Insecurity

H Street in Washington, DC was bustling at lunchtime. I pressed my back against the building behind me so I was out of the flood of pedestrians and stared across the street at the modern building that housed the World Bank. As one of the major power organizations in the world, I knew it had to be part of the patriarchal puzzle, but which piece? It was the World Bank, but it didn't feel like part of the banking system.

It was a sunny autumn day with a gusty breeze. People came and went through the building's main entrance. They looked harmless enough—just ordinary people on their lunch hour.

I walked to the end of the block, crossed the street, and entered the World Bank's bookstore. Once inside, I hesitated. The smiles of developing country peasants greeted me from hundreds of pamphlets, books, and posters. Babies received vaccinations as mothers beamed at the camera; small children sang in front of newly constructed schools; farmers happily displayed their abundant harvests...but something just didn't feel right.

I flipped open one of the books.

"The World Bank's primary focus is on helping the poorest people and the poorest countries...onto paths of stable, sustainable, and equitable growth...bringing finance and/or technical expertise toward helping them reduce poverty.... [It] works to...turn rich country resources into poor country growth.... [It] supports the efforts of developing country governments to build schools and health centers, provide water and electricity, fight disease, and protect the environment."[58]

This description of the World Bank was far more altruistic than the one I had uncovered in my research: World Bank policy—policy that causes widespread poverty, inequality, and suffering among the world's peoples, as well as damage to the world's environment— principally benefits international investment bankers, multinationals, and corrupt politicians.[59] One study showed that in the 1990s, in areas utilizing World Bank adjustment programs, the number of people living in poverty actually *rose,* and the World Bank had a 65-70% failure rate in the poorest countries.[60]

Which description is more accurate?

I threaded my way through the aisles of smiling peasants. They certainly looked pleased with the World Bank—maybe a little too pleased. Were they really happy, or were these portraits simply the end-products of the World Bank PR machine?

I closed my eyes, trying to feel behind the façade in order to penetrate the core of the World Bank. No psychic perceptions came. Frustrated, I focused my attention on my teacher and projected a thought:

Show me what is going on here.

I waited, but he was apparently unavailable. My frustration grew to annoyance. Finally I strode to the entrance, shoved the door open, and merged with the crowd on the sidewalk.

As I walked down 19th Street, the lunchtime throng thinned to a handful of sightseers. After several blocks, I approached Constitution Avenue, and a giant obelisk came into view. I stopped short, thinking, *What, in God's name, is that?*

Of course I knew what it was physically. I knew it was the Washington Monument. I had seen it on a childhood trip to DC. I had seen it in a thousand pictures. It wasn't the monument that stopped me; it was its energy. It felt like the rock island off the coast of Scotland before it was freed. I gazed at it for a few moments.

Why is its energy so dark and distorted?

No answers came.

I could have hiked over to the monument to investigate but opted instead to turn onto Constitution Avenue. The Washington

Monument wasn't on my agenda. I had come to the East Coast to investigate banking, to follow the flow of money. Besides, my feet were tired. I stuck to my agenda and made my way to the Federal Reserve.

When I arrived the grounds were deserted. Traffic whisked along Constitution Avenue behind me, but there were no sightseers, no pedestrians, and, from the looks of the place, no one inside, either. I was standing in front of a white stone tomb. The wide walkway, the steps ascending to the entrance, the angular, two-story building—all were constructed of massive white stone blocks...and iron. The front door and the windows were barred.

I sat on a bench beside a large fountain that had been shut off for the season. The basin that normally held water now provided a refuge for autumn leaves. Gusts of wind sent them shuffling around the base.

I pivoted on the bench and studied the bank again, one of twelve around the country that comprised the Federal Reserve System. Not a government institution, as I had been taught in school, the Fed was actually a privately owned corporation.[61] Congressional committee documents compiled in the 1970s revealed that its ownership included the most prominent banking families: the Rothschilds, the Rockefellers, and the Warburgs.[62] Through the years, stock had been passed down through inheritance.[63]

It looked like a fortress—so solid, so gigantic, so impenetrable— and I felt so...so small. I suddenly felt exhausted, drained of energy. I turned my back on the building, and my body slumped on the bench.

What am I doing here?

The dead leaves rustled in the fountain, and the sound was annoying. I shook my head.

I can't do this. I can't do this task. It's too big.

I stood up and hurried back down Constitution Avenue, back to the crowded, impersonal streets, telling myself that I would feel better tomorrow, that the other places on my itinerary would bear more fruitful experiences. But that was not to be.

I visited two conference hotels where the Bilderbergers had met, and I made a quick tour of the United Nations in New York, but I had no psychic perceptions at any of the venues. By the time I arrived in Bretton Woods, New Hampshire, only to discover that my psychic apparatus was still out of order, I felt desperate.

I sank down on a red velvet chair in the palatial ballroom of the Mt. Washington Hotel, birthplace of the World Bank. *The Bretton Woods Agreement was signed here when the World Bank and the International Monetary Fund were born*, I thought dully.

As I scanned the Spanish Renaissance architecture and the majestic Presidential Mountain Range beyond the wall of glass windows, the World Bank and IMF were the farthest things from my mind. I closed my eyes and allowed myself to really feel what was going on. After a few moments, I realized that I was angry.

Why was I angry? Who was I angry at? I went through the past two months in my mind, reviewing everything that had happened since Scotland, up through my conversation with Anders…. *Anders! Anders had said I lacked humility. I'm angry at Anders!*

I sighed and opened my eyes. He had been right, though. I had become egotistical. I banged my forehead with the palm of my hand.

It had been a reoccurring problem throughout my life. Years before, my teacher had addressed it.

"What is your biggest obstacle to enlightenment," he asked me.

"My ego?"

He nodded. "Your parents programmed you to be a star, didn't they?"

How did he know that? I had never discussed my childhood with my teacher, but he was right. My father had told me, on a daily basis, that I was superior to other people. Elitism had systematically been woven into the fabric of my consciousness. My mother had escorted me to my first dance class when I was three, then spent the warm-up period holding my hand because I couldn't yet reach the ballet bar to hold onto it. Singing, piano, and acting classes followed, culminating with a Fine Arts degree in drama. With the certain knowledge that stardom awaited me in New York, I had embarked on my acting career.

"An ego that large," my teacher had told me, "must indicate a lot of insecurity underneath, don't you think?"

This had been a revelation. A handful of people through the years had confronted me about my egotistical behavior, but I had never examined what lay beneath it. Hesitantly I began exploring the foundation blocks of insecurity on which my ego was built, and I made steady progress as I worked with my teacher through the years. Eventually I was able to stand back and view the two aspects of my ego as a polarity of feelings: overbearing pride and worthlessness. Now, in the ballroom of the Mt. Washington Hotel, I closed my eyes again and processed my feelings about the incident with Anders.

Reconciling Opposites

Most human beings perceive the world in terms of duality, their consciousness polarized into pairs of opposites: good/bad, right/wrong, arrogance/insecurity. We all have a tendency to play out one side of a polarity while keeping the other side hidden in the unconscious. I played out self-importance and was unconscious, until my teacher's comment, of my feelings of worthlessness. Some people do just the opposite. They play out worthlessness and are unconscious of their egotism. It is possible to recognize, embrace, and reconcile polarized states of mind. It is ultimately possible to find the underlying unity inherent in all of the pairs of opposites within us. To move beyond duality into unity is to become enlightened.

My teacher had spoken at length about the reconciliation of opposites and how polarities intertwine in our awareness field to create the ego. "You must clear all your egoic patterns in order to become enlightened: Final clearance sale—everything goes!" he told us, but he never gave his students processing techniques with which to tackle the problem. Maybe, if you've been enlightened in hundreds of past lives, you don't need techniques to wake up in this one.

I didn't think the resume of my past lives was quite that stellar. When my teacher passed away in 1998, I was still wrestling with my arrogance and a fair amount of emotional baggage, as well, and I set out in search of help. I found three enlightened women.

Leslie Temple-Thurston[64] had developed processing techniques for reconciling polarities through a system called The Marriage of Spirit. Gangaji[65] and Pamela Wilson[66] advocated self-inquiry as taught by Ramana Maharshi, an Indian sage who taught Advaita, or *not two*. My teacher's school of hard knocks had focused on warrior skills, an arena where emotions were always supposed to be kept under control. These female teachers, who investigated polarities held in the emotional body, made me weep with relief. They welcomed and accepted me just the way I was, emotional baggage and all.

Now in Bretton Woods, using the processing techniques I had learned, I relived my conversation with Anders. He had said that I lacked humility. *Who does he think he is to throw my teacher's recorded words at me? How arrogant can he be?*

I stopped myself mid-complaint and gritted my teeth. Slowly, painfully, I took the finger I was pointing at Anders, turned it around, and pointed it at myself.

How am I arrogant?

That was the important question. I had to be honest. I had projected my own arrogance onto Anders. Anders was a mirror. I had simply seen my own ego reflected back to me.

Tears filled my eyes. I sat in the ballroom of the Mt. Washington Hotel and embraced each of my pent-up, previously unconscious emotions.

My arrogance had actually been triggered before my conversation with Anders. It went back to Scotland. My ego interpreted Scotland as an important success that I had achieved. How stupid was that? I'd had nothing to do with the success in Scotland! The mystical work of the Bilderbergers had been undone only because I had moved my personal ego aside in order to let Spirit come through my heart and do the work; but my ego had taken credit and had grown, unchecked, during the subsequent two months.

I shivered. The vibration of arrogance that had ensnared my attention gradually lifted. I sighed and looked around me. Suddenly I was able to register the Mt. Washington Hotel ballroom. I could see the beautiful mountain range outside the window, and, on the mystical planes, I could see a sort of energetic grid. Like on a giant computerized map in a military war room, lines ran out in all directions, connecting the World Bank with hundreds of dots. What are these dots…the countries that the World Bank loaned money?

The Fed

The following day I traveled to Jekyll Island, Georgia, birthplace of the Federal Reserve System. As soon as I arrived, a wave of excitement enveloped me. I knew that mystical work had been done on the island. I didn't yet know what it was, but I was determined to find out.

It was a sunny afternoon. October in the deep south was surprisingly hot, and I stripped down to the tank top under my blouse as I stood on the manicured, emerald green lawn of the Jekyll Island Club and scrutinized the grand white façade. During its heyday it had hosted many of the nation's most influential financiers, industrialists, and politicians. Now the Jekyll Island Club was a private hotel, and I had a room on the top floor.

I walked under a shade tree, settled into one of the white wooden lawn chairs, and leaned back. What had the place been like in the early 1900s? I tried to visualize it.

From 1886 until 1942, the Jekyll Island Club had been a private hunting resort for the nation's elite families. Founded by a group of millionaires who'd bought the entire island, it was a closed social unit with a strictly limited membership. Members included families like the Rockefellers, the Vanderbilts, the Pulitzers, and the Goodyears, as well as J. P. Morgan, one of the most influential bankers in history.[67] Morgan's private bank, J. P. Morgan & Company, was so powerful that the US government solicited its help in the depression of 1895 and the financial crisis of 1907. He also dominated two other industries: He helped consolidate the railroad industry in the East and formed the United States Steel Corporation, which became the world's largest steel manufacturer.[68]

The Jekyll Island Club members built lavish homes that they referred to as cottages. Wives moved to the island with the children after the Christmas holidays each year to escape the winter weather in the cities farther north. Husbands visited as their schedules permitted.

The clubhouse, with its wide, wraparound porches, was the central attraction. The first floor contained a formal dining room, where the chefs and waiters had been recruited from New York City's best restaurants. In the evening the millionaires dined together and discussed business deals. After dinner they adjourned to the smoking room or played billiards. Upstairs were guest rooms for people who had been invited to visit the club.

Highly secretive meetings to formulate the Federal Reserve had been held exactly ninety-two years before my visit. J. P. Morgan had arranged for seven men to use the off-season clubhouse in October, 1910. They began by carefully crafting the name Federal Reserve System. *Federal* implied that it was part of the US government. *Reserve* suggested that it had large reserves of cash or gold. *System* diverted the attention away from the fact that it was privately owned.[69] The deceptive name, coupled with underhanded political and legal maneuvers over the next three years, enabled this small group of bankers to achieve a financial coup.[70]

Earlier attempts to impose central banking in the United States had been repelled by Presidents Madison, Jefferson, Jackson, Van Buren, and particularly Lincoln, whose writings revealed a deep understanding of banking.[71] President Woodrow Wilson, who signed the Federal Reserve Act of 1913 into law, later deeply regretted his decision, confessing that the American banking system was now dominated by a small group of men.[72]

The seven attendees represented an incestuous web of the largest banking concerns in the United States and Europe.[73] If there had been any question in my mind as to whether the descendents of the goldsmiths were alive and well, G. Edward Griffin, in his six-hundred-page book on the Federal Reserve, had dispelled it:

> "Centralization of control over financial resources was far advanced by 1910. In the United States, there were two main focal points of this control: the Morgan group and the Rockefeller group. Within each orbit was a maze of commercial banks, acceptance banks, and investment firms. In Europe, the same process had proceeded even further and had coalesced into the Rothschild group and the Warburg group."[74]

Together, they represented one-fourth of the world's wealth![75]

The bankers joined forces on Jekyll Island with a common business objective: reduce competition, decrease risk, and increase profits. What emerged was the banking cartel of the United States, an entity that would eliminate competition from newer and smaller banks; get control of the reserves of all the banks so the more reckless ones wouldn't be exposed to bank runs and currency drains (when a bank cannot meet its obligations to another bank); obtain a franchise to create fictitious money for lending; and secure a license to print dollars so it could artificially expand the money supply in order to ensure that taxpayers would absorb the cartel's banking losses through inflation.[76]

As a privately held moneymaking concern, the owners of what's become known as "The Fed" have pursued the aggregation of as much private and government debt, with interest, as possible.[77] What has the scorecard of the Federal Reserve been through the years? The dollar has fallen in value more than 95% since its inception.[78] As US Representative Ron Paul states, "From the Great Depression, to the stagflation of the seventies, to the burst of the dotcom bubble in 2001, every economic downturn suffered by the country over the last eighty years can be traced to Federal Reserve policy."[79]

The first central bank, the Bank of England, was established in 1694. Since that time, the wealth of nation after nation has been harnessed by central banks.[80] Today the Federal Reserve is merely one component of a global network of central banks.

President Bill Clinton's mentor, Dr. Carroll Quigley, a prominent historian and professor of history at the Foreign Service School of Georgetown University, summarized the strategy of those behind the global banking system:

> "The powers of financial capitalism had [a] far reaching aim, nothing less than to create a world system of financial control in private hands able to dominate the political system of each country and the economy of the world as a whole. This system was to be controlled in a feudalist fashion by the central banks of the world acting in concert, by secret agreements, arrived at in frequent private meetings and conferences.

The apex of the system was the Bank for International Settlements in Basle, Switzerland, a private bank owned and controlled by the worlds' central banks, which were themselves private corporations....[81] It must not be felt that these heads of the world's chief central banks were substantive powers in world finance. They were not. Rather, they were technicians and agents of the dominant investment bankers of their own countries, who had raised them up and were perfectly capable of throwing them down. The substantive financial powers of the world were in the hands of investment bankers...who remained largely behind the scenes in their own unincorporated private banks. These formed a system of international cooperation and national dominance which was more private, more powerful, and more secret than that of their agents in the central banks."[82]

I rose from my lawn chair. Despite the fact that my body had grown stiff with sitting and peering into the past, a sense of excitement bubbled up inside me. Somehow the experiences that awaited me at the Jekyll Island Clubhouse, where the secret Federal Reserve meetings had taken place, were going to help me feel more deeply into the pockets of the supremely wealthy, the international investment bankers.

Asking Nature for Help

I strolled down the path to the tram station where the island tour started. The place evoked a sense of elegant Southern ease. It rose from the earth, came up through my feet, and made me sway a little as I walked, like a Southern belle in a hoop skirt. The giant live oaks, with their sweeping boughs, expressed it, too, as their wispy strands of gray moss swayed in the breeze.

The little tram wound its way through the millionaire cottages as its driver regaled us with the history of Jekyll Island. When we passed the oldest tree, his tinny-sounding voice crackled over the loudspeaker.

"If trees could talk, just imagine the stories that tree could tell!"

I looked from the driver to the tree. *Why not?* If the driver was open to the concept of a talking tree, why shouldn't I be? It might be worth further investigation.

At the completion of the tour, I explored the ground floor of the Clubhouse hotel. In one hallway I discovered a brass plaque: *The Federal Reserve Room.*

Well, the meetings may have been secret in 1910, but they aren't now.

I eased the door open and peered in. The polished wood floor gleamed in the shafts of sunlight coming through the western windows. It was a fair-sized room with wood paneling. It looked masculine. It appeared to be a sort of shrine, with portraits of the seven men who had attended the meetings.

I entered and read excerpts from the memoirs of each, exhibited beside his picture. After a few minutes, my mind felt distorted, like an out-of-focus camera lens. I tossed my head back and forth, trying to throw off the sinister feeling coming from the pictures. Everywhere I encountered the energy of the global elite, it was always the same—the colonial fort in South Africa, the rock island in Scotland, the Washington Monument in DC, and now here.

I left the Federal Reserve Room and took a brisk walk around the hotel to clear my head. Then I had afternoon tea and scones in the dining room. Fueled with caffeine, I tripped off to see the oldest tree on the island.

It was a live oak. I read the plaque at its base. *Three hundred and fifty years old!* I backed up and gave the massive tree a thorough inspection. It felt dignified and serene...and distinctly masculine. Its enormous trunk, its majestic limbs, the undulating moss... *Gorgeous!*

I remembered my teacher saying that the key to understanding nature was to admire it. "That's all things in nature want, really—just to be admired, to be appreciated. Nature is not something to conquer but to learn from. Everything has consciousness."

I smiled. *You are so beautiful,* I said telepathically to the tree. *Wow...unbelievably beautiful!*

"Why don't you come up and sit so we can have a talk," the tree said in a deep, resonant voice.

I froze. *Was that my imagination?* I had always been a lover of nature, but I had never had a tree talk to me. Celeste crossed my mind. I had observed her communicating with the animals in South Africa.

Perhaps I should maintain an open mind. I stopped my thoughts and remained absolutely still.

After a few moments, I heard the voice again. This time it contained a hint of amusement. *"Come up, if you like."*

I took a deep breath and approached the trunk. It was about five feet up to the cradle where the gigantic limbs extended out in all directions. I found a couple of handholds and boosted myself up. *I'm not as good at this as I once was,* I told it telepathically.

"You seem pretty agile to me," replied the tree.

I found a wide hollow in a limb and seated myself comfortably. A man and his wife approached, looking first at the tree, then at me. I smiled, nodded, and tried to convey the impression that everything was perfectly normal. Once they departed, the conversation began in earnest.

I can't get over it, I began. *You are so beautiful. Magnificent!*

"Thank you," the tree replied.

You must be very wise at this point. You've lived a long time.

"I've seen my share," it said.

I paused. *What were the people like who lived on Jekyll Island at the turn of the century? All of the wealthy families?*

"Good people, many of them. Good hearts. Some were very ruthless."

I nodded. *Do you remember the seven men who came to create the Federal Reserve System?*

"I remember them well."

What were they up to on a mystical level?

The tree was silent.

You're going to hold out on me? I asked.

"No, but you have to work a little for the information. You need to still your mind in order to see it."

I closed my eyes for a few moments. My attention was drawn down into the Earth. Slowly the image of a channel running north and south appeared. Energy circuited through it much like electrical current circuits through an electrical line. The land around the line was empowered. It vibrated at a higher frequency. *There's an energetic line here, right?*

"*Correct,*" it replied. "*There's a line under the island that extends up through Washington DC and New York City. Why do you think they bought this island?*"

My eyes opened wide. *Of course.*

"*Lines aren't good. Lines aren't bad,*" the tree told me. "*They just are. They bought the island in order to take control of the line. They coated it with their own sort of energy, used it for their own purposes. J. P. Morgan was well aware of the impact that energy would have on the political and financial sectors farther north.*" There was a pause, and then the tree continued. "*I stand on the very middle of the line. Why do you think I'm so old and wise and beautiful?*"

I chuckled. *I see.*

We were both silent for a moment.

"*The lines are there for anyone to use,*" the tree said pointedly. "*They belong to Mother Earth, but anyone can use them. Do you understand?*"

I let this soak in a moment. *Yes, I understand.* I bowed. *Thank you. You've been most helpful, my beautiful friend.*

"*My pleasure, my beautiful friend.*"

I went to my room. My conversation with the tree had convinced me that the line needed to be cleared, that whatever energy the Jekyll Island crowd had laced it with needed to be eradicated. It was one thing to tap into an energetic line in the Earth and use it for spiritual evolution. It was another thing to harness its energy as a way of forcing your agenda on others in a game of power.

Sitting on my bed that evening, I petitioned my teacher and the Lineage to assist me in clearing the line. I quieted my mind, moved my personal ego out of the way as I had done in Turnberry, and asked Spirit to come through me and do the work.

Upon entering the mystical plane, I saw that the line was coated with a black, gooey substance. I concentrated all my attention on it, but I suddenly grew hopelessly tired, and it was impossible to stay awake. *Oh, well,* I thought, *I'll do it in the morning.*

In my meditation the next morning, when I focused on the line,

I immediately started dozing. I wanted to clear the line, but I was so sleepy.

Although I felt depleted, I toured the Rockefeller cottage later in the morning. In the afternoon, the regularly scheduled tour of the Jekyll Island Club Hotel was cancelled. I drifted outside, onto the porch, and drooped into a high-backed wicker chair. My body felt weak. It had been that way since attempting to work on the energetic line. Why? I strained to recall something my teacher had said.

"There are three things that indicate a lower mystical attack," he'd explained on numerous occasions. "Either you become really tired, or you become depressed and start having strange thoughts, or you become nauseated. In each case, the symptoms appear suddenly."

The first time he spoke about it, I was skeptical. "I occasionally experience one of these symptoms," I told him, "but I've never been aware of anyone attacking me in another dimension."

"It doesn't matter if you're aware of it or not," he told me, shaking his head. "It happens. Never underestimate people. People have a lot of evolution. They may have acquired mystical skills in other lifetimes, and when your mystical body executes a maneuver, your conscious mind isn't necessarily involved. They may deny doing anything, and they're right—from the vantage point of their conscious mind—but their mystical body knows exactly what it's doing. So, in answer to your question, just because you are unaware of someone attacking you doesn't mean it doesn't happen. That's why you need to learn to see. Never be afraid of people. There's no need to be paranoid, but be street smart. The world is a tough place, and your naiveté isn't going to protect you."

Now I stood up and walked down the steps to the lawn. Someone didn't want me to proceed; there was no other explanation for the sudden fatigue. Who, then? Someone connected with the banking industry? Who would be tracking my movements? Who would not want this line to be cleared?

At 6:00 P.M. I returned to my room, sat on my bed to meditate on the line, and was again overcome with fatigue. I surrendered, turned on the television, and watched the news. A movie came on. I called for room service; I couldn't make it to the dining room. When the movie finished, I switched off the television.

What's the use? It's impossible to do this.

I lay down on the bed, curled up on my side, and stared blankly at the wall. Was the line even relevant to my spiritual assignment? Maybe my conversation with the tree had just been in my imagination. Maybe I was feeling arrogant again. But my psychic perception about mystical foul play on the island had been so strong when I arrived. I glanced at the clock. It was 10:00 P.M. I had to get up early in order to make it to the airport on time.

I can't believe I've failed like this when my mission seemed so clear. I sighed and closed my eyes.

"Sit up and meditate."

My eyes sprang open. It had been my teacher's voice. I continued to lie there, listening, not breathing.

"Sit up and meditate," he repeated.

I propped myself up in bed against my pillows.

"Intend the act of blowing this energy line clean," he commanded.

The Lineage immediately came into focus above me. I struggled to compose a prayer to invoke their help.

"Don't pray," he snapped, *"just do it!"*

All right, all right! I replied, summoning all of my will power.

Just as in Scotland, energy descended from above, passing through the Lineage and entering my being, but this energy did not circuit through my heart. It was more like the pure power of intention pouring through all of my chakras at once. Concentrating my will, I focused on the line with unbending intensity and watched, amazed, at what was happening in the mystical realms. The line writhed, shook, and convulsed like a snake until finally the black began to peel away.

After ten minutes, when exhaustion threatened to overcome me again, I appealed to the trees on the island. Speaking to the oldest tree first, then to all of the trees—the oaks, the pines and the other varieties whose roots extended down toward the line and drew strength from it—I called for help. I could see them with astonishing clarity. An entire army of trees answered the call, dignified but militant. In one deep, unified voice they intoned, *"We stand ready!"*

As we all struggled together, the reverberations shook the line from Jekyll Island to Washington DC. When the work was finally done—when all of the black gunk was gone—I had used every ounce of will I possessed. I thanked the trees, collapsed, and immediately fell asleep.

The East Coast Line

The next morning, while eating a quick breakfast in the dining room, I took stock of what I had learned over the past week.

During my entire trip—Jekyll Island, the two Bilderberg hotels, the sites in DC, New York, and Bretton Woods—I had been traveling up and down the energetic line. *It must start at Jekyll Island, or maybe even somewhere south of the island, then run all the way up the East Coast.* In my mind's eye I could see that the line had been cleared from Jekyll Island to Washington DC. I could also see that more work needed to be done in order to clear the energy of the line as it extended north.

In addition, I had been introduced to something new with regard to clearing energy. My experience on Jekyll Island had differed from that in Scotland in one significant way: the type of energy that had come through me. In Scotland the energy was gentle and caring. The previous night it had been fiercely transformational. In each instance I had merely opened my being and volunteered to be of service to Spirit, so I could only assume that Spirit had taken a different form, the form that was appropriate for each situation.

There were still many puzzle pieces that I needed to assemble and put into place, but I felt proud of my work with the energetic line and with my reconciliation of the arrogance/insecurity polarity. I had also learned that I could communicate with trees, that I could call on Nature for help with my task!

When I finished breakfast, I checked out of the hotel and rolled my suitcase down the hall toward the exit. I hesitated at the Federal Reserve Room. Turning, I swung the door open and confronted the portraits. The urge was irresistible. I thumbed my nose.

7

ONE WORLD GOVERNMENT

My field trips—first to Scotland, then to the East Coast—had increased my appetite for spiritual sleuthing. I was definitely making progress, assembling clues in the mystery of the energetic structure underlying the Patriarchy, but I still couldn't see the connection between the Bilderbergers and the bankers, if indeed there was one. I was disappointed that I'd had no psychic perceptions at the two Bilderberg conference hotels on the East Coast, but perhaps that was because the group—formed by the royal families of Europe—didn't do mystical work in the United States. Was it beneath their dignity? Was it not necessary? Did they reserve their mystical work for their own continent? The Sherlock Holmes inside of me sensed a mystery: The Case of the Bilderbergers.

It was November. In December I could travel to Europe and find out. What better way to wrap up six months of research? I asked Anders if he would like to join me. Sleuthing took a toll—physically, emotionally and psychically—and Anders' lighthearted approach to life always made me laugh. He would bolster me. I offered to pay his expenses if he would watch my back while I talked to trees and freed rocks. The idea of spending his Christmas recess in Europe couldn't have pleased him more. He loved traveling almost as much as he loved meditating, and this trip would provide the opportunity to indulge in both, so it was agreed.

I splurged on a large suitcase and began debating what to take. I knew it was early to start packing, but a month's worth of bulky winter clothes, research material, and organic snacks for two people required serious planning. Anders, the military strategist, insisted a good first-aid kit was essential. I argued that my research journals took precedence.

"Do you think I should take my cocky pants?" he asked one evening when we were discussing the trip.

"What?" I responded. Anders spoke fluent English, albeit with a thick Norwegian accent, but he sometimes confused words. This time I was puzzled.

He repeated his question more slowly. "I said, do you think I should take my cocky pants?"

Suddenly the light dawned. "Oh!" I smiled. "You mean your *khaki* pants?"

He thought about it a moment, then smiled sheepishly. "Right, right...my *khakis.*"

"Yeah," I told him, "I think you ought to take them."

He nodded.

"But take your cocky ones, too," I added. "You may need them."

Propaganda

During November, when I was not scheduling our travel (or packing), I read. I had already studied how the global elite rewrote history and controlled education; but now, having grown wiser through my research, I knew that it went deeper than that.

We have had freedom of the press in the United States. Thousands of books are available that present information not covered in school. Why do so few people investigate alternative views? Why do so few people know about the Bilderbergers? Why do most people sneer when you say that corporations own the government and dismiss it as conspiracy theory, as though it were fantasy?

I wanted to examine how the educational system related to the media and how the media's depiction of today's public policy became the rewritten history in tomorrow's textbooks. Somehow, it was all interrelated. My curiosity led me to propaganda as a method of control.

Throughout patriarchal times, the ruling class has developed ways to control the so-called ignorant masses. In totalitarian states, they simply use force, but with the upsurge of modern democracy in the seventeenth century, the ruling class faced an interesting challenge: How do you control people in a democracy? How do you retain the façade of freedom while manipulating the masses towards your own self-serving ends? Their solution was propaganda.[83]

Propaganda is defined as the deliberate, systematic attempt to shape perceptions, manipulate cognitions, and direct behavior of people to achieve a response that furthers the desired intent of the propagandist.[84] The word *propaganda* originated in 1622 when the Catholic church founded the *Congregatio de Propaganda Fide* (Congregation for Spreading the Faith) for the propagation of Christianity by missionaries.[85]

Prior to plunging into my research, I had largely identified propaganda with the political practices of oppressive regimes such as Hitler's Germany, Communist China, and the Soviet Union, but I discovered that the United States government has also had a definitive history with propaganda.

President Woodrow Wilson was the first to use propaganda on a large scale. He was elected president in 1916, in the midst of World War I, by promising "Peace Without Victory," a platform that appealed to Americans who saw no reason to enter a European war. Once in the White House, however, Wilson did an about-face and had to devise a way to garner public support for getting involved. In 1917 he created a Committee on Public Information (CPI), the first American propaganda agency.

The CPI used a variety of methods to influence the public, including journalism, commercial art, entertainment, advertising, and even school essay contests. Within six months it turned a pacifist population into a war-hungry, patriotic force ready to save the world.[86] Oddly, the effectiveness of American propaganda was later an inspiration to Hitler, who referred to its success in *Mein Kampf.*

Following the First World War, in the 1920s, a number of propaganda pundits emerged in the United States.[87] Edward

Bernays, the nephew of Sigmund Freud, published *Propaganda*, a public relations manual detailing how to manipulate the habits and opinions of the masses, something he believed to be the essence of the democratic process. He felt the "intelligent minorities" had the right to "regiment the public mind every bit as much as an army regiments the bodies of its soldiers" by making use of propaganda "continuously and systematically."[88] Walter Lippmann, the influential American journalist, argued that a properly functioning democracy has two classes of citizens: a specialized class—those who analyze, make decisions, and run things in the political, economic, and ideological systems—and "the bewildered herd."[89]

I felt my jaw sag. Here it was again: men of the global elite declaring with blatant arrogance that they had a right to manipulate people to their own ends. I was horrified, but politicians and corporate leaders of the day apparently had no such reaction. They absorbed the information in these PR/propaganda manuals and eagerly began putting their newfound knowledge to work.

For example, as part of a PR campaign created for his client, the American Tobacco Company, Bernays paid ten debutantes to walk down Fifth Avenue in New York smoking Lucky Strike "torches of freedom" while the already alerted media took their pictures. This event marked the first time women had smoked freely in public, and, during the days that followed, women were seen smoking on the streets all across the nation. Lucky Strikes went on to become the fastest growing brand in the country, and it wasn't until much later that the stunt was traced back to Bernays and American Tobacco[90].

Another example occurred during the 1930s when labor unions went on strike. Corporate leaders fought back with a PR campaign.[91] They systematically promoted the concept that there are normal, hardworking Americans (the industrious father going to work with his lunch pail, the devoted mother taking care of the home, the happy banker looking for someone in need of a loan, and the benevolent corporate leader working for his community) and, on the other hand, those out-of-control labor unions (striking workers aligned with Communism, bent on tearing apart the fabric of society). I could clearly remember my father, who was exposed to that campaign while growing up in the 1930s, railing against labor unions when I was growing up in the 1950s. Now I understood how his views had been molded and how propagandized views got handed down from one generation to the next.

In the years that followed, this us-against-them attitude continued to permeate television shows, films, print media, and advertising. The result was that everyone began focusing on themselves and their own families. Their mantras became "every man for himself" and "me first." [92] It didn't matter if the people down the street had healthcare or not.

Through the years, as Capital Hill evolved into a government of, by, and for corporations, political PR and corporate PR worked hand in hand. Increasingly sophisticated corporate advertising transformed citizens into consumers. The government was pleased. If people were isolated in their own homes watching television or out at the shopping malls consuming, they weren't interfering with politics. When they did focus on political issues, increasingly sophisticated political PR was broadcasting a frightening message about "The Red Scare of Communism." It was enough to drive people back to the safety of sitcoms.

As Communism waned, during the late 1980s, the government began to hype its "War on Drugs," but this new war failed to be sufficiently menacing. They needed a more immediate threat, a "new Pearl Harbor," as the Project for the New American Century (whose signatories include Dick Cheney, Donald Rumsfeld, Paul Wolfowitz, Scooter Libby, and others of the Bush administration) blatantly admitted.[93] After 9/11, they struck gold with the "War on Terror," a war that could never end until every terrorist in the world had been thwarted.

I evaluated the effectiveness of the War on Terror PR by checking Wikipedia, the online encyclopedia. It detailed no less than thirty different flavors of propaganda: meaningless slogans, suppression of facts, repetition, intentional vagueness, oversimplification, glittering generalities, patriotic flag-waving, encouraging people to jump on the bandwagon....[94] I went down the list. Meaningless slogans: Bumper stickers encourage us to "Support our Troops" in order to distract us from a meaningful investigation of whether or not we should support our country's policy of preemptive war. Suppression of facts: The fact that The Islamic Militant Network—the forerunner of Al Qaeda—was created by the CIA is not discussed.[95] Repetition: "Iraq has weapons of mass destruction" was chanted so often that, despite well-circulated evidence to the contrary, half of the population still believes it is true.[96]

It appeared that the PR machine had improved with age. It now pumped out propaganda through news reports, government reports, historical revision, junk science, books, leaflets, movies, radio, television, and posters.[97] The size of the current PR industry made my head spin. A billion dollars was being spent each year in the United States to ensure that those who owned the country could govern without dissent.[98]

So what about television? Wasn't it created as a public servant? What about investigating both sides of a story? Weren't journalists free to write whatever they wanted? The answer in many cases is yes, but the majority of journalists, like the rest of us, have been schooled and propagandized by the global elite. They are products of the system. They wouldn't be hired for high-paying media jobs if they weren't. Most journalists do indeed write freely about the system—within the limits of their perception.[99] Others who attempt to investigate and reveal a deeper level of the truth are either dismissed or kept in line by propagandized bosses. Occasionally a truth-seeking journalist breaks rank and joins the alternative media.

The problems with media go beyond limited journalism. The major media are large corporate entities, owned by multinationals. As such, they are happy to march to the beat of the globalization drum. Additionally, media corporations sell advertising to the corporate world. Why should they bite the hand that feeds them? Last, the elite factions of the media, such as the *New York Times*, cater to a relatively privileged audience and slant their news accordingly. Small fry media simply follow their lead. So much for freedom of the press.

As J. Liebling, an American journalist, said, "Freedom of the press is guaranteed only to those who own one."[100]

It all began to make sense to me. The Carnegie Endowment set out to control education in the 1920s. They knew that few people actually double-check what they learn at school. They were aware that disinformation would be repeated over and over—by students, by teachers, by parents—constantly reinforcing the idea that the disinformation was really a well-known fact, even though no one could point to an authoritative source. They knew that the disinformation would be recycled through the media and then right back into the educational system and that this would occur without the need for direct governmental intervention. The system was a self-perpetuating loop of carefully crafted propaganda that kept the herd bewildered—so bewildered that it never occurred to most of us to inquire beyond textbooks and the evening news.

In fact, our society appears to have exceeded Lippman's idea of a properly functioning democracy with a permanently bewildered herd. The American propaganda campaign was so successful that the entire nation would swear that we have no propaganda. "Propaganda? Ridiculous!" people would say. "We have freedom of speech. We have the Bill of Rights."

In my heart, I now knew that simply wasn't true. Thanks to our well-oiled propaganda machine, we had become totally controlled.

I winced. My teacher would have called this what it is: lower mysticism. These men were manipulating energies, using money and influence to control people, and propaganda was just one small facet of their system. They had global institutions. They owned central banks. They sat on the boards of each other's multinational corporations. They used revolving doors between government and business. They conferred at Bilderberger meetings. It appeared that they would not be satisfied until there was One World Government.

No, I corrected myself, *that name is outdated.* When the so-called ignorant masses had started to catch on, the PR machine had spit out a new name: the *New World Order.*

The Mystical Structure

My research was nearing an end. I stood in my office with the late afternoon sun pouring through the window onto my bookshelf like a spotlight. I dusted off the shelves, then stored all my books in a neat row. An unexpected wave of awe passed through me. These authors had completely changed my understanding of the world. In Europe I would round out the left-brain, intellectual knowledge I had gained during these months of research with right-brain, psychic perceptions at Bilderberg hotels and institutions like the WTO. Maybe after absorbing both types of knowledge I would be able to identify the underlying mystical structure of the Patriarchy that I had been asked to take apart.

I had returned to the idea of the mystical structure again and again over the past months. After each phase of research, I would stop and ask myself, *Now, do I possess enough knowledge to delve behind the physical constructs of the Patriarchy and identify the underlying energetic structure?* The answer was always *no.* I knew I was looking for a structure, some sort of architecture made up of energy, but no pictures coalesced in my mind. Was it hierarchical? Was it some sort of network of intertwining energies? I still had no idea. My mind was awash with facts—so much miscellaneous data—that I simply could not see the big picture.

I scanned the bookshelf. One book caught my eye, and I pulled it down. It contained a section on the Illuminati. The Illuminati was another secret organization, long shrouded in mystery.

One theme that had surfaced repeatedly during my research was the idea that those who seek to rule the world are members of a present-day Illuminati, a term which in Latin means *enlightened ones.* Illuminati concepts can be traced back in history, but the Illuminati were first publicly identified as a group in 1776, when Adam Weishaupt, a professor of canon law at Ingelstaad University in Germany, formed the Bavarian Illuminati.[101] Weishaupt's writings reflected the same elitist, power-obsessed views as the men I had been sensing behind the scenes:

"Do you realize sufficiently what it means to rule—to rule in a secret society? Not only over the lesser or more important of the populace, but over the best men, over men of all ranks, nations, and religions, to rule without external force, to unite them indissolubly, to breathe one spirit and soul into them, men distributed over all parts of the world?"[102]

Weishaupt devised a pyramid structure comprised of degrees, his key personnel being located within the top nine. Through his chain of command, he was able to wield power and effect change:

"I have two immediately below me into whom I breathe my whole spirit, and each of these two has again two others, and so on. In this way I can set a thousand men in motion and on fire in the simplest manner, and in this way one must impart orders and operate on politics."[103]

I froze. The book tipped flat in my hands as I had a clear flash of intuition: the One World Government was being built, step-by-step, using esoteric Illuminati principals passed down through history. The man in the South Pacific...I had seen that he had two male secretaries. Was the man in the South Pacific the head of the present-day Illuminati? If so, what did that mean with regard to the underlying mystical structure? Was it something like Weishaupt's pyramid?

How Close Are They?

As our departure date grew near, my excitement about traveling to Europe turned into agitation. I very much wanted the trip to be a success. The Lineage had instructed me to use the time between the summer and winter solstices to research what was going on in the world, then identify the underlying mystical structure. Now the winter solstice was just around the corner. I wanted to identify the structure, but I'd still only had glimpses of the elusive powers behind the Patriarchy. How much time did I have left to figure it out?

The evening before our departure, I sat in my tidied office, staring blankly out of the window. *One World Government.* The phrase kept running through my mind. *Perhaps, if I could understand more clearly the mindset of those creating this world government, I would be one step closer to knowing the underlying structure.*

Actually, I could see nothing inherently wrong with a world government. If one worldwide government were presided over by benevolent, spiritually oriented leaders, it could be a positive development. Wasn't a peaceful world, where all nations respected each other and lived together in harmony, what most of us wanted? There was nothing wrong with a world government, but one had to look behind the *concept* and consider the *intention* of those administrating it. Of course if the intention was the complete subjugation of the world's population to satisfy the arrogant desires of feudalistic rulers obsessed with power…well, that was another matter.

"One world government," I whispered aloud.

What kind of person would come up with a scheme for enslaving the entire world?

Of course I had already discovered the answer: someone who was arrogant and obsessed with power. I had direct experience with both of those characteristics. I understood arrogance. Since childhood, I had been programmed for success, believing myself destined to be a star. I also understood obsession with power. I had at times, during my mystical training, become obsessed with power and the thrill of wielding it for my own gain.

A sick feeling crawled inside my stomach. I understood these men better than I cared to admit. I stood up and began walking aimlessly through the house. I was getting warm, warmer than ever before. I gritted my teeth and forced myself to investigate more deeply.

What did I feel like when I was arrogant? When I was feeling arrogant, I was convinced I was right. I took a rigid stance and held it. I expected others to conform to my version of the truth. More important, I didn't realize that I was being arrogant. I often didn't realize it until someone pointed it out—like Anders telling me I lacked humility. It had been the same when I was obsessed with power. I didn't know I was obsessed. My teacher had pointed it out and had coached me back to a more balanced state of mind.

I shook my head. *Of course! These men don't know they are arrogant and obsessed with power!* I had been assuming their intentions were malevolent, that they were evil men who wanted absolute control, but that wasn't the way they saw it at all. They were seeing the world through the glasses of arrogance and power. In their minds, they were *entitled* to rule the world. In their minds, they would be doing the world a service. In their minds, the world was filled with ignorant masses that would benefit from a world government run by elites.

I headed back for my office. My mind felt like it had turned inside out. I had been standing on the outside of the Patriarchy, judging the intentions of these men! In order to understand them, in order to see the underlying mystical structure of their system, I needed to put myself in their shoes.

Rounding the corner of my office, I walked to my whiteboard, picked up a marker, and stared at the shiny surface. Then I asked myself a question I had never considered asking:

If I wanted to rule the world, what would I need?

The answers poured out effortlessly, as a jumble of research facts suddenly ordered themselves like a Rubik's cube clicking into place:

1. World Unions—Hundreds of nation-states around the world will be a pain to rule. I need to simplify things. I need to create a handful of super-national unions that will combine all of the nation-states. I already have a European Union; I'll expand NAFTA into an American Union and then work towards an African and a Pacific Union. Four unions will certainly be easier to rule than nation-states, each with its own president or dictator.

2. Resources—I'll need control of all natural resources. Do I have that? I'm not sure. This merits further consideration.

3. Goods and Services—I have a network of corporations and multinationals. I won't need the World Trade Organization anymore. There won't be anyone left to oppose me.

4. Workforce—I'll need to have a productive workforce to keep

things running, a labor pool composed of young, strong workers. I can pare down the population. The elderly will be useless—an unnecessary waste of food. Conveniently, the Rockefeller Foundation has studied eugenics for years, so I'll have all of the knowledge at my fingertips and will simply have to implement a few extermination processes. These are worker bees, after all—a dime a dozen. Do they even have souls, these worker bees? Probably not.

5. Workforce Tracking—I will need to track and control my workers. Why not use a centralized computer system? I can expand my Homeland Security database to include data on workers around the world. Maybe if I implant microchips in everyone, it will simplify matters.

6. One Currency—It will make my life easier if all monetary transactions occur in a single currency and if I can eliminate paper money and just issue debit cards. Lucky me! I have a network of central banks and control of the global banking system.

7. Police—I'll need to police the workers. I can implement a standing army of NATO or UN peacekeeping forces.

8. Subordinates—I will need a dependable management team, men "into whom I breathe my whole spirit" in order to "set a thousand men in motion and on fire." I can draw on the ranks of trusted royal families, politicians, and CEOs.

9. Mind control—As the victor, I'll be entitled to rewrite history. I have everything I need to accomplish that: an educational system, a public relations industry, and the global media. Perfect! Textbooks will extol the way I saved the world, brought peace in troubled times, and ruled with calm efficiency.

I replaced the marker in the whiteboard tray, backed up, and sat down, my burst of energy dampened by the cruel reality of what I had written. I scanned the list, considered the state of the world, and shook my head.

They are close, very close.

By Their Own Admission

Later that night of December 13, 2002, I gathered my research journals and tucked them into the suitcase alongside the first-aid kit. We were boarding a plane the next day, setting off to take psychic snapshots of One-World-Government locations. Was it really possible? Could these men really pull off a coup and institute a world government?

The answer, I believed, was yes. I knew it from my research, and I knew it from the speeches I had read, passages from over the decades that had slipped through the cracks of a sellout-media blackout, unsettling quotes that hinted at the truth. Throughout the night I tossed and turned in my sleep as they advanced through my dreams in succession, each searing itself on my mind like a brand:

1913—Woodrow Wilson (US President): "Since I entered politics, I have chiefly had men's views confided to me privately. Some of the biggest men in the United States, in the field of commerce and manufacture, are afraid of something. They know that there is a power somewhere so organized, so subtle, so watchful, so interlocked, so complete, so pervasive, that they better not speak above their breath when they speak in condemnation of it."[104]

1922—John F. Hylan (Mayor of New York City): "The real menace of our republic is this invisible government which like a giant octopus sprawls its slimy length over city, state and nation. Like the octopus of real life, it operates under cover of a self-created screen.... At the head of this octopus are the Rockefeller Standard Oil interests and a small group of powerful banking houses generally referred to as international bankers. The little coterie of powerful international bankers virtually runs the United States government for their own selfish purposes. They practically control both political parties."[105]

1928—Edward Bernays (author, architect of modern propaganda techniques): "We are governed, our minds are molded, our tastes formed, our ideas suggested, largely by men we have never heard of...who understand the mental processes and social patterns of the masses. It is they who pull the wires which control the public mind, and who harness social forces and contrive new ways to bind and guide the world."[106]

1933—Franklin D. Roosevelt (US President): "The real truth of the matter is, as you and I know, that a financial element in the large centers has owned the government of the US since the days of Andrew Jackson."[107]

1936—Joseph Kennedy (father of US President John F. Kennedy): "Fifty men have run America, and that's a high figure."[108]

1950—James Paul Warburg (part of the Warburg banking family, CFR Chairman 1921-1932, participant in the Federal Reserve meetings on Jekyll Island): "We shall have World Government, whether or not we like it. The only question is whether World Government will be achieved by conquest or consent."[109]

1953—John Swinton (Chief of Staff, *The New York Times*): "There is no such thing, at this date of the world's history in America, as an independent press. You know it and I know it. There is not one of you who dare to write your honest opinions, and if you did, you know beforehand that it would never appear in print.... We are the tools and vassals of rich men behind the scenes. We are the jumping jacks. They pull the strings and we dance."[110]

1961—Edith Kermit Roosevelt (columnist and granddaughter of US President Franklin D. Roosevelt): "The word 'Establishment' is a general term for the power elite in international finance, business, the professions and government, largely from the northeast, who wield most of the power regardless of who is in the White House. Most people are unaware of the existence of this 'legitimate Mafia.' Yet the power of the Establishment makes itself felt from the professor who seeks a foundation grant, to the candidate for a cabinet post or State Department job. It affects the nation's policies in almost every area.... What is the Establishment's view point? Through the Roosevelt, Truman, Eisenhower and Kennedy administrations its ideology is constant: that the best way to fight Communism is by a One World Socialist State governed by 'experts' like themselves. The result has been policies which favor the growth of the superstate, the gradual surrender of United States sovereignty...."[111]

1962—Nelson Rockefeller (Governor of New York State, Vice President select under US President Gerald R. Ford): "[There is] a new and free order struggling to be born.... The nation-state is becoming less and less competent to perform its international political tasks.... These are some of the reasons pressing us to lead vigorously toward the true building of a New World Order."[112]

1964—General Douglas MacArthur (Commander of Allied Forces in the Southwest Pacific during World War II): "I am concerned for the security of our great nation; not so much because of any threat from without, but because of the insidious forces working from within."[113]

1966—Dr. Carroll Quigley (historian, professor at Georgetown University): "There does exist, and has existed for a generation, an international anglophile network which operates, to some extent, in the way the radical Right believes the Communists act. In fact, this network...has no aversion to cooperating with the Communists, or any other groups, and frequently does so. I know of the operations of this network because I have studied it for twenty years and was permitted for two years, in the early 1960s, to examine its papers and secret records. I have no aversion to it or to most of its aims and have, for much of my life, been close to it and to many of its instruments. I have objected, both in the past and recently, to a few of its policies...but in general, my chief difference of opinion is that it wishes to remain unknown, and I believe its role in history is significant enough to be known."[114]

1970—Curtis Dall (Son-in-law of US President Franklin D. Roosevelt): "The Depression was the calculated 'shearing' of the public by the World Money powers, triggered by the planned sudden shortage of supply of call money in the New York money market.... The One World Government leaders and their ever close bankers have now acquired full control of the money and credit machinery of the US via the creation of the privately owned Federal Reserve Bank."[115]

1970—Baron Edmund de Rothschild (grandson of Mayer Anschel Rothschild, head of the House of Rothschild): "Western Europe is going to form a political union. The structure that has to disappear, the lock that has to be burst, is the nation."[116]

1971—John Rarick (US Congressman from Louisiana): "The Council on Foreign Relations is 'the establishment.' Not only does it have influence and power in key decision-making positions at the highest levels of government to apply pressure from above, but it also announces and uses individuals and groups to bring pressure from below, to justify the high level decisions for converting the US from a sovereign Constitutional Republic into a servile member state of a one-world dictatorship."[117]

1972—Richard M. Nixon (US President): "There must be a thoroughgoing reform of the world monetary system.... For its part, I can assure you, the United States will continue to rise to its world responsibilities, joining with other nations to create and participate in a modern world economic order."[118]

1974—Richard N. Gardner (US Ambassador to Spain, State Department functionary, and Columbia University Professor of Law and International Organization): "In short, the house of world order will have to be built from the bottom up rather than from the top down. It will look like a great booming, buzzing confusion...but an end run around national sovereignty, eroding it piece by piece, will accomplish much more than the old-fashioned frontal assault."[119]

1976—Larry P. McDonald (US Congressman from Georgia): "The drive of the Rockefellers and their allies is to create a One World Government combining super-capitalism and Communism under the same tent, all under their control.... Do I mean conspiracy? Yes I do. I am convinced there is such a plot, international in scope, generations old in planning, and incredibly evil in intent."[120]

1990—Mikhail Gorbachev (President of the Soviet Union): "A New World Order is taking shape so fast that governments as well as private citizens find it difficult just to absorb the gallop of events...."[121]

1991—George Bush (US President): "We have before us the opportunity to forge for ourselves and for future generations a New World Order, a world where the rule of law, not the rule of the jungle, governs the conduct of nations.... When we are successful—and we will be—we have a real chance at this New World Order, an order in which a credible United Nations can use its peacekeeping role to fulfill the promise and vision of the UN's founders."[122]

1991—Dr. Henry Kissinger (US Secretary of State, Chairman of Kissinger Associates, Inc. consulting firm): "Today, America would be outraged if UN troops entered Los Angeles to restore order. Tomorrow they will be grateful! This is especially true if they were told that there were an outside threat from beyond, whether real or 'promulgated,' that threatened our very existence. It is then that all peoples of the world will plead to deliver them from this evil. The one thing every man fears is the unknown. When presented with this 'scenario,' individual rights will be willingly relinquished for the guarantee of their well-being granted to them by the World Government."[123]

1991—David Rockefeller (Son of John D. Rockefeller, Jr., chairman of the Chase Manhattan Bank, member of CFR, founder of the Trilateral Commission): "We are grateful to *The Washington Post, The New York Times, Time Magazine* and other great publications whose directors have attended our [Trilateral Commission] meetings and respected their promises of discretion for almost forty years. It would have been impossible for us to develop our plan for the world, if we had been subject to the bright lights of publicity during those years. But, the work is now much more sophisticated and prepared to march towards a world government. The supranational sovereignty of an intellectual elite and world bankers is surely preferable to the national auto-determination practiced in past centuries."[124]

1994—David Rockefeller: "This present window of opportunity, during which a truly peaceful and interdependent world order might be built, will not be open for too long…. We are on the verge of a global transformation. All we need is the right major crisis and the nations will accept the New World Order."[125]

1994—Government of Morocco full-page advertisement in the *New York Times*: "The Final Act of the Uruguay Round, marking the conclusion of the most ambitious trade negotiation of our century, will give birth—in Morocco—to the World Trade Organization, the third pillar of the New World Order, along with the United Nations and the [World Bank/]International Monetary Fund."[126]

1996—Walter Cronkite (news anchorperson): "If we are to avoid catastrophe, a system of world order—preferably a system of world government—is mandatory. The proud nations someday will…yield up their precious sovereignty."[127]

1997—Bill Clinton (US President): "There are a lot of very brilliant people who believe that the nation-state is fast becoming a relic of the past."[128]

2000—Project for a New American Century (Washington-based think tank founded by US Vice President Dick Cheney, Defense Secretary Donald Rumsfeld, and Defense Policy Board chairman Richard Perle): "The process of transformation, even if it brings revolutionary change, is likely to be a long one, absent some catastrophic and catalyzing event—like a new Pearl Harbor."[129]

2001—Gary Hart (US Senator from Colorado): "There is a chance for the President of the United States to use this [9/11] disaster to carry out…a New World Order."[130]

2002—David Rockefeller: "For more than a century, ideological extremists at either end of the political spectrum have seized upon well-publicized incidents, such as my encounter with Castro, to attack the Rockefeller family for the inordinate influence they claim we wield over American political and economic institutions. Some even believe we are part of a secret cabal working against the best interests of the United States, characterizing my family and me as 'internationalists' and of conspiring with others around the world to build a more integrated global political and economic structure—one world, if you will. If that is the charge, I stand guilty, and I am proud of it."[131]

I had no problem with the idea of creating a new order for the world. The world, sadly, needed one…but not one governed from the South Pacific.

Boarding the plane the next day, I knew that things had gone too far. Too many political and social structures were in place. It would be impossible to turn the tide of events in the physical world. The solution lay in the mystical realms.

8
TRACKING THE BILDERBERGERS

As Anders and I stood in the ticket line, waiting for our first-class, one-month Eurail passes to be validated, I took in the Copenhagen station: the mighty trains queued up on their tracks, the babble of multiple languages, the fluttering sound of the mechanical arrival/departure board updating trains, tracks, and times. I was no longer in the good old US of A and a wave of excitement enveloped me.

On the way to our train, Anders purchased a supply of Scandinavian candy. We found our track, wrestled our suitcase into our train compartment, and settled into our seats. The rumbling train lurched forward, then groaned its way out of the station.

I smiled as I gazed out the window and listened to the methodical clicking of the train wheels against the tracks. The adventure was beginning. Before it was over, we would pass through nine countries and visit seven hotels that had hosted Bilderberg conferences over the past decade. If I managed to disconnect that much of their mystical web of ideas, what would happen?

The circumstances at the first Bilderberg hotel we visited were almost identical to those at the hotel in Scotland. The Bilderberg mystic had woven a mystical web of ideas, then anchored it to a rock, using an energetic line. By aligning myself with the Lineage and with Spirit, I was able to facilitate the dissolution of the line and free the rock. While I didn't learn anything new, the experience made me confident that I was onto their lower mystical devices and more practiced in my higher mystical method of undoing them.

My experience at the second Bilderberg hotel yielded more in-depth insights. It was on Stenungsaund Island, off of the west coast of Sweden. Soon after we arrived, Anders and I took a long walk around the island. Despite her gentle beauty—her smooth, flat rocks that sloped down to the caress of the water, her evergreen trees with patches of snow nestled in their shadows—I sensed a strange depression underfoot. She felt like a radiantly powerful woman in her prime, garbed in the bedraggled funeral dress of someone twice her age.

I told Anders I would like to pause for awhile, then strode to the water's edge and sat down. The presence of the Lineage above as well as the power of the Earth below was unmistakable.

When I asked for permission to clear the Bilderberg mischief, energy descended, collected momentarily in my heart chakra, then moved down through my feet into the island; but this time I wasn't sitting in a dining room, viewing an island beyond the Scottish coastline. I was sitting on the very rock the Bilderbergers had used! *Stenungsaund* translates as *rock*. Rock Island. They had placed an entire, populated island in bondage!

The heart energy merging with the island set off a huge explosion in the mystical realms. *Boom! Boom!* With each explosion, the island heaved a great energetic shudder. I felt like an acupuncture needle, as one shockwave after another rose through me. My first experiences of doing energetic work had, by comparison, been like watching TV. Now I found myself in the middle of a battlefield. Finally, just as my body was on the verge of collapse, the explosions climaxed, and the island below my feet broke apart into infinitesimal particles of ecstatic consciousness. Suddenly the island began to dance in celebration.

I took Anders' arm to steady myself, and we walked back toward the hotel. I was exhausted. As I shambled along the path, I wondered why the Bilderbergers had met so many times in Sweden. The group had held conferences in Stockholm three times—in the sixties, seventies, and eighties—then came to Stenungsaund Island in 2001. Meeting four times in one country didn't follow their normal pattern.

I stopped dead in my tracks, seeing clearly what had happened. A mystic living in Stockholm hadn't fancied the Bilderbergers defiling his city. Three times they'd met in Stockholm, and three times he'd unhooked their energetic lines. But Sweden was important to them, the key to Scandinavia. In the end the Bilderbergers resorted to holding a fourth conference, this time on Stenungsaund Island in a three-star hotel where, under normal circumstances, they would never have met. They hoped to establish a line that wouldn't be noticed. Evidently they had succeeded.

Until now.

All at once I felt as though someone had plunged a knife into my stomach. If the Bilderberg mystic could see the disconnected Stockholm lines, he would see my work, as well. How many times had my teacher told his students, "Never underestimate your opponent?"

"Is everything all right?" Anders asked.

I nodded, took a long, deep breath, and resumed walking. I had to be careful, very careful. The last thing I wanted was a confrontation with the Bilderberg mystic on the inner planes.

First Meeting Place of the Bilderbergers

From Stenungsaund we journeyed by train to the Hotel de Bilderberg in Oosterbeek, Netherlands. For the mystic, beginnings and endings are important, and the Hotel de Bilderberg was the first place the Bilderbergers had met.

I trembled with anticipation as the taxi dropped us off. If I was going to peer more deeply into the inner workings of the Bilderbergers, this was where it would happen.

It was evening, and the hotel looked like a cozy Dutch inn, only larger. Turn-of-the-century gas lamps illuminated the perimeter. Quaint cut-glass windows adorned the ground floor, and its white wooden exterior was complemented by a two-story Christmas tree trimmed with white ornaments.

Inside, the décor was modern and tasteful. When we got to our room, I poked around in the antique Dutch writing desk and the white marble bathroom, giggling to myself like a young girl. For the past five months, I had scoured books and Internet articles for the tiniest tidbit about the Bilderbergers. Now the name of this highly secretive group was plastered everywhere. We had Bilderberg stationery, Bilderberg pens, Bilderberg hand lotion, and Bilderberg soap.

Anders said he had a stomach virus (although numerous bags of Scandinavian candy had suspiciously disappeared), so he stayed in bed and ordered soup through room service. I checked on him periodically but had most of my time to myself. I swam in the pool, took long walks along rhododendron hedges, and finished the book I was reading. No mystical work had been done on the grounds, so I was able to rest for a couple of days and steep myself in the beginning-energy of the hotel. On the evening before our departure, I asked my teacher to help me perceive the inner workings of the Bilderbergers, and he obliged. The doors of perception flew wide open.

The Royal Strategy of One World Government

During my research I had repeatedly come across the fact that European royalty created the Bilderberger group—that Prince Bernhard of the Dutch royal family had formed it in 1954. I had also read that the Dutch and the British royal families had a close friendship and that Prince Bernhard often visited Queen Elizabeth II of England. Now my psychic perception was that Queen Elizabeth and the Bilderberg mystic actually invented the Bilderberg concept. The Queen, perhaps preferring to remain in the shadows, had used Prince Bernhard as her front man.

Some authors speculated that Prince Charles, the heir to the British throne, was being groomed to head the One World Government.[132] Looking into the psychic planes, however, I saw that the Prince was only one of several candidates for this prominent post. Charles was being groomed and *nominated* by his mother, Queen Elizabeth. She was using him, the rightful heir to the British throne, as a pawn in a chess game of power.

There were a number of groups that desired world government; royalty was only one. Certainly, international bankers were another group. Power-hungry politicians, corporate CEOs... All the groups considered their contribution to the New World Order of vital importance, and all believed that someone from their group should head the world government when it finally came to power. The groups frequently had power struggles. When necessary, they worked together to cross a hurdle in the race toward world government, but only because each lusted after ultimate control.

The royals were undoubtedly practicing superb gamesmanship on the global chessboard. Each year they used the Bilderberger conference to rub shoulders with the most prominent bankers, politicians, businesspeople, educators, media owners, and military leaders from around the world. They promoted their ideas, exerted their influence, and took the pulse of the other groups. At the end of the conference, they revised their plan for world domination—with someone of royal blood as the ultimate ruler, of course—then used mysticism to weave their web of energetic concepts in an alternate dimension. Over time those concepts would manifest as reality in the physical world, and hovering over their base of power in Europe, the web continually expanded.

I had underestimated the Bilderbergers. The royals wielded tremendous power in the world while operating almost completely behind the scenes and the most influential player, aside from the Bilderberg mystic, was Queen Elizabeth.

The Queen came from a long line of powerful monarchs. Her ancestors had amassed the British Empire, once the largest empire in history. Their maritime explorations in the fifteenth century resulted in numerous colonies, and by 1921 they ruled almost a quarter of the world's population.[133]

Great Britain was now depicted as a second-rate power and the Queen as merely a figurehead, but I psychically perceived that the British royals had never really renounced their goal of world domination. They were willing to endure the current perception that they were second-rate as long as they could head the world government of the future. This meant that they had to find a covert way to manipulate the domestic and foreign policy of the United States—the most powerful country of the day—to their own ends.

Their first method of attaining this goal was a mystical one. To that end, they employed the Washington Monument. The Bilderbergers didn't need to weave their mystical web above their meeting places in the United States or Canada. It was more effective to connect their European web to the energetic line that ran up the East Coast, then use the Washington Monument, which sits on the line, as their broadcasting tower. The distorted energy I had experienced in Washington DC was due not only to the bankers who had usurped the line, but to the Bilderbergers.

Their second method was to affect American policy through the Council on Foreign Relations. The British citizen who made that possible was Cecil Rhodes. During the late 1800s, Rhodes became enormously wealthy as the result of his diamond and gold prospecting in South Africa.[134] In 1890, Queen Victoria, Queen Elizabeth's great-great-grandmother, named him prime minister of Africa's Cape Colony, the place where I had my first immersion in patriarchal energy. Soon after, he began forming semi-secret Round Table groups. Each was a maze of corporations, institutions, banks, and educational establishments. Each had an inner circle called the Circle of Initiates and an outer circle called the Association of Helpers.[135] In his writings, Rhodes' called for "the establishment, promotion and development of a secret society, the true aim and object whereof shall be the extension of British rule throughout the world…[to include] the ultimate recovery of the United States of America."[136]

By the end of World War I, the Round Table system had become so extended that the Royal Institute of International Affairs was created in London as an umbrella organization, and substantial contributions began coming in from organizations associated with Andrew Carnegie, J.P. Morgan, and the Rockefellers.[137] When I had researched the Council on Foreign Relations, I had read that the Royal Institute was its *sister* organization. Now my psychic perception was that the CFR actually falls *under the umbrella* of the Royal Institute. Rhodes' mission had been accomplished. The United States had been "recovered" by Great Britain by using the Royal Institute to control

American policy, via the CFR.

So, European royalty led by the Queen of England, operating through the Bilderberg group, the Round Table, and the Royal Institute of International Affairs, had covertly gained control of the United States, the military heavyweight of the world—not an insignificant move in the New World Order game of chess! Celeste had said that she sensed a group running things, and it was not the US government. Perhaps it was the Bilderbergers. Perhaps that was why I had been drawn to visit Bilderberger hotels and disassemble their energetic work.

I had a picture of Prince Charles in one of my books in the suitcase, and I found a postcard of the Dutch royal family in the hotel gift shop. Placing them side by side, I studied the eyes. It was difficult to do a psychic reading. They seemed multi-layered. All at once I smiled. Of course! As royals, they had been trained since birth to project a certain image. They possessed varied layers of psyche but wore an exterior mask. It was not unlike one of my teacher's concepts, something he had called the "caretaker personality."

Spiritual Teachings on the Impeccable Warrior

In the early eighties my teacher began talking about the caretaker personality of the impeccable warrior, a subject that was so important that he was still talking about it the last time we saw him in 1998. A caretaker personality was a uniform we wore, only it involved more than clothing. It was a sort of personality that we could put on or take off.

"You are formless," he explained. "You are made up of pure Light. But in the early stages of self-discovery, you can't expect to balance your formlessness with your daily activities. You need a personal form to deal with the world. I suggest the caretaker personality of the *warrior.*

"You need to understand that you are affected by everything in your environment more than you realize. You may not see the effects physically, but things affect you psychically. They affect your spiritual development. The warrior pays attention to *everything.* Even the minutest things affect us, and we pay attention to them."

Following our teacher's instruction, we took on the arduous task of scrutinizing every aspect of our lives. To begin, we weeded, pruned, and manicured our physical environments. The places we lived—our bases of power—were of supreme importance. We brought our homes into perfect order. We got rid of anything we didn't need. Our closets were organized, our paperwork was caught up, and we always had fresh flowers.

The next step involved doing a careful analysis of our lives. If our careers weren't in order, we fixed them. If they weren't the right careers, we changed them. Then we examined our relationships to ensure they were healthy, happy, and progressive. As the years passed, we progressed to addressing more subtle aspects of our lives: mental laziness, attachment to emotions, personal ideas and beliefs, and polarized states of mind.

The goal was to become what my teacher liked to call *impeccable*—an *impeccable warrior*—a term he borrowed from the writings of Carlos Castaneda.[138] The impeccable warrior was calm, unemotional, and efficient. She possessed courage, cunning, and discipline. She developed humility, and she learned to be impeccable as a way of advancing herself spiritually.

The trick was not to be rigid about it. The order needed to grow out of the balanced awareness of meditation, not an inherent inflexibility. Initially I found this challenging.

"You're so anal-retentive!" my teacher teased.

I went to the library, found a Freudian psychology book, and studied the anal-retentive personality trait. The next time I saw him I told him that, after reading about it, I agreed with his assessment.

He broke into peals of laughter. "Well, you didn't need to bother looking it up," he said . "If you wanted to know the meaning of anal-retentive, all you had to do was look in the mirror!"

As our study progressed, he explained the more sophisticated aspects of the warrior. One involved maintaining a keen awareness at all times. We learned to remain composed, stand back from life, and always scan for danger—danger in the form of physical violence as well as danger in the mystical realms. If we found ourselves in a problematic situation, he advised, "Never underestimate your opponent. The day you do is the day you lose the battle. Respect your opponent, but always know that you can win if you're clever, if you have enough power, and if you learn the art of patience." To develop the trait of keen awareness, he suggested we study martial arts.

Another advanced aspect of the warrior was *inaccessibility*, a term also coined by Castaneda.[139] This trait required humility. It was the art of blending in and moving through life quietly.

"Most people who stand out in a crowd," my teacher explained, "do so because they are fixated in their egos. You may think it's nice to be the center of attention, but when you stand out, people focus on you. And whenever someone focuses on you, they direct a vibratory force toward you on a subtle physical level. When people dislike you or are envious of you, that emotion touches you and damages your subtle physical body. When the subtle physical body gets damaged, your energy leaks out. When it becomes damaged enough, you die.

"Never be afraid of people, though. A warrior isn't afraid, but a warrior has street smarts. Be aware that this is the way the world works, and be intelligent about it. By remaining inaccessible, you insulate yourself. Instead of losing energy, you retain your energy and can use it to move into higher states of consciousness."

The warrior's strategy of bringing her physical life into perfect order was executed with one sole purpose in mind: to let go of it. "Creating order in the physical," my teacher said, "frees you from the physical. It allows you to access more of what lies beyond the physical. The more impeccable you become, the farther you can hurl yourself into the Light of Spirit. As warriors, we hurl ourselves into the Light again and again until we become the Light itself."

The next two Bilderberger hotels Anders and I visited taught me valuable lessons about the price a warrior pays by failing to be impeccable, keenly aware, and inaccessible. At the second hotel, I was the one paying the price.

The Bilderberg Mystic Is Not Impeccable

When we arrived at the Chateau du Lac in Genval, Belgium, I knew something was seriously amiss. The first indicator was the hotel staff. They were automatons. The doorman, the bellman, the clerks at the check-in desk—everyone executed his or her job in a mechanical stupor. Just entering the lobby was like walking into a science fiction movie.

I didn't know quite what to do, so Anders and I decided that an exploratory walk around the lake was our best bet. While we realized that the zombie zone might envelop the whole area, we also felt that I certainly wasn't going to be able to hoist my psychic antenna inside the hotel. We hastily stowed our luggage in our room, returned to the lobby, and then walked back outside.

After a few hundred yards, I turned around and studied the hotel, a crème-colored castle with a red tiled roof and medieval turrets. It had been built on generous acreage with a small lake as its centerpiece. All of the Bilderberger hotels had felt distorted—their energy was fuzzy and out of kilter, with a dark vibration—and the energy of the Chateau was all of those things, but it also seemed violent. It had a sort of payback feeling, as though someone had gotten angry and hurled a huge lightning bolt, and everything still vibrated with the violence of its impact.

The poor staff had been steeped in the hotel's dark energy since the departure of the Bilderbergers in 2000. On an intellectual level, they were oblivious to the effect it was having on them. On a psychic level, they had shut down in an effort to defend themselves. Every day, their state of mind deteriorated a little more. After two years they had become robotic. I wondered if it was possible to fix the problem.

We walked slowly along the gravel pathway that flanked the water. The lake felt dead. I didn't feel great, myself. The violent energy muddled my mind and jammed my third eye. I couldn't think, and I couldn't see.

Halfway around I became exasperated, glared at the hotel on the other side of the lake, and felt like a bull preparing to charge. Fighting to control my agitation, I made my way to the edge of the water and focused on the lake instead.

I felt so sorry for her. Water is normally bubbling with emotion, but there was no feeling whatsoever.

I asked the Lineage to intervene. Energy immediately began flowing through my heart and into the lake. Miraculously, my third eye began to feel open and receptive, and I was able to quiet my frustration. Lifting my eyes, I gazed steadily at the hotel and, gradually, I was shown what had transpired.

The Bilderberg mystic had sent his trusted scout to evaluate the Chateau du Lac. As a prospective meeting place, it had to be a suitable five-star location and have the right mystical properties. The scout had approved the hotel, and the conference had taken place. The Bilderberg mystic had arrived at the end, as was his custom, but there was no rock there. How was he supposed to anchor his web of ideas? He had become infuriated—with the scout, with the hotel, with the conference, and with the lost opportunity. In his rage he had cursed the resort.

Usually the Bilderberg mystic was impeccable: calm, efficient, cunning, and disciplined. Usually he was inaccessible—doing his mystical work quietly, behind the scenes, so no one would notice. This time he blundered. He allowed his emotions to spiral out of control. His ego took over. Someone was going to pay, and he didn't care who saw his curse in the mystical realms.

His curse had left a faint trace of energy, a mystical imprint. Now the face of the Bilderberg mystic appeared superimposed over the hotel.

I suddenly stopped breathing. I recognized that face.

It's the man in the South Pacific!

My body went numb. The only thing I could feel was my heart heaving in my chest. If the Bilderberg mystic was the man in the South Pacific, I had pitted myself against a more sophisticated opponent than I had imagined.

I took a couple of deep breaths to steady myself, then shook my head in confusion. What did this mean? Was the man in the South Pacific royalty? I had assumed he was an international financier. Was he so powerful that he played multiple roles in the One World Government game? I was at a complete loss.

I waited a few minutes until I felt calm again. Then I asked the Lineage to lift the curse on the Chateau du Lac. I pushed aside my concerns about the man in the South Pacific, stilled my mind, and let the Lineage do their job.

When the work was complete, Anders and I returned to our room and slept soundly. By the next morning when we awoke, the energy at the hotel was crystal clear; and as the first rays of sunlight sparkled on her water, the lake was vibrant.

I Am Not Impeccable

The second hotel we visited, in my ongoing lesson about impeccability, was the Royal Hotel in Evian-les-Bains, France, the home of Evian mineral water. We arrived by boat across Lake Geneva, then hiked up the hill, passing numerous hotels, restaurants, and tourist shops, until we approached the Royal.

We paused some distance away so I could gaze at it, and I was startled. In the mystical realms, an undulating wave of energy flowed across its modern exterior and the surrounding grounds.

The Bilderberg snake!

In Scotland I had been sitting inside the hotel when my teacher had pointed it out. Now I was seeing it from a distance. Like clockwork, the Bilderberg energy undulated about once every half minute.

After we walked onto the hotel grounds, I could sense that the man in the South Pacific had attached his web of energy to a rock inside the mountain, a rock that had a fissure through which the hot Evian mineral water flowed. In doing so, he had laced the roots of tall fir trees with his malevolence. He was so uncaring! My heart went out to the majestic firs.

I tried to channel energy into the rock, the hotel, the grounds, and the trees. I stilled my thoughts and focused my attention, just as I had done at other hotels. But then the Bilderberger snake would undulate across the grounds. Its distortion would pass through my awareness field, break my concentration, and send my mind careening off into a convoluted train of thoughts.

It happened again and again. The more it happened, the angrier

I became. Rain drizzled on us, and I was getting cold, but no matter how hard I concentrated, the snake outmaneuvered me. My irritation grew. I cursed at the Bilderberg mystic and his damned snake, and I was less than pleased with Anders, who kept looking from his watch to the boat schedule and then glaring at me.

I shut my eyes tight and absolutely refused to be beaten.

You have no right to use this mountain for your malevolent purposes, I said inwardly, as though the Bilderberger energy could hear me, *and you definitely have no right to interfere with my meditation!*

A half minute passed. The snake undulated again.

That's it!

My teacher had taught his students a defensive technique—something I called the energetic hand grenade—to be used when we were under severe lower mystical attack. I decided to employ it. I focused on the Bilderberg snake, using all my will power. I visualized hand grenade after hand grenade hitting the length of its body and blowing the snake to bits. And I kept it up—one minute, two minutes—straining to hold my concentration.

I paused and waited. Nothing moved. Two minutes passed, and still, everything was quiet. I opened my eyes. To my immense relief, instead of drizzle, it was raining gold light. The Bilderberg energy was eradicated. The trees felt happy, the mountain felt happy, and the Earth felt ecstatic.

I nodded to Anders. "We're done here."

He rolled his eyes, checked his watch, grabbed my arm, and hustled me down the mountain. We arrived at the pier just in time to board the boat.

"Anders," I said, reaching for him, "I'm dizzy."

He put his arm around my waist to steady me. Stooping over slightly, he searched my face. "What's wrong?" he asked.

"I don't know. My equilibrium is off. I can hardly walk."

Anders helped me to a wooden bench on the deck of the boat as it pulled away from the dock. The upper part of my head had a frenetic energy running through it. My sense of balance was so disturbed that I feared I might fall off of the bench.

"I've got to close my eyes," I whispered.

As soon as I did so, I had the clear psychic perception of a man and a woman yelling at each other. The image was so clear that I might have been standing in the room with them. They were in the midst of a heated argument.

"You are completely and utterly inept!" the man shouted.

"Me?" the woman retorted with indignation. *"You were the one who was supposed to take care of it!"*

"You bitch!" he raged. *"How dare you accuse me...?"*

I was horrified. I recognized the woman. It was Queen Elizabeth. And I had a sick feeling about the man. I opened my eyes. I must have looked like I had seen a ghost.

Anders stared at me. "What is it?"

"I believe..." I paused to swallow, "that there are two Bilderbergers who have seen that their mystical work is being unraveled. I don't think...." I faltered and bit my lip. "I don't think that they have identified me." I shook my head forcefully. "Damn! I attracted their attention when I got angry and used explosive energy. I let my ego and my personal desire take over, instead of allowing Spirit to do the work. How stupid could I be? I was completely un-impeccable!"

"Do you know who they are?"

"One is Queen Elizabeth, and the other," I said, lowering my voice, "is the man in the South Pacific."

Now Anders bit his lip. "You're sure? Not Prince Bernhard? He founded the Bilderbergers."

I stared absently at the wooden deck below my feet, feeling out the possibility, hoping that he might be right, praying that I hadn't really attracted the attention of the man in the South Pacific. Finally, I sighed.

"No, Prince Bernhard is not that good a mystic. I don't think he could see this on the mystical planes." I looked at Anders. "I remember reading somewhere that Queen Elizabeth's servant said there is only one person the Queen is afraid of. It's a man. I think the person she's afraid of is the man in the South Pacific. I'm sure they are the ones who know. They don't know who I am yet, but now they will be watching, scanning the mystical planes, trying to find me."

9
TAKING A BREAK FROM
THE BILDERBERGERS

My teacher had said, "In order to be inaccessible, you need to break up your routines. Human beings are creatures of habit. It's very easy to stalk a person once you learn their routines. A moving target is harder to hit."

Now I took his advice to heart as never before. I decided to break up my routine of visiting Bilderberg hotels. Fortunately I had a Eurail pass that allowed me to be on the move constantly. Some of the world's most powerful organizations were in Europe. I wanted to visit them so that my mystical body could fully log their energy.

For the next ten days, Anders and I hit one patriarchal hotspot after another—NATO, the World Court, EU buildings, central banks, the royal residences of the Netherlands, Belgium, and Liechtenstein—where I tapped into the arrogance and power-obsession of the people behind them. While each of them taught me something, my most important psychic observations occurred at the WTO, the UN, and the Bank for International Settlements.

The World Trade Organization

Anders and I checked into a hotel on the Rue de Lausanne in Geneva, home to the WTO and the UN, and I opened the double French doors onto our third-floor balcony and walked outside. The World Trade Organization building was visible through the trees across the street.

I leaned on the ornate balcony railing and released a deep sigh. I was dead tired. Perhaps the traveling was taking a toll.

Anders, who had always yearned to see the samurai swords at the Collections Baur Museum, headed off for the bus stop, leaving me solo for the morning. I took a shower, hoping it would give me a boost of energy, then left the hotel and walked across the street to the entrance of the WTO.

The massive black iron gate was wide open, and I surveyed the long, gray, four-story building with its row upon row of windows. Two enormous bronze statues flanked the front entrance. There was no guardhouse. Could one just walk in?

Slowly I picked my way down the long cobblestone driveway to the wide front steps leading to the entrance. I hesitated. From this close vantage point, the bronze statues were gigantic, and the double oak doors looked impossibly heavy.

You haven't come all the way to Europe to be timid, I told myself. *Just open the door.* But I stood motionless on the steps, my pulse quickening.

A car clattered down the drive behind me, jolting me out of my deliberations. Placing my hand on the oversized door, I pushed hard.

I wasn't sure exactly what I had expected from the lobby of the world's most exalted center of trade, but this certainly wasn't it. Inside the anteroom, an elderly guard was seated in a highly polished wooden booth, reading a newspaper. He wore an official navy-blue uniform, but it looked as though it had seen better days. He finished his paragraph before looking up.

"Do you speak English?" I asked.

"Yes," he said quietly, with what sounded like a German accent.

"Is it all right to walk around the grounds?"

He nodded. "There is a nice walkway in the back by Lake Geneva, madam. It's a popular spot." He turned back to his newspaper article.

"Ah, thank you."

When I rounded the corner of the building, I was pleasantly surprised. The trees had no leaves at that time of the year, but the lawn was a vibrant green, decorated with artfully placed bronze statuary. I ambled along the sidewalk, which an earlier rain had left dotted with puddles, until I found a bench overlooking the lake and sat down. A couple strolled past, walking a well-mannered Scottish terrier.

The lake looked clean and crisp in the morning light, but I was preoccupied. Why was I so tired? I could barely walk. Was I under mystical attack? No. The fatigue had not come on suddenly. It had been building steadily since my arrival in Geneva. I leaned back and closed my eyes.

After a long rest, I turned to look at the grounds. Two enormous fir trees loomed in the distance. One of them had a queenly air, with long, graceful boughs that swept the ground. She was taller than all the other trees and even the WTO building. Her reign by the shores of Lake Geneva had doubtless begun long before the WTO was built.

I walked over to her, stooped under the low-hanging branches, and placed my hand on her trunk. The feeling she exuded—deep, wise, and majestic—was almost enough to make me forget my fatigue.

What a stately being you are, I told her telepathically. I luxuriated in her still beauty. Then, after a few moments, I ventured a question. *Is there anything you can share with me about this place?*

There was a long pause. When she finally responded, her words were simple.

"Stop them."

My eyes opened wide. Her candor made me catch my breath. I didn't know how to respond. Finally I said, *"I'm trying to do just that."*

"We've heard about you...," she told me, the cadence of her words slow and unperturbed.

I scowled and took a step backward. Was that the tree talking or my ego? If there was one thing I didn't need on this trip, it was a bout with arrogance. I straightened myself, stopped my thoughts, and waited.

"...from the trees on Jekyll Island," she continued, seemingly oblivious to my turmoil. *"We have a network. We communicate...*

through the water that comes into our roots and from the whispering of the wind. We know that you are working on our behalf, and we're willing to help you in any way we can."

My heart softened. *I appreciate your offer. If you'd allow me to, I'd like to tap into your consciousness when I'm back in the United States. You stand here as a silent witness to everything that happens. May I contact you inwardly in the future so I can monitor what is going on?*

"Yes," she replied. "I'd be honored."

I hesitated, then decided to put the question to her one more time. *Is there anything else you can share with me about this place?*

There was another long pause. I stood at attention, listening intently. I thought perhaps the conversation was over, but then she spoke.

"Stop them...before they destroy everything."

Upon hearing her words, what little energy was left in my body drained out. Her answer was so direct, so final. A feeling of hopelessness consumed me. Was the situation that desperate? Was there so little time left? Perhaps this tree saw the world situation with a clarity I didn't. What was it exactly that she perceived?

I dragged myself back to the hotel, deep in thought. I had researched the WTO but had never stopped to really feel the extent of the destruction inflicted by the corporate world. The environmental degradation was overwhelming: air pollution, acid rain, chemical fertilizers, pesticides, soil erosion, strip-mining, deforestation, oil spills, sewage sludge, industrial waste.... As I walked down the block, the dismal list trailed on and on in my mind. But that was just the beginning, just the damage to Mother Earth. Pollution affected plants, animals, and humans. Multinationals bulldozed their way through countries, leaving behind them endangered species, chronic health effects, premature deaths, deformed babies.... And what about the destruction within the very souls of the people, people used only as tools in a game of profit? How was it possible to stop this power-hungry global elite?

In the hotel bar I ordered a double espresso from the bartender, then seated myself at a small table by the window so I could see the

WTO across the street. The coffee gave me a boost and cleared my head. I observed the building for some time. Finally a pattern emerged. Over and over, a sheet of dark, hazy energy cascaded off of the building, and I became enveloped by fatigue, which I then struggled to throw off. The fatigue was not caused by our travels. It was caused by the energy of the World Trade Organization!

One of my teacher's mystical secrets popped into my mind: "When you throw a stone into a lake, it creates two ripples. Everyone knows about the first ripple. It moves from the stone to the shore. Mystics know about the second. It moves from the shore back to the center of the lake. Always look for the second ripple."

At the time my teacher said it, I hadn't really understood. Now I stopped my thoughts and held perfectly still, like a rabbit observing its predator, waiting for it to make a move.

The first half of the mystical formula became clear. The World Trade Organization—a stone thrown into the lake, an organization that exerted influence on the world—created a ripple going out. It was a mixture of distortion and fatigue in an alternate dimension, as though some sinister force was whispering, "Consume! Surrender to the lure of worldly possessions. There Is No Alternative." The corporate PR campaigns I had read about had this lower mystical energy running through them, and it was being felt, whether consciously or unconsciously, by every human who was subjected to advertising.

The second part of the formula, the ripple that comes from the shore back to the center of the lake, was the end result of the WTO's activities. It felt something like a pulling type of energy.

I paused to get a better sense of it, locked onto it in the mystical planes, and felt my hand go to my heart. The corporate world, using the WTO to break down global trade barriers, was pulling in money. The second ripple, the one my teacher had said that mystics should look for, expressed the true motives of the corporate world. It was greed...pure, unadulterated greed.

The United Nations

Anders joined me in the bar for a late lunch of sandwiches.

Afterward, when we had settled the check, he said, "On my way back to the hotel, I spotted a public laundry down the block. I thought I might do our laundry if you can get along without me for a while."

"How lovely!" I exclaimed. "Just be sure not to mix the lights and the darks." I knew from watching Anders do his laundry at home that this was a distinct possibility. "Do you want me to come up to the room with you and separate the clothes?"

"No, no," he said impatiently, heading for the door. "It'll be fine."

"Are you sure?" I asked, but he was already out of earshot.

The Palais des Nations, the European branch of the UN, was several blocks beyond the World Trade Organization. I set out hoping that lunch would fortify me, but the WTO excreted endless waves of fatiguing energy. I trudged along, stopping often to rest.

Once I turned off of the congested Rue de Lausanne and entered the UN complex, the streets were quiet. I checked my map frequently, not wanting to waste energy on a wrong turn.

At last I reached the iron gate at the main building. It was locked, the UN deserted for holiday recess. I grasped the bars and pressed my face against them, the metal cold against my cheeks. I could see the building's portico with its enormous, white, four-story pillars. Hundreds of national flags lined the driveway leading up to it. They snapped in the wind, their metal ropes clanging against the flagpoles, a haunting percussion chorus on the otherwise silent grounds.

The UN charter speaks of human rights, respect for international law, social progress, better standards of living, and peace. Opponents say that, although most people who work for the UN believe in its benevolent purpose, it is really the vehicle through which the world government and world army are being manipulated into place, that the public is being convinced, via propaganda, that the UN is the only way to create peace and stability in the world.

The planning of the UN was done by secret steering committee. All but one committee member belonged to the Council on Foreign Relations, and the Rockefellers donated the money to build the UN facilities, both in New York and Geneva.

Again and again, as I studied the building, the energy wavered between pristine clarity and sinister darkness. Standing there, I understood for the first time why I had repeatedly found it difficult to take a psychic reading of the United Nations. There were both light and dark forces at work inside of it, various factions vying for control. Again and again the thought arose in my mind: *middle ground, middle ground*—equal positive and negative energies.

If the UN was on middle ground, which way would it ultimately go? The agendas of the global elite seemed so far-reaching, so far advanced. My head drooped, and I rubbed my eyes.

I dragged myself back down the street. My feet were killing me. My body ached. It had been a difficult day: first the greed at the WTO; now the precarious balance of the UN.

By the time I arrived at our hotel room, exhaustion had overwhelmed me. To make matters worse, I opened the door to the room only to discover that Anders had included one of his new black T-shirts in the white laundry.

"All of my beautiful, silky long underwear!" I moaned. "I spent a bloody fortune on these before the trip, and now they're metallic gray!" I sorted through the pile of clothes. "And look at these underpants and socks! I thought you said you had everything under control!"

"I'm sorry," he responded, wide-eyed, moving back.

"I can't believe this," I hissed, flinging the dingy underwear at the suitcase. Tears filled my eyes. "I'm going to bed," I told him, stumbling across the room and turning down the bed covers.

"Without dinner?" he asked tentatively.

"I don't care about dinner," I snapped, starting to undress. "I care about getting some sleep. I can barely stand up."

Anders cautiously approached the bed and began to tuck me in, trying to smooth things over. "Since they're metallic gray," he said soothingly, "can't you just think of them as a suit of armor, like Amazon underwear? Who knows? In the end it could be helpful."

"Leave me alone!" I shouted, turning away from him. "Can't you see I'm exhausted?"

Anders straightened to his full height, then marched to the door, turned defiantly toward me, and said, "You've been saying you'll write a book about all of this. Well, I'm going to write my own version. I'll call it..." He paused. "I'll call it *Kundalini, Living with a Coiled-up Snake*. And I'm going to tell everyone what really happened on this trip!"

The following morning I slept in, hoping to get rested. When I opened my eyes, Anders was lying on his twin bed, looking at me. I closed my eyes again. I had behaved horribly. Regret flushed through my body. Opening my eyes, I reached my hand out to him.

He took my hand and squeezed it. After a long pause he said, "You're very condescending to me sometimes. Do you realize that?"

I didn't reply.

"Do you think it's easy for me—always being your sidekick, having you call all the shots, always being expected to support your spiritual mission? And it really drives the knife in and turns it when you're arrogant."

I withdrew my hand. His words stung, but he had only spoken the truth. I finally nodded.

"You're right. I am disrespectful to you sometimes. It's my ego. I was trained to be a star—to be *the* star—but I really don't want to play that role anymore. I apologize." I sighed and turned onto my back. Would my arrogance never loosen its hold on me? I glanced at him. "Can you forgive me for being a coiled-up snake?"

He slid out of his bed and into mine.

I touched his cheek. "I'm really sorry, sweetheart. I appreciate your support more than I can tell you."

He nodded, and we kissed.

We decided not to rush to the train.

The Bank for International Settlements

Later that morning, two days before Christmas, we traveled to Basel, Switzerland, where we stood in front of a tall, round, glass building. A brass plaque by the entrance bore its name: *The Bank for International Settlements*. Such a tiny plaque to identify the world's most powerful financial institution![140]

The BIS is the central banks' central bank. It is controlled by a small, elite circle of bankers, representing the world's major central banking institutions.*

I had traveled with my teacher to many places of power in nature, and I considered myself a connoisseur of energy, but standing next to the BIS I was dumbfounded. Never had I encountered a manmade structure that exuded that much power. It felt intensely grounded, as though it had massive roots that anchored it deep inside the Earth.

I closed my eyes in order to take a precise reading of my teacher's first ripple. The power rolling off of the building was almost audible, like the deep, bass purring of an overweight cat: *"We Own Everything."* I shivered in spite of the sun shining down on the Basel streets.

I made my mind quiet so I could feel the second, more elusive ripple. Was it greed, as it had been at the WTO? No. If you already own everything, greed is redundant. The second ripple was a pulling action, as it had been at the WTO, but what was being pulled was different.

All at once I saw it: The BIS pulled life force! During my research into banking, I had gained an intellectual understanding that the world's people were being held in slavery by money, and that knowledge had saddened me. Now, experiencing directly the consciousness of international bankers and their ruthless disregard for humanity broke my heart. They were literally sucking the life force out of people, and they didn't care. The global banking system was a giant, unfeeling, sucking vacuum that pulled the heart and soul out of every one of us.

Anders and I checked into a hotel next to the bank, and when I opened the large wooden window in our room, the entire view was filled with the Bank for International Settlements. I propped myself up against the pillows on my twin bed, the one nearest the window, and regarded the building. My broken-heartedness had changed into determination. If I could play a part in dismantling this type of patriarchal power, I was glad. It was an honor. I was ready to move forward.

---

* Although we didn't know it at the time, the Bank for International Settlements would soon release a policy paper calling for one global currency.

Immediately upon asking for guidance from them, the Lineage began speaking to me. Aside from asking them for help with the energetic work, I hadn't communicated with them since receiving my assignment initially, and I thrilled to the sound of their voices speaking slowly and distinctly in unison. Every cell in my body stood at attention, ready to absorb their instruction.

"Feel the line from the bank down into the Earth, and merge with it," they told me. *"Follow it as it extends out in many directions, networking all of the central banks in the world."*

As they spoke the words, I could feel all of the lines extending out like the spokes of a wheel. Each central bank acted as a wheel, as well, networking private banks in each country. They formed a giant grid.

"Your job," they continued, *"will be to raise the vibration of the structure, to cause it to vibrate in a faster, more refined way. There is nothing wrong with the structure, only with the energy that animates it."*

There was a pause. Then they resumed more quietly, almost as though they were taking me into their confidence. *"Raising the vibration is the last thing they will expect."*

Then all was silent, and I relaxed.

How brilliant! The last thing the bankers would expect was someone infusing the banking system with more light. In approaching the problem this way, I would not be opposing them. I would actually be helping to elevate their consciousness without their even knowing it. Every day, they worked within the structure and were affected by it. If the vibration of the structure became uplifted, so would their energy.

I began meditating, but not so much with the intention of raising the vibration of the banking system. I knew that I didn't possess the power to do that on my own, that it would require the focus of a team, the strength of the collaboration promised by the Lineage. I meditated in order to fixate the feeling of the banking system solidly in my psyche while I had the opportunity to sit at its core.

Self-Love

At the end of my meditation, which went long into the night, I experienced moving up into the sky and behind my body. From that vantage point I could see a small golden figure sitting on a bed in a hotel room in Basel, Switzerland. A distant thought drifted through my silent mind: *My God…that's me!*

I peered down at the little female form sitting perfectly still, attempting to do an impeccable meditation. She was trying *so* hard, bringing all of her spiritual training to bear on the task she had been assigned. She didn't realize it, but she had become a warrior, and at that moment she would have made her teacher very proud.

My heart melted. Tears rolled down my cheeks. I watched her for a long time in silent awe. It was the first time that I had ever felt love for myself…accepted myself exactly as I was…acknowledged the perfection of my own soul. Finally I lay down to go to sleep, wrapped in a blanket of profound peace.

When we awoke the following morning, it was Christmas Eve, and Anders insisted we take a holiday. I donned my metallic gray underwear for the first time. As we strolled through the lobby and checked out of the hotel, I found that I rather liked wearing it. No one knew that secretly, underneath my street clothes, I was an Amazon.

After a short jaunt on the train along the border of France and Germany, we disembarked in Strasbourg, France, checked into a pretty inn off of the church square, treated ourselves to a boat tour of the city's canals, and ate a late lunch of duck *à l'orange* on a bed of wild rice, the closest we could come to turkey and dressing. When we emerged from the restaurant, a delicate snow had begun to fall.

We drifted through the cobblestone streets, two phantoms from another land observing the French celebrating Christmas. The church square was lined with vendor booths and Christmas lights. We joined the villagers as they bought last-minute gifts, laughed, drank hot mulled wine, and laughed even more. Anders wanted to watch the children ride the "jolly-go-round," so we stood arm in arm as the brightly colored wooden horses paraded through the snow, accompanied by a Mozart Sonata.

Spiritual Teachings on Love

Throughout all of the years I knew him, my teacher rarely used the word *love*. He said that it had too many connotations and that it cheapened the concept to talk about it. He defined love as "quiet commitment" and, more often than not, used the word *commitment* instead of *love.*

One night, however, he spent the whole evening talking about love, actually using the word repeatedly. But that was like him—always doing something unexpected for the shock value it would have.

"We live in a world obsessed with love," he told us. "Everyone is always looking for someone to love. Yet it would seem that for all people go through in order to experience love, very few find real happiness. Why is this?"

The question was rhetorical, and he settled into his topic. "Most people suffer in love because of attachment. We are interested in getting a net return on our investment. Not only do I want back what I invested, but I want more. This is the capitalist notion of love. This doesn't work very well. In fact, it destroys the very nature of love.

"In its essence, love is a free, formless strand of luminosity. Most people think of love as an emotion, but what I am describing is a light that uplifts our awareness, transforms our consciousness, and kindles in us the flame of self-giving, knowledge, and power. Love is about giving. It doesn't seek to please itself. It knits together families, friends, lovers, societies, nations, and perhaps, one day, a world.

"There are many different expressions of love. The gradation of love is determined by what you direct your love toward. As young children, we feel the immature love of the ego and our own satisfaction. As we mature, we love others, the world, or God. As we advance spiritually, we don't love for any reason. We just love for the sake of love. Love teaches us that what is most important is self-acceptance."

My teacher paused to scan his audience, and I leaned forward in my seat, interested to hear what he would say. I had no experience with self-acceptance. I continually judged myself as insufficient, always berated myself to do better.

"You must love yourself," he continued, "even when you don't measure up to your own expectations. You have a certain idea of who you should be and what you should become, but these are only ideas of the mind. You have many different selves inside of you, many different voices that speak through you. You have to accept that you will often do the exact opposite of what you think is right. You need to accept that and still love yourself.

"Ultimately, love teaches us that everything is an extension of our deepest self. Those around us are extensions of ourselves, and we are extensions of them…not only the people, but the plants, the animals, animate and inanimate objects. All things have life, form, and existence, and we learn to love them all. Beyond what we call existence is nonexistence. Beyond form is formlessness. Beyond matter is Spirit, and in Spirit there is nothing but love. Its very nature is love. If we examine the nature of existence very closely, we find that it is made up of love." He paused, and everyone became even more attentive.

"The real test in your evolution is this: Are you willing to give up *everything* for what you love? No one can tell you who or what to love, but you must have the willingness to follow your love as far as it will take you. Whether it is practical or impractical, whether it brings you salvation or destruction, it doesn't matter. Love is the strongest force in the universe, and once you harness yourself to that force, it will carry you all the way to nirvana."

The evening that my teacher spoke so eloquently about love was very precious because it allowed me to see a tenderness he rarely shared. The majority of the time, he was anything but tender. He was something more akin to a military general—aloof, tough, and exacting. It forced me to really evaluate what he meant by love: not emotionalism but a quiet commitment. He lived quiet commitment when it came to his students.

When I looked at it that way, I could see that he was the embodiment of love. He would do anything to further his students' evolution. He constantly used his psychic skills to assess where they were at, where they needed to go, and how to get them there in the most effective way. He was hands on and one hundred percent engaged, and he was certainly not hesitant to give someone an adjustment if they were spiritually off kilter or caught up in ego.

My first spiritual adjustment had come in 1983 in front of three hundred people. I had taken a brief sojourn back into the world of theatre by co-authoring a play with one of my teacher's other students, Robert, and had asked a question about our success. My teacher immediately cut me off.

"Listen to her voice! There is so much ego in her voice these days!" he shouted. "You were a pretty nice person when you first came here to study. Now just listen to you! It's embarrassing! You must think you're important. I can assure you that nothing is farther from the truth...."

The assault lasted ten minutes. I felt like a deer staring into the headlights of an oncoming truck.

My teacher's method was to yell someone down, then soften his tone to one of encouragement. "After tonight you'll have a decision to make," he said, his eyes looking directly into mine. "Either you can take offense and decide not to come back, or you can examine your ego, learn some humility, and continue your spiritual education."

I continued...although it wasn't easy to attend my teacher's next event; I was completely humiliated and couldn't meet anyone's eyes. But as the years passed, I learned that his yelling bouts, far from being cruel or damaging, were really priceless moments of change. I gained the ability to open my being and breathe his harsh words into my heart, confident that his surgical knife would pare away another layer of ego and catapult me forward in my spiritual evolution. I gradually came to the realization that he yelled out of love.

Occasionally my teacher dropped his military persona to give someone a compliment. It didn't happen often. In all the years I studied with him, I could count on one hand the number of times he said I had done a good job. Each time, my heart melted in gratitude, and the endless struggle to be a good student seemed justified. He would straighten to his full six-foot-four-inch height, hold himself perfectly in countless dimensions, and say, "You know, of course, that I've always loved you."

10

THE BILDERBERGERS
MEET THE LINEAGE

On the last phase of our European trip, Anders and I sped through the German countryside on a high-tech train bound for Baden-Baden, the location of the final Bilderberg hotel on our itinerary. Anders dozed in the seat beside me while I read.

The train slowed as it approached a station. I closed my book, checked my watch, and scanned the timetable. The Germans were always on schedule, and today was no exception. Precisely on time, the train pulled into the orderly-looking village of Ingelstaad.

Ingelstaad? Why did that sound familiar? Suddenly I remembered: Ingelstaad University was the birthplace of the Illuminati, the esoteric organization formed in 1776 by Adam Weishaupt!

"Wake up, sweetheart" I whispered frantically to Anders. "We're getting off!"

He stumbled from his seat and grabbed the suitcase, still half-asleep. "Girls!" he mumbled. "They're like mini world wars."

The Lineage Hands Out Clues

It was only because Anders spoke fluent German that we managed to find the one remaining building of Ingelstaad University, buried in the heart of the village on a narrow cobblestone street. We circled it, then sat on a park bench in the adjacent square. It was a cold, dreary day and had started to rain in a fine mist. I adjusted the brim of my hat and scrutinized the building with curiosity.

At all the other locations we had visited, I had been able to prepare myself through research. This was different. Almost nothing had been written about the Illuminati because researchers knew almost nothing about them. They were highly secretive—so much so that I didn't even know if they still existed. Perhaps we were on a wild goose chase, perhaps we should have remained in the warmth of the train, but I had been so intrigued by Weishaupt's pyramid structure before leaving home. My six-month research deadline had come and gone on December 21st, and I still had no idea what the underlying mystical structure of the Patriarchy was. Perhaps Ingelstaad held a clue.

On the side of the salmon-colored building was a faded eighteenth-century painting of a professor standing behind a lectern, speaking to a handful of students, but it was overpowered by the husky black and white lettering of German graffiti below it—an odd mixture of old and new worlds. I told Anders that I'd like to sit quietly for a few minutes, although I didn't have much expectation of discovering anything.

Anders stood guard. I sensed that the teenagers setting off fireworks at the end of the block made him a little nervous. Maybe it sounded like gunfire to him. For me, it was not the most conducive environment for psychic perceptions, but it was worth a try.

If my impulse to come here was correct, I said telepathically to the Lineage, *if there is something you would like me to see, please help me to be open to it.*

After a few moments, much to my astonishment, I felt the assembled Lineage clearly. I straighten on the bench.

"The Illuminati was an important group at one time," they told me in their usual even cadence, *"but the organization has changed and evolved into something else."*

There was a pause, and I felt slightly disappointed. On the other hand, I knew that the Lineage didn't indulge in idle chit-chat. If they were speaking, that meant they had something important to communicate. Reminding myself of this helped me to remain calm, but nothing could have prepared me for what they said next. They resumed speaking with more intensity than I had ever heard. Their sentences unfolded as a protracted revelation.

"There are twelve rings functioning on the planet. They intersect, and there is much overlap. There is a royalty ring, a banking ring, a government ring...."

They caused an image to form in my mind. It was similar to the five interlocking rings of the Olympics logo, only this image had many more rings and was multidimensional. It turned deliberately, like an orbiting spaceship, so I could view it from all angles.

My breathing became shallower. I couldn't believe what I was seeing. *Rings! The mystical structure I've been groping for all of these months is composed of rings of power!*

It had actually been staring me in the face all along. The first week of my research, I had seen that the man in the South Pacific was part of an Egyptian ring of power. I had read about Cecil Rhodes' Round Tables, his Circle of Initiates. Adam Weishaupt had nine key positions at the top of his pyramid. I was willing to bet those nine positions had something to do with nine rings of power. Elation swept through my body. The energetic structure I needed to disassemble was composed of rings!

My teacher suddenly appeared in my mind's eye, as though he had been waiting offstage in the wings of the theatre, heard his cue, then stepped center stage into the spotlight.

"Remember when I had you read the Lord of the Rings trilogy by J. R. R. Tolkien?" he asked me, grinning like a Cheshire cat. The epic adventure revolved around a ring of power coveted by a Dark Lord because it controlled a number of other rings. *"Tolkien,"* he continued, *"wasn't so far off."*

I nodded, and my teacher gradually faded from view. The download was over.

I sat for a few moments longer. The noises of the street became apparent again as I stared in amazement at Inglestaad University.

Thank goodness I had followed my intuition to jump off the train. I had now confirmed that although the Illuminati organization had evolved into a different configuration, its philosophy still manifested in the actions of the global elite. The One World Government was being built using esoteric Illuminati principals. In addition, I had received two important clues to guide my future detective work: There were twelve rings of power functioning on the planet, and I could use Tolkien as a guide.

The Royalty Ring Meets Its Fate

The word *baden* is German for *bathe*, and Baden-Baden was famous around the world for its mineral waters. Long ago, the Romans had built baths there, and during the nineteenth century, royalty from all over Europe congregated there to take the waters. Now the city exuded old-money elegance.

Anders and I managed to arrive in Baden-Baden before dark. The luxurious Steigenberger Hotel had been the meeting place of the Bilderbergers in 1991. After checking in and showering, we walked to the back of the hotel and sat under the covered porch. The sound of mineral water splashing in the nearby fountain wafted through the evening air.

I was so tired—not because of mystical attack or Bilderberger energy rolling off the building (although there was always some of that) but because all the energetic work had finally taken a toll. Each time I encountered the Bilderberger energy, I took it through my body, and it left me fatigued. Over the past month, the work had worn me down.

Please give me the strength to do this, I said to the Lineage.

Then I simply channeled energy through my heart, and the Bilderberger energetic line was dissolved. What had taken me hours to accomplish at the beginning of the trip now took ten minutes. I had finally realized that I didn't need to understand anything about what had transpired at a location, how to proceed with the energetic work, or which type of energy was suitable to use. All I had to do was put my body there, align with Spirit, and make myself available as a conduit.

The next morning as I awoke, I noticed that something was radically different...but what? I examined my awareness field in all directions. I was amazed. I could feel no boundaries. I scanned myself again, taking an even more careful inventory. There was no trace of the personality structure I normally felt all around me. I let myself relax into the experience. It was exquisite. I felt as if I were floating in a sea of gold light. There were no thoughts and no impressions, just the divine sensation of oneness with all things. I was like a tiny droplet of water that had always mistakenly assumed it was separate from the ocean when, all along, it had been the ocean itself.

The ecstatic oneness was beyond description. Tears of gratitude streamed down my face. My heart filled with love for my teacher and the Lineage. It was obvious that the task I had embarked upon was causing unprecedented spiritual growth. In over thirty years of spiritual practice, nothing I had ever imagined had even come close to this experience.

For the next three days, Anders and I rested in Baden-Baden, spending our days at the peaceful, blue-tiled Caracalla Therme Baths and our evenings drinking German lager with our meat-and-potatoes dinners. Then we moved on to Wiesbaden, nearer to the Frankfort airport where we would depart the following day, to soak in their Roman baths. At last the mineral water seemed to be washing away some of my fatigue.

On the day of our departure, at the end of my morning meditation, I suddenly opened my eyes. The Bilderbergers had met in Wiesbaden! My hunch was that they had held their conference at the five-star Nassauer Hof Hotel we had walked past the day before.

Anders rolled his eyes when I told him I'd like to stop by the Nassauer Hof on our way to the airport.

"Please," I begged him. "Please be patient with me a little longer."

As we entered the lobby, I spotted a gray-haired man who appeared to be in his seventies standing behind the concierge desk.

"Excuse me, sir. Do you speak English?"

"Yes, madam."

"Have you worked at the hotel a long time?"

"Yes."

I made my voice sound casual. "Did the Bilderberg group meet here some years ago?"

He smiled. "Yes, the Bilderberg Conference…I remember well."

He paused. "Let me see. Schmidt attended and also...what was his name? Prince something...."

"Prince Bernhard?" I ventured.

"Yes, that's it, Prince Bernhard of the Netherlands. And Kissinger came from the United States. The Bilderbergers had very tight security. I've never seen so many secret-service men. There were gunmen on all the rooftops. It was quite an experience."

"Do you remember when it was?" I asked.

"Oh, quite a long time ago." He thought for a moment. "It was some time after Kennedy's assassination. In the late sixties, I should think."

"Thank you," I said, patting his arm gently. "You've been very helpful."

"It's my pleasure, madam. No one has ever asked about the Bilderbergers."

Anders and I entered the lobby, sat at a small Victorian table, and ordered coffee. As we waited for it to arrive, I took stock of my Bilderberger progress. I had visited the Hotel de Bilderberg, where the Bilderbergers first met in 1954, as well as most of the hotels from the last decade where their energetic lines that had been attached to rocks had been disconnected. Now I was at the Nassauer Hof, where they'd met in the late sixties. That was right in the middle. If I disconnected the energetic line here, what would happen?

As soon as the waiter brought our coffee, I tuned out the hustle and bustle in the lobby and entered the mystical planes. My heart opened, but this time an unusually large volume of energy poured down through the Lineage and flowed into the earth. After about five minutes, I sensed the Bilderberger line anchored to the thermal-water rock formation and disconnected it. The line vanished.

Still, something remained. I looked more closely. The anchor line was gone, but the encoded Bilderberger information still hovered above me. Had this been the case at the other hotels? Was I noticing this only now?

As if in answer to my question, my vantage point suddenly shifted. I found myself high above the European continent, looking down. It was true! The Bilderberger web of encoded information overhung all of the places they had met. Some of the lines that had anchored the information to rocks were gone—from the hotels used during the last decade as well as from the Nassauer Hof—but the information they wanted to broadcast to the world was still there. It formed a giant ring!

Suddenly it felt as though the whole universe stopped. Everything became eerily still. Then, without warning, the entire ring shattered. It looked like a formation of glass that had suddenly broken into ten thousand pieces. It exploded, then hung weightlessly in the air.

Everything was silent for a long moment. Then I could suddenly see a number of the royals turning their heads in confusion.

"*What just happened?*" one asked.

"*Something has shifted,*" another said.

There was a moment of disorientation, the awareness that something extraordinary had taken place. Then slowly, ever so slowly, a wind originating at the center of the ring began to blow. It blew from the center in all directions. It blew the shattered pieces of information outward in an ever-widening circle. It blew the royals away from each other, dissipating their intention to work together toward a world government.

All of a sudden I was jolted from my vision by the sound of clapping. At first I was puzzled. Then I realized that the Lineage was simply jubilant. No longer above my head, they were clustered about me, and a celebration had broken out.

They're applauding, I thought to myself. *They are pleased!*

I took a very deep breath, then let it out slowly. I had accomplished what I had come to Europe to do. I hadn't known that it was what I had come there to do, but I had facilitated the destruction of the Royalty ring, as I now thought of it. Of course, as my teacher had said countless times, nothing can ever really be destroyed. When something dies, it changes form and is transmuted into something else. What, I wondered, would the Royalty ring change into?

Is there any other information you wish to give me before I leave Europe? I asked the Lineage.

They replied, as always, in one voice, "*Not at this time. Job well done!*"

At the airport I asked a man to snap a picture of Anders and me. I smiled proudly and gave the camera a big thumbs-up. The initial six months of the project had been a sterling success. For the first time in my life, I was on track. This was what I had prepared for and prayed for. After the years of training with my teacher to become an impeccable warrior, after additional years learning the art of processing from female instructors, and after so many years of begging to be of service to humanity, I was finally doing what I was meant to do.

After we boarded the plane and started the long trip home, however, the euphoria ebbed away. By now the man in the South Pacific must have been aware that his carefully constructed web of ideas had been destroyed. How was he feeling that day as he walked through the rooms of his island home? Had he identified the mystic who had outmaneuvered him, or was being challenged by an insignificant female simply outside his personal range of possibility?

I was certain that, sooner or later, my assignment would lead me to the man in the South Pacific. I could feel it deep in the marrow of my bones. I wondered how long I would be able to outmaneuver him before we squared off on the battlefield of the mystical planes.

PART TWO

THE INNER
WORKINGS
OF THE
PATRIARCHY

11

RINGS OF POWER

Back home in New Mexico in January and February, I was like a high-strung racehorse held in check at the starting gate. I had done my research. I had been given clues about the underlying mystical structure of the Patriarchy I was to take apart. I had learned to do energetic work in an efficient and effective fashion. Why was I unable to move forward?

I could sense a collaboration looming but didn't know how to assemble the team. I spent hours standing in front of my whiteboard, attempting to name the "twelve rings of power functioning on the planet," but always ending up tossing the marker back on the tray in frustrated failure. I hiked in the high desert around Los Alamos, scouting for a tree that could help me rally the other trees around the world to assist with the project, but I never found one.

Much later I was able to look back with objectivity, see that my spiritual growth had accelerated after accepting my marching orders, and realize that a time of rest allowed changes in consciousness to take effect. Later I could see that the project had an ebb and flow, times of action and personal growth and times of integration, but during the first two months of 2003, I was a horse chomping at its bit.

Then, around the first of March, the phone rang. It was Alexandria.

"Jackie is coming in from California for a two-week vacation in Santa Fe."

Alexandria's pronouncement was a gunshot signaling the start of the race. The waiting was over.

"I haven't seen Jackie for years," I told her. "Do you think the three of us could spend some time together?"

"Oh, I definitely think we should spend some time together," she assured me.

Jackie had also been a student of my teacher. We had never been close friends but had socialized from time to time, and I admired her immensely. She was a psychic perceiver extraordinaire.

My teacher had once said, "Some of my women students have been born and bred, lifetime after lifetime, to be seers. They can see *on demand*." Jackie was one of them. She was so psychic that the constant influx of psychic impressions she received from the world was often overwhelming for her. She had solved this problem by taking one of my teacher's suggestions—studying martial arts as a way of cultivating the mindset of a spiritual warrior—to the extreme. She earned a fourth-degree black belt in Shotokon karate. This mindset created a psychic suit of armor that buffered her from the world. I had studied karate, and although I had never achieved a high rank, I understood how much discipline was required to do so. Jackie had not only earned four black belts, but had traveled to Japan to participate in Shotokon karate seminars, an honor few women could claim.

I counted the hours until I could meet with Jackie and Alexandria. I felt sure that Jackie's sudden appearance meant collaboration was just around the corner. We would certainly make a fine team. We had all graduated from my teacher's mystical boot camp and spoke a common language. And there was something else, something that might prove to be even more important. We had all been part of the ring of power at his mystery school in ancient Egypt.

The Egyptian Ring of Power

In the late eighties, my teacher singled out twenty-four women—including Jackie, Alexandria, and myself—separated us from his other students, and set us on a different course of study.

"There are three past-life profiles in this group," he explained to us. "Some of you have incarnated repeatedly as sovereigns—members of royal families. Some have been seers who served as advisors to those who were sovereigns. The rest have been what you might call heavy hitters, or soldiers. You were trained for these profiles in ancient Egypt. I'm not referring to Egypt during the time of the pharaohs. I'm talking about a period of Egyptian history that was much earlier. During that lifetime, you studied with me in a mystery school...." He paused. "...and, you took a spiritual fall there." He turned his head slowly, meditating intently on each of us in turn. "It is *imperative* that you remember what happened."

I was stunned. I hadn't the slightest inkling of a past life in Egypt. Aside from my high school history classes, I had no knowledge of Egypt whatsoever.

I decided that the best course of action was to contact a psychic who did past-life regressions. With her help, the story of my Egyptian life emerged.

When I was six years old in that lifetime, I had been taken to a mystery school situated on Philae Island in the middle of the Nile River. I became part of a group of twenty-four little girls. In our early years we played games, took classes, and helped the older priestesses. When we matured, our mystical training began.

Our training was highly technical and extremely exacting. My teacher taught us many advanced mystical skills. He gave all the young priestesses a well-rounded spiritual education but also cultivated special skills in each of us.

Our skill sets fell into three broad categories: seers, sovereigns, and soldiers. Seers were schooled in the intricacies of psychic perception. Sovereigns were taught leadership skills: how to rule using the energy of the heart, strategize solutions to problems, negotiate peace, and hold a spiritual alignment—something that involved modeling a balanced state of awareness so that those under a sovereign's guardianship could feel that balance on the inner planes and align themselves with it. Soldiers were trained to enter into alternate dimensions, gather knowledge, transmute energies, and effect change.

As a group, our job was to constantly monitor and raise the collective consciousness of the province where our temple was located.

By fusing these three skill sets, we were highly effective. When the seers saw a problem, the sovereigns devised a solution, which the soldiers implemented.

There was no need for verbal communication within the group. We were all psychic, and we worked with a complete absence of personal ego. Our inner beings were very still. There was no emotion, but there was no lack of emotion either. We were simply at peace. The group executed one activity after another in a calm, fluid state of attention. Over the years, we perfected our skills, solidified our bond, and evolved a sophisticated ring of power.

In my past-life regression, one episode at the temple emerged as pivotal. As we prepared for an evening festival, I descended into a storage area to retrieve sacred grain. When I lifted the lid from the basket where the grain was kept, I jumped back. There was a snake inside, which was a bad omen. It was not that the snake was bad. We kept snakes in one of the underground temple chambers. They were used in our mystical training. The problem was that the snake was somewhere it should not have been. The energy of the snake and the sacred grain were incompatible, so I attempted to negate the omen with a prayer.

In the evening the festival commenced on one of the temple's outside terraces. It was a perfect night with a balmy breeze. A full moon had just risen on the horizon, and a million stars shone in the heavens. The flames from the sacred fires, which burned in massive stone dishes on the terrace, threw fanciful shadows on the temple walls. People were dancing, eating, and having a good time.

My teacher pulled me aside and said he wanted me to help him. He had to go away to attend to some business the next morning. He wanted all of us to take care of things for a few days.

The next morning everyone in the mystery school assembled in the main courtyard to say goodbye to my teacher. Suddenly I had the feeling that something dreadful was about to happen. I ran after him, imploring him not to go, but he couldn't be dissuaded.

Once he had gone, a strange quiet descended. I walked slowly through the rooms of the temple. It was like walking inside a huge bell and waiting for it to ring. Entering the chamber where the snakes were kept, I found that one of them had died—another bad omen: first the snake in the sacred grain, now the dead snake. I walked out onto a terrace, trying to figure it out. What did the omens mean?

An old beggar woman suddenly emerged from behind the temple wall at the edge of the Nile. My heart immediately opened to her because she was so elderly and decrepit, but as she approached, I studied her more intently.

There was something odd about her. Her outer appearance was feminine—she wore a dress—but underneath, I sensed a masculine energy, as though a male mystic had changed himself into a woman but didn't feel at home in the body. I tried to perceive at a deeper level what was going on. Slowly she mounted the steps onto the terrace. Then, unexpectedly, her head jerked up, and she looked straight into my eyes. It was not the movement of an old woman! Before I could react, she performed some magic. Suddenly it felt like there was a snake wrapped around my heart. I fell to my knees, grasping my chest in agony.

"Take it away," I commanded her.

"I will if you grant me one wish."

Something inside me knew that this was a trick, but my mind felt confused. "Please," I begged, "take it away. Undo the magic."

"Grant me the wish, priestess."

I hesitated.

"I'm just an old woman," she insisted. "I couldn't possibly do you any harm."

It was a lie. Despite my pain, I could see her clearly now. She was a powerful mystic, and she had the ability, on another plane of reality, to change her form into a cobra. I confronted her with this.

She examined me carefully. "Yes," she purred finally, "you have seen, and it is true." She cocked her head. "Perhaps I could fight the snake around your heart, kill it, and make it let go."

"No!" I knew she was lying again.

Then all at once we became entangled. I wrestled—with a beggar woman in the physical, with a cobra in an alternate dimension—

battling for my life. The snake bit my heart, and I gasped for air and then collapsed. The last thing I remembered was the feeling of the cool stones of the terrace floor against my cheek. Then I lost consciousness.

I entered a sort of dream. In the dream I was shown many things. Initially I experienced taking a fall, a spiritual fall in consciousness. Everything around me began to rumble and shake until the floor beneath my feet crumbled. I went through, falling and falling. I called out for help. I called to my teacher, but my teacher never came.

Then I was taken through a hundred future incarnations— my awareness becoming progressively more dense, my emotions becoming more and more caught up in the world of human dramas, my memory of Egypt fading into oblivion—until finally I incarnated in the twentieth century, when I met a tall, lanky American man. He looked at me, and suddenly there was golden light. I vaguely remembered this light. It reminded me of something from a long time ago.

Fascinated, I stayed with this man. As I studied with him, my mystical powers returned, the light returned, and in the end I remembered who I was.

Then all at once I awakened from the dream to find myself lying on the temple's terrace, alone.

After this, life at the temple went on, but everything changed. One of the women in our ring of power became involved with a man—a priest from a different temple, a member of another ring of power. Having a sexual relationship was taboo for priestesses, so she slipped out at night to see him. He was extremely powerful, and she became fascinated by the concept of power. She began to realize that *she* was powerful. She found that she could control the priest by using the skills that my teacher had taught her. She could control her environment. She could get whatever she wanted.

She shared her experiences with our small group. We listened, enraptured, not realizing we were being pulled toward destruction. We longed to experience the world outside the temple walls. We longed to test our powers.

One by one, each of us began having relationships with the priests at the other mystery school. Gradually we became confused. We wanted to stay with my teacher but we also wanted to go. It was frustrating. We turned our frustration on him. We blamed him for our unhappiness. We grew vindictive and the energy we directed at him affected his health.

Finally the situation became so abusive that my teacher took action. He divested us of our powers. He took away our mystical powers so our ability to harm others would be minimized. Then he sent all of us away. We were dispersed to different provinces throughout Egypt.

In the early days of my teacher's mystery school, my being had been light and free. Now, I went from light to dark; there was a dark aura surrounding me. I dressed in black. My being became dark and sinister.

I ended up living alone. I had no compassion, only desires and a love of power. I hated my teacher, and I corrupted all his teachings. I found someone else to instruct me, a master of the dark arts. Using my mystical skills, I pulled experiences into my life. I pulled in people, manipulating them without their knowledge, preying on their weaknesses, and gaining control over them.

All the women in our ring of power entered this mode. From our various locations in Egypt, we all pulled. We pulled things away from our teacher: other students who were still at the mystery school, opportunities that might have come to him. We destroyed his work. We shredded the fabric of his temple. In the end there was no one left for him to teach.

After the past-life regression, guilt consumed me. My consciousness at the mystery school had been so high, yet I had made decisions that caused me to plummet in consciousness, become obsessed with power, and turn against my teacher, the one being in the universe who always stood by me. Why? Who was the strange beggar woman who initiated the cycle of events? Why hadn't I heeded the omens, made better decisions, and taken a different path?

In the years that followed, I went over and over the Egyptian life in my mind, struggling to assemble more facts. Eventually I saw that ancient Egypt had been a major turning point, a time when a shift took place in the Earth's energy field. After the shift, little by little, darkness began to dominate, and the masculine/feminine energies grew more and more out of balance.

At our mystery school, our female group had turned from the light and aligned with the darkness. I tried to convince myself that we had simply made a mistake, but that didn't ring true. There was more to it than that. Our alignment with the darkness was intimately tied to the pivotal shift in the planet's energy.

Could I have the sequence of events backwards? Perhaps it wasn't that the shift occurred and caused us to align with the darkness. Perhaps when we aligned with the darkness, it helped *cause* the shift to occur! That *did* ring true—sickeningly true—and my heart almost stopped beating as the ramifications poured over me.

The shift had precipitated the rise of the Patriarchy. Could we really have played a part in that? It felt as though our spiritual fall had helped create an opening in time, like a crack in an egg, through which the Patriarchy—with all its repression, domination, and bloodshed—had entered the world.

My teacher had told us to remember. I had to remember more! Egypt was pivotal. Egypt was part of a larger saga.

The Egyptian Ring of Power Re-forms

I arrived early at the Longevity Café in Santa Fe, a bohemian tea shop known for its exotic brews, and waited for Jackie and Alexandria. When I saw them enter, I could barely contain the wave of love that swept through me. The bond I had with both of these women was overpowering. We were a family reunited. I had come home.

Jackie flashed a smile and strode forward to give me a warm hug. For a moment I closed my eyes and lost myself in her red-brown curls. When we separated from our embrace, I gave her a good once-over.

Jackie was younger than Alexandria and me, in her mid-forties. She wore a tailored, winter-green pantsuit that perfectly complemented her long red hair. Her green Irish eyes flashed—eyes that seemed happy to see me, eyes that peered beyond the relative world, registering a hundred different inter-dimensional planes at once. Jackie was complex—a clear psychic, a martial artist, a former musician, a brilliant computer analyst—all contained in a robust, big-boned, Celtic package.

There had been twenty-four women in my teacher's Egyptian mystery school. Fate had drawn three of them together in Santa Fe, and the synchronicity was undeniable: Jackie was a seer, Alexandria was a sovereign, and I was a soldier. Immediately the one mind we had shared in Egypt clicked into place.

We claimed a corner booth with a cozy assortment of overstuffed pillows, ordered tea, and immediately fell into a deep discussion of world events. I was no longer alone in my Los Alamos office, struggling for answers. The answers were coming fast and furious. Now my challenge was trying to keep up.

Jackie and Alexandria were well versed in the areas I had researched and skilled in the type of energetic work I had learned in Europe. As I summarized the recent results of my detective work, they were not surprised to hear that there were rings of power functioning on the planet. When I told them that our teacher had suggested using the *Lord of the Rings* trilogy as a guide and asked if they had read the books, it was Jackie who responded.

"Read them?" She laughed. "I've got them memorized!"

I grinned. Jackie had always been studious. I might have guessed that back when my teacher had given all us students the assignment to read Tolkien's trilogy, she had read them more than just once.

Tolkien's Rings

One of the most popular and influential works in twentieth-century literature, *The Lord of the Rings* is an epic fantasy written by English philologist J. R. R. Tolkien. The title refers to the story's main antagonist, the Dark Lord Sauron, who creates the One Ring of Power as the ultimate weapon in his campaign to rule all of Middle-earth. The tale begins in the Shire, a land of diminutive hobbits, or "hole-dwellers," similar to Tolkien's own English countryside, and follows the course of the War of the Ring as it rages across Middle-earth. In addition to hobbits, the lands are populated by humans and other humanoid races, including elves and dwarves, who have in their possession nineteen other rings of power.

"What is the verse about the rings?" I asked Jackie. "I've been trying to remember it."

Jackie nodded slightly from her seat on the opposite side of the table, cleared her throat, and began:

"Three Rings for the Elven-kings under the sky,
Seven for the Dwarf-lords in their halls of stone,
Nine for Mortal Men doomed to die,
One for the Dark Lord on his dark throne
In the Land of Mordor where the Shadows lie.
One Ring to rule them all, One Ring to find them,
One Ring to bring them all and in the darkness bind them
In the Land of Mordor where the Shadows lie."

We all pondered the verse.

"Seven rings were given to the Dwarf-lords," I mused. "Seven rings that have something to do with halls of stone. Could they be rocks? Mountains?"

Oh," Alexandria said, excitedly. "Are they places of power on the Earth?"

"You're right!" Jackie agreed. "They are power places. Every person has seven chakras. So does Mother Earth. The seven rings of the Dwarf-lords must be the seven chakras of the planet."

I nodded at Jackie. "What else does Tolkien say about the seven rings?"

"In the story," she began without hesitation, "three of the seven were captured by the Dark Lord. The other four were consumed by the dragons."

"Consumed by the dragons," I said, frowning. "What do you suppose that means?"

She hesitated. "Frankly, I've never thought about it."

There was silence.

"If nobody has any ideas," Alexandria mused from her seat at the head of the table, between Jackie and me, "what about the nine?" She turned to me. "Are the Nine for Mortal Men the rings you've been pursuing on the East Coast and in Europe? Are they rings of the New World Order?"

"That's my sense," I told her, "but I keep trying to come up with twelve. The Lineage told me there are twelve rings functioning on the planet, but whenever I make a list, I think of seven or eight, then get stuck. Tolkien says there are only nine rings of men." Suddenly, a tumbler dropped into place in my mind. "Oh, my God! Nine and three makes twelve!"

"Right, right!" Jackie exclaimed, psychically perceiving what I was thinking. "Nine for Mortal Men and three for the Elven-kings makes twelve rings functioning on the planet!"

Alexandria applauded politely. "So the twelve rings are functional, and the seven Earth chakras are out of commission, either captured by the Dark Lord or consumed by the dragons...whatever that means."

Our chai arrived, and Alexandria ceremoniously filled our cups. The teapot and cups were a funky pottery style, but with Alexandria performing the honors, we might have been having high tea with a sterling silver tea set.

The Three Rings—Spiritual Knowledge

Alexandria replaced the teapot on the table. "So, what does Tolkien say about the Three Rings for the Elven-kings?"

"The Elves were the spiritual ones in the *Lord of the Rings*, the keepers of the ancient wisdom."

Alexandria straightened. "Then that's us, right? Spiritual seekers around the globe?"

Jackie raised her eyebrows. "It would seem so."

"Well, what do we have knowledge of?" I asked. I looked at Jackie, the seer of our threesome. "One of the three must be psychic perception."

"Right," Jackie agreed. She returned my gaze. "Another is power, knowledge of the kundalini, the root chakra ability to soldier."

I nodded. "And the third?"

Alexandria placed her tea cup on the table, leaned forward, and said softly, "Love—the third type of spiritual knowledge represented at this table."

We all looked at each other and burst out laughing.

Jackie took a small leather journal out of her briefcase, printed the title *Three Rings* on a blank page, and then wrote:

Seeing

Love

Power

"So these three rings," she said, tapping her mechanic pencil on the page, "have a very high vibration. They resonate with three different strands of ancient spiritual knowledge, and they've never been lost from the planet. They've been under the keeping of spiritual masters and their students for eons. Women may have been burned at the stake during the Inquisition for looking into their crystal balls, but the art of scanning the psychic planes to perceive things beyond the physical has never gone out of style."

"And it's the same with the spiritual art of love," Alexandria interjected, smoothing the wrinkles in the napkin on her lap. "The open heart gives one the ability to view the world through the eyes of love, with respect and compassion for all living things. It's the art of spiritual balance—holding yourself perfectly in multiple dimensions and remaining poised in the still-point of existence, no matter what happens."

I nodded and smiled. "I guess that leaves me to sing the praises of power. Wow! After the insights I've had about the global elite during these past months—and about myself, for that matter—all I can say is that power is something to be wielded carefully. The person who enters the mystical planes to transmute energies better have humility as her middle name." I smiled and eyed both of them. "And it never hurts to collaborate with a sovereign and a seer."

The Seven Rings — Mother Earth's Chakras

In order to identify the chakras of Mother Earth, we tried to remember things our teacher had said about important power places. One evening he had spoken at length about Machu Picchu in Peru, Ayers Rock in Australia, and Mount Kailas in the Himalayas. Intuitively we felt that Machu Picchu was the root chakra of the planet, Ayers Rock was the second chakra, and Mount Kailas was the crown. These three seemed to be the ones that had been captured by the Dark Lord. Somehow they had been enslaved so their energy was no longer as accessible as it once had been. The other four—the ones that had been consumed by the dragons—were more perplexing.

"This may sound strange," I told them, "but I wonder if these four Earth chakras are more like groupings of power places. If you focus on some of the various power spots in the world and feel the energy of each one, they vibrate in a similar way. For instance, think about the energy of the third eye and psychic perception. Then think about Mount Fuji in Japan. Think about Greece. I've visited Greece, and I guarantee its energy is the third eye."

"And certain parts of Hawaii are places of seeing," Alexandria added. "Also Mount Shasta in California...."

"I think we're onto something," Jackie said. "A few years ago, Spirit told me that I'm responsible for 'holding' the Pacific Rim. There are a number of places of seeing that are strung out along the Pacific Rim in an oblong configuration." She shook her head and grinned. "I'm suddenly realizing that, all this time, I may have been holding the third-eye chakra of the planet!"

"This is an amazing theory." Alexandria smiled. "The places where Celeste has been asked to do energetic work over the past ten years—Blyda Canyon and the Cape of Good Hope in South Africa, Giza in Egypt, and the Temple Mount in Jerusalem—form an oblong configuration as well." Her eyes rested on her teacup for a long moment. "They feel like the navel chakra to me. They're all places of immense power." She looked up and smiled. "And how perfect that Celeste was born in South Africa."

Suddenly my trip to the East Coast came to mind. "Maybe," I

continued, "the places I was drawn to on the East Coast—Jekyll Island, Georgia, Washington, DC, and Bretton Woods, New Hampshire—are part of the throat chakra, but I don't know where else."

"The throat chakra is about the expression of the truth," Jackie suggested. "DC is the expression of government, New York of finance, Boston of science and technology. And London...I've always thought that London is the stronghold of the One World Government. These are all places that broadcast information."

"So, I was told to clear the energy of the East Coast line. Do you think the line is part of the throat chakra?"

Jackie's eyes went slightly out of focus. "The download I'm getting is that the throat chakra is round."

"Round? I asked.

"It appears to run up the East Coast of the United States," Jackie continued, "then across to London, passing through Europe, cutting through northern Africa, clipping the top of Venezuela, and intersecting some of the Caribbean islands."

I stared at her, struggling to take in this new information.

"And what about the heart chakra?" Alexandria asked.

"Ireland," Jackie said. "Different parts of the UK."

"And Hawaii?" Alexandria mused. "Parts of Hawaii are definitely keyed to the heart, like Haleakala on Maui. Also Monument Valley. I visited there recently, and it felt like pure heart. Not heart in the way most people think of it...not emotional. Monument Valley radiates silent strength. The same with the lions of South Africa—the heart is the energy of the mother lion defending her cubs. That's an important aspect of the heart. It's the Kali aspect. Many people have trouble seeing the fierceness of Kali as love, but it is."

"In the psychic realms," Jackie said, "the heart chakra looks like a flower. Its base rests at the core of the Earth, and the tip of each green-colored petal breaks through the surface at different places: Monument Valley, Alaska, Hawaii, the British Isles, Vietnam, Cambodia, Bhutan...." She added the heart chakra to her list, entitled *Seven Rings*, then pushed her journal to the center of the table so we could read the entire list:

Crown Chakra—Mt. Kailas
Third-eye Chakra—Oblong Pacific Rim locations
Throat Chakra—Circular East Coast/London locations
Heart Chakra—Flower petal points around the globe
Navel Chakra—Oblong South Africa/Egypt/Jerusalem locations
Second Chakra—Ayer's Rock
Root Chakra—Machu Picchu

I studied the list, then saw a connection.

"Ah! Wait! I've just seen what happened. I've just figured out what 'consumed by the dragons' means."

They both stared at me.

"These four Earth chakras—the navel, the heart, the throat, and the third eye—were fractured. During the Atlantean cycle, these four Earth chakras were intact and stood as singular major power places, but when the explosion occurred that caused the continent to sink under the water, they were shattered into pieces and blown across the globe. In other words, they were 'consumed by the dragons,' consumed by the fire of the explosion."

"Oh...." Jackie gasped. "You've hit it! Absolutely." She knitted her eyebrows. "I can remember being in Atlantis, trying to prevent it from happening, trying to stop the guys who were playing around with gravity. What assholes! I've always felt bad that I failed."

"Well, you know," Alexandria said, patting Jackie's hand soothingly, "some days are like that."

We all laughed.

"I wonder if each of us is responsible for holding one of the fractured chakras," I ventured. "Celeste seems to have been assigned the navel chakra. Jackie has been told she holds what we now know is the third eye. And my intuition has been telling me to move to the DC area. Perhaps I'm supposed to move there and hold the throat chakra."

"That leaves the heart chakra," Alexandria said, scowling.

"It seems logical," Jackie said, now patting Alexandria's hand. "You're our royalty, the sovereign...someone who has been trained how to rule using heart energy."

Alexandria sat up a little taller at the head of the table, fingered her teacup thoughtfully, and smiled.

The Nine Rings—The New World Order

We took a bathroom break, ordered more tea, and reconvened.

Alexandria called the meeting back to order. "What about the nine rings..." She frowned with distaste, "...the components of the New World Order? Can we try and name them?"

Jackie resumed her role as keeper of the lists. "Government, the military, and industry, for sure."

"There's a royalty ring in Europe," I told them, "or at least there used to be."

"Media and the arts," Alexandria offered.

"Banking," I added.

Jackie wrote them all down, then looked up at us. "Religion."

"Absolutely," Alexandria agreed, feigning banging her fist on the table. "Over the past five thousand years, religion has suppressed the concept of a self-sufficient human being with the capacity to evolve toward enlightenment and has instituted a church hierarchy that people are told they must use in order to approach God. In Christianity, Jesus is not just a brilliant, enlightened, human teacher, but a divine savior. It's the He-can-do-it-but-you-can't approach." She looked over at Jackie's list. "So, how many is that?"

"Eight."

We all looked across the table at the list and thought for a minute.

"Where does the World Bank fit into all of this?" I asked finally.

"That's the ninth!" Alexandria said, tapping Jackie's journal. "Natural resources—at a mystical level, the World Bank is all about control of natural resources."

I looked at Jackie.

"I have to say I agree," she added, writing it down.

I rubbed my forehead. "I have struggled to understand the World Bank for months. I'm not sure I get it."

"Ever notice," Alexandria explained, "how interested the World Bank is in water? They build dams. They irrigate crops. What is the most precious commodity on the planet? Water. If you are planning a coup to take over the planet, you need control of all of the vital natural resources, right?"

"Wow," I murmured, suddenly feeling the energy behind her words. "Things fall into place really quickly when you collaborate."

Alexandria lifted her eyebrows then turned to Jackie. "Let's see your list. Have we gotten all of them?"

Jackie slid her journal to the center of the table:

Government
Military
Industry
Royalty
Media
Arts
Banking
Religion
Resource Management

"So," Alexandria mused, "these nine rings of power exist on the mystical planes. They form the energetic underpinnings of the New World Order, and their energies manifest in the physical world. They touch our personal lives every day when we read the newspaper, when we pay our bills.... But it goes further than that. Most of us have intimate knowledge of one ring via our career. We gain life experience, learn lessons, and evolve through our association with a given ring."

Our waitress arrived with a fresh pot of tea.

The One Ring—the Man in the South Pacific

After the waitress left, Jackie leaned forward. "Of course, we can't forget about the One Ring." She frowned. "The various rings are controlled by the One."

"'One Ring to rule them all,'" Alexandria added somewhat

mournfully. "So the Dark Lord, whoever that is at the moment, holds sway over all the other rings."

Alexandria reached for the teapot. While she filled our cups, I filled them in on the man in the South Pacific. At the end of my explanation, I shuddered involuntarily. "I wonder how the man in the South Pacific is going to react to us moving ahead."

Jackie shrugged, closed her journal with a snap, and put it back in her briefcase. "I say if we piss him off, so be it."

"Absolutely," Alexandria agreed, raising her teacup for a toast. "When did we ever back down from a challenge?"

We toasted and sipped our tea.

Alexandria smiled primly at her teacup. "After all, he's only the head of the Patriarchy."

Jackie laughed. "Right. And if he gets pissed off and nukes us, well…hey, it can't feel much worse than being burned at the stake! We've all got to die sometime."

We raised our teacups again to toast the completion of a long day's work. The clues given by our teacher and the Lineage in Ingelstaad had paid off. We were three exhausted detectives, but we now had the lay of the patriarchal land: There were twelve rings functioning on the planet. Three were spiritual qualities that had been kept safe throughout the Patriarchal Age. Nine were rings of power that comprised the New World Order and its support system. There were seven Earth chakras—some intact, some fractured—that were somehow being used by the global elite in their game of power. And, somewhere in the South Pacific, there was an ultimate controlling force: the One Ring of Power.

12
A SYSTEMS ANALYSIS
OF THE PATRIARCHY

On a summer evening in 1983, my teacher had strolled into the lecture hall where his students were assembled. We were living in Los Angeles, but that evening, wearing a three-piece, pinstriped suit, his appearance was unmistakably Wall Street.

"Tonight I'd like to talk to you about the world of business," he began. "If you don't already have a career that is making you money, I suggest you begin to give your career serious thought."

I was disappointed and slumped back in my seat. I wanted to hear about mysticism, but my teacher wasn't going to talk about that.

"We are standing on the threshold of an information age," he told us. "It's not unlike the days when human beings first learned to write, and scribes were in high demand. Today computers are in their infancy. They're going to become crucial to business. Everything will one day be run on computers. If you enter the field of computer science now and get in on the ground floor, you'll be able to do extremely well."

The sound of people rustling filled the hall.

"A lot of you have the idea that your meditation and your experiences in other dimensions are all that is important. You think that those experiences are spiritual and that working in the physical world is not. That's simply not correct. You need to engage your mind during the day. You need to challenge yourself. Your work in the world balances out your experiences during meditation. The two go hand in hand. The more crisp you can be in your work, the better you can meditate. The better you can meditate, the more successful you can become in the world. Your work stabilizes your awareness field. It allows you to bring psychic perceptions down from other dimensions and into the conscious mind. You can't walk around like a space cadet. Spiritual seekers work. That's what we do.

"When we used to lived in monasteries, we worked...in the kitchen, in the garden, copying manuscripts. There was always work. The only difference is that today our work is in the city." He tilted his head and smiled. "You've actually worked with computers before. Can you remember that? We used to work with computers in Atlantis, but in Atlantis our computers were extremely advanced. They were made with crystals and operated on light. We programmed them with our minds. The reason there have been recent advances in computing is that the old Atlantean souls have started to reincarnate. We are approaching the techno-chic era we experienced near the end of the Atlantean cycle. Don't you understand? You'll be really good at this."

He paused and scanned his audience. Then he leaned forward and spoke more intimately. "This computer business is not as scary as it sounds. Just start by learning to type, get a temp job doing word processing, then take a university course at night, an introduction to computer science, in order to explore the idea. Then enroll in a technical school that offers an intensive, six-month computer training program, a crash course in writing software code. Then, after landing your first job, take university classes at night in order to flesh out a degree in computer science. Take it one step at a time." He shook his head. "I think you may be very pleased."

Some of my teacher's students held higher degrees and had built successful careers in the fields of law, medicine, mathematics, and science, but they were in the minority. Most were just trying to make ends meet. Many of the women had artistic backgrounds. I had been an actress, Alexandria a dancer, Jackie a musician, Celeste a painter. Computers sounded dry and boring to us. Sensing this, my teacher encouraged his female students, telling us that it was a field especially suitable for women: there was not a lot of discrimination, we could increase our personal power and make the money we needed to have an independent lifestyle, we could cultivate our masculine side and balance our internal masculine/feminine energies.... So, over the months, as my teacher continued to market computer science to us, we gradually warmed to the idea.

"One of the biggest benefits that comes from designing and writing software is that it will strengthen your mind," he told us. "In order to work in computers, you have to learn to hold a variety of information in your awareness field simultaneously. It's not unlike what we used to do in Tibetan monasteries when we meditated on *thankas*. First you would meditate on the face of the Buddha. When you could hold that image perfectly in your mind, you would add his hat, then the lotus flower in his hand, and so on.

"When you perform a systems analysis, you break a problem into components, then systematically refine your understanding of each. It's called stepwise refinement. You hold the big picture in your mind, but you drill down into each component until you have completely refined your understanding of it as well as its relationship to all of the other components. In the end you know all the details of the system and have a comprehensive understanding of the whole.

"Once you develop that skill, you can apply it in a lot of different ways. You can apply it to your everyday life. If things aren't going well, you'll be able to do a systems analysis of your day. 'Where did I lose energy today?' Ultimately you'll be able to hold all the components of your life in your mind and see which ones are not bright and shiny, which ones need to be changed. You can also apply it to your meditation practice. You know, your awareness has to be very strong to become enlightened. Eventually you hold the entire universe in your mind."

He paused. "I can't say enough good things about a career in computers, really. There are so many benefits for spiritual seekers." He laughed and shook his head. "Let's face it. This is America, a country high on technology and hedonism. We seem to need a new brand of spirituality. This is it. This is the way to be spiritual and live in the world."

I decided to follow my teacher's suggestions. I took an aptitude test for computer science and scored high. I was amazed and felt encouraged. Once I enrolled in computer classes, however, reality set in. My mind was an out-of-shape muscle that resisted exercise. Struggling through each programming assignment, I worked what seemed like endless hours. Finally I managed to graduate and landed a job for $24,000 a year...an amount that seemed huge to me in 1983.

Over the next few years, more and more of my teacher's students followed suit. In the end, everyone who studied long-term with him became proficient in computer science and had a highly successful career. In doing so, we developed strong, analytical minds that could be applied to any problem.

In the next phase of the Patriarchy project, Alexandria, Jackie, and I performed an in-depth analysis of the nine rings of the New World Order. We had named them and had the overall picture in our minds. Now it was necessary to refine our understanding of each ring, to drill down into each ring's energy, to figure out how they all worked together, and to see how the whole system had come into being. In order to take the Olympic-logo configuration of the nine rings apart, we needed to understand how it had been constructed. In computer terminology, we needed to reverse-engineer the Patriarchy.

The Order of the Nine Rings

In the aftermath of our meeting at the Longevity Café, I kept dreaming about the nine rings. I would see all of them stacked up, one on top of the other. Then, without warning, they would flip positions, my stomach would churn, and I would wake up feeling nauseated.

In one dream, my teacher said, *"Everything is reversed in this age. You live in a world obsessed with power."* This information was not new. He had made this sort of statement many times throughout the years, but I couldn't see how it applied to the nine rings.

After many dreams, meditations, and fruitless hours at my whiteboard, I finally had a breakthrough: each ring vibrated with the energy of a different chakra! By listing the seven personal chakras in their proper order—with the crown at the top and the root at the bottom—I was able to connect each chakra to one of the nine rings and describe it in its purest state, devoid of the influence of the Patriarchy:

Royalty ring (crown chakra)—composed of highly evolved, enlightened people who have fully opened their crown chakras so they can receive information from the higher spheres. This ring would hold the uppermost position in society and function from a place of complete purity and humility. Its role would be to see the correct direction for humanity, to guide, inspire, and enlighten.

Arts ring (third-eye chakra)—peopled by those who have developed their third eyes and who possess the ability to see into hidden dimensions, pull from them inspiration and ideas, and translate these into works of art on the physical plane. This ring would be given one of the most prominent positions in society. Artists would create art with the intention of educating, uplifting, and celebrating the evolution of humankind.

Media ring (throat chakra)—populated by those who have developed the qualities of the throat chakra, have the ability to communicate, and possess a love of expressing the truth. The Media ring would provide the dissemination of enlightened information, giving humanity as much information as it could handle in order to encourage evolution.

Resource Management ring (heart chakra)—comprised of individuals who naturally reside in their heart chakra, feel a kinship with the Earth, and can work with nature to provide abundance. This ring would help ensure the abundant supply and preservation of all natural resources and would provide/distribute the basic raw materials needed by the Industry ring.

Banking ring (navel chakra)—composed of people who easily align themselves with will power, have a gut feeling for the operation of society, and can structure a fair method of barter and exchange in order to keep society running smoothly. This ring would create a currency based on gold, which carries the vibration of the higher spheres, to enable people to purchase their basic goods and services.

Industry ring (second chakra)—populated by those who express the energy of birth and creativity, who can invent, design, and engineer ways of improving society. This ring would include industry, science, and technology. Its job would be to supply all the goods and services needed for the comfort and well-being of humanity, taking care of the basic necessities, so people could focus as much attention as possible on their growth and evolution.

Military ring (root chakra)—comprised of individuals who are well grounded in the natural order of society, who can feel when things get out of balance, and have the discipline and power to restore it. The Military ring would be used defensively and only as a last resort.

I stepped back from my whiteboard and thought, *Now that seems like a sane society! Perhaps that is how the rings will function in the golden age that my teacher predicted would commence at the end of 2012.*

As I gazed at the list, my teacher's words echoed in my mind: *"Everything in this age is reversed."* What would happen if the order of the chakras remained the same but the order of the rings was inverted?

I grabbed a red marker and scribbled a second list. As the ink flowed onto the whiteboard, I could feel I had hit upon the order of our present-day patriarchal debacle:

Military ring (crown chakra)—composed of the powerful US armed forces, the FBI, CIA, NATO, and various other military organizations, it implements maneuvers in order to bring about more fascist states. This ring holds a prominent role in society, implementing policies of domination and repression, enforcing the concept of martial law throughout the world.

Industry ring (third-eye chakra)—working through the Global 1000 and the World Trade Organization, it is concerned with the production of goods and services for profit—profit before people. This ring represses consciousness by distracting people with consumerism.

Banking ring (throat chakra)—less visible in society but wielding incredible influence through the funding of the other rings, it is responsible for the creation of worthless fiat money, control of wealth, and the taxing of the common people via inflation in order to equalize developed and developing countries. This ring harnesses people to the grindstones of their jobs, forces them into servitude to currency, and broadcasts the message that money is true wealth.

Resource Management ring (heart chakra)—acting through the World Bank/IMF, it grabs control of water and other natural resources in preparation for the One World Government. This ring convinces people that all resources—not only natural resources but their own optimism, inspiration, and strength—are limited.

Media ring (navel chakra)—its ringleaders, in bed with other corporate management, politicians, and royalty via the Bilderberger conferences, limit and sanitize news and related media, endorsing and channeling the propaganda necessary for the control of the masses.

Arts ring (second chakra)—demoted to the near-bottom of the social order as an unnecessary luxury and consists, for the majority of audiences in developed and developing countries, principally of television, pop music, and the commercial cinema. Like the Media ring, it promotes conformity, consumption, and a "me first" attitude.

Royalty ring (root chakra)—composed of the crowned heads of Europe, who claim to be mere figureheads as their respective governments rule, but are keener than ever on world domination via lower mystical methods and embody the image of spiritual leaders gone bad.

I backed up and leaned on the edge of my desk. This list felt sad... sad, but true.

I took a deep breath and scanned the two lists. They included only seven of the nine rings. The government and religion rings and their connections with chakras were missing. I honed in on them. They were somehow different.

Suddenly the light dawned. They too could be related to chakras—*transpersonal* chakras. Most of the transpersonal chakras are located *outside* the human body—below the root chakra and above the crown.

In the Patriarchy, the government and religion rings must hover above the other seven and serve as the ultimate control mechanisms!

Religion ring—provides the overarching method of oppression. It endorses a polarized set of moral rules to encourage guilt and includes demonic spheres to instill fear; it preaches that God is outside us and that only special savior beings can become enlightened; it dissuades people from investigating self-knowledge and tells them that they need church elders and special intercessors to interpret the divine. The Religion ring caps a person's spiritual aspiration.

Government ring—composed of misused power, manipulation, and repression. It is not representative of the people but of the powerful corporations that steamroll the planet. The Government ring puts a lid on society in order to hold the masses in check and protect the minority of the affluent.

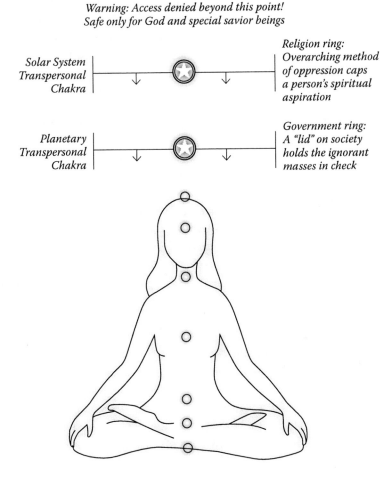

Warning: Access denied beyond this point!
Safe only for God and special savior beings

Solar System Transpersonal Chakra

Religion ring:
Overarching method of oppression caps a person's spiritual aspiration

Planetary Transpersonal Chakra

Government ring:
A "lid" on society holds the ignorant masses in check

In a golden age and in their proper order, these two rings will *underlie* society. They will function in a very different way but will be equally impersonal:

Government ring—an out-of-sight coordinator, like an entity organizing a conference attended by all of the other rings. If the government is doing a good job, working quietly behind the scenes, all people are aware of is the brilliantly run society it supports.

Spirituality ring (currently known as the Religion ring)—
works silently behind the scenes, as well. The Christian Bible
says that man shall have dominion over the Earth and all her plants
and animals. In the proper order, the Religion ring's dominion over
the Earth becomes the Spirituality ring's oneness with everything,
reverence for the Earth and all the life she fosters. In a golden age,
humans recognize that everything is infused with Spirit.

By determining the order, I had made a good beginning, but I
knew I had only scratched the surface. The combined energies of
the rings were much more complex, and I was incapable of doing a
complete systems analysis on my own. An array of skills needed to be
applied to the problem.

I phoned Alexandria and Jackie. They were ready and willing, and
Celeste also offered to help. Because the Patriarchy project dovetailed
with the energetic work she was doing with her students, she agreed
that it made sense to join forces.

The four of us embarked on a systems analysis of the New
World Order.

The Polarized Energies of the Patriarchy

We met the following day at Celeste's home, amid vases of fresh
flowers and statues of Buddhas. As we chose our seats at her long
wooden dining table, Celeste floated around the room pouring cups
of tea and laying out a plate of cookies. When she took her place at the
head of the table, I showed them the fruits of my previous day's labor.
My final version combined my two lists side by side:

Golden Age	Chakra	Chakra	Patriarchy
Royalty	Crown	Root	Military
Arts	Third Eye	Second	Industry
Media	Throat	Navel	Banking
Resource Managment	Heart	Heart	Resource Management
Banking	Navel	Throat	Media
Industry	Second	Third Eye	Arts
Military	Root	Crown	Royal

Jackie's eyes lit up. "Woo-o-o-o-o! Look at the polarities!"

Everyone leaned closer.

"This is the configuration I've been able to come up with thus far," I told them, "but I don't know what it means." I looked at Jackie hopefully. "Do you?"

She pulled the diagram toward her and gazed at it without saying anything. I held my breath. I could tell that she was about to leave this physical world and go into a place of pure seeing.

"The men who run the planet from behind the scenes have purposely designed this," she began slowly. "They have consciously inverted the energies of the rings to construct their patriarchal system. If you pull back from the diagram a bit, focusing on just the two columns of chakras, you can feel the polarities. They form an enclosed space—it almost feels like a prison camp." She grimaced. "It *is* a prison camp. People today think they are free, but that's only because they've never been beyond the perimeter."

She pushed the diagram back to the center of the table so everyone could see it and tapped her finger on the top row.

"First," she continued, "look at the polarities created by reversing the energies of the crown and the root chakras. The root chakra is about survival. The crown chakra acts as the gateway to higher knowledge. In the world today, these two energies have been reversed. So what does that mean to the average human? How does that play itself out in the world around us?

"The military should be used defensively, as the last resort when under attack, a way of preserving survival. Instead, it acts as the crowning glory. So the system that we live under programs us to believe that might makes right and martial law rules. It tells us, 'Let's bomb Iraq to protect the American way of life!'

"The job of royalty," she said, glancing at Alexandria, "is to guide, serve, and protect the realm. But today, royalty has taken a position at the root of society—out of sight, using mystical methods to control the world. So that mode of operation forms the foundation of society. Anything that gets built on top of that foundation, therefore, is built on the energies and desires of the royals. From that position, they dictate the rules for humanity. It's the classic feudal system, only our feudal system today is undercover. The people of the world, the peasants of the realm, don't know it, but they live by the grace of the royals. Basically this means that we work our asses off on their behalf. The ancient royal motto was 'To rule is to serve.' With the energies reversed, it becomes 'To rule is to *be served.*'"

She shook her head slowly and pointed to the next set of polarities.

"Next comes the inversion of the second chakra, associated with birth and creativity, with the third eye, which is the ability to see into the invisible realms.

"Industry should be finding more and more creative ways to serve humanity, but today industry is about consumerism. 'What's good for General Motors is good for the world.' When people look around, they see not with their third eyes but with their physical eyes, and what their physical eyes see are bigger and better things to buy, compliments of the corporation-run industrial sector.

"Artists use their third eyes to peer into the invisible realms and then create pure art that captures what they see, but today art is used in the service of commerce. We have artists who sell out to the public relations machine, artists who have to be businesspeople in order not to starve, painters who need a gallery to show their work. Hollywood is the movie *industry*, show *business*."

Her finger inched down the page.

"Then we have the inversion of the throat and navel chakras. The throat is the expression of the truth. The navel is will power, the drive to implement your dharma—to follow the path that is right for you.

"Money should be used to manifest and support the dharma, but in the world today, the planetary agreement is that money is the truth, money is real wealth. Money has become the expressive medium, and bankers are dictating the truth. So the belief system is that money can be used to buy the things that express who you are: 'a material girl in a material world.'

"The media should be reporting the truth, but the media today— these multi-national corporate giants—report not the truth but whatever the other eight rings need reported. It's sort of the difference between *thy will be done* and *my will be done*. Maybe that's why they call it the *me*-dia."

Jackie paused, studying the next polarity for a long moment. I looked up from the list, wondering why she had stopped. Tears filled her eyes.

"Finally," she continued, flicking off the emotion with a shake of the head, "we come to the heart chakra that represents love and compassion. It's in a sort of double bind. It's upside down and inside out. The heart, which should be expressing infinite love, is imploded. So in today's world, we have been programmed with the belief system that the heart is the expression of finite love. And in terms of the rings, we're dealing with natural resources. That means limited, polluted, depleted, and controlled resources. Life is constricted. 'Don't use the water, because there isn't enough.'"

She sat back in her chair.

Everyone stared at the diagram and was silent for a long while.

"It's fairly depressing, isn't it?" I ventured.

"Absolutely," Alexandria agreed and sighed. "And all *we* have to do is disassemble their work."

"Right," Jackie said. "No problem."

There was another long pause.

"Well," Celeste said in a soothing tone, "there's one positive thing about it. We've got the Divine Feminine on our side. Remember the story of the *Bhagavad Gita*? Remember how Arjuna, before he begins the great battle to reclaim his kingdom, is given two options? Either he can have vast armies to add to his military might, or he can have Lord Krishna as his solitary advisor? Of course, he chooses Krishna and then goes on to win the day. Well, we're in a similar situation. We're facing off with the patriarchal behemoth, and our solitary advisor is Mother Divine, the divine feminine energy in the universe." She smiled. "Personally, I think we should feel optimistic." She scanned each of our faces. "Please..." She smiled, gesturing to the plate on the table. "...have some cookies."

We ate everything.

The Schematic of the Patriarchy

A couple of days passed, and again we gathered around Celeste's dining room table. Jackie extracted new diagrams from her briefcase and laid them out. She quickly swept back her long red curls, took a hair band from her pocket, and made a pony tail. My hunch was that it was to be a no-nonsense session, that we were finally going to get to the bottom of things.

"Look at this!" she exclaimed, bringing her flattened hand down on the paper for emphasis. "Look at the architecture these guys have created!"

We studied her diagrams.

"This is what Spirit showed me last night while I was meditating on the Patriarchy. Its architecture is a perversion of the true alignment in consciousness of the planet! Her rightful energetic form is the Diamond Body—in other words, the integrated double-pyramid helix...."

I was familiar with the Diamond Body from Tibetan Buddhism. It was also called the *vajra* body. *Vajra* meant wisdom—hard and sharp as a diamond—that could be used to cut through erroneous conceptions. It was the subtle physical body that the spiritual seeker developed, after long years of practice, when on the verge of enlightenment...the gateway for reaching the subtlest primordial Clear Light.

As for "the integrated double-pyramid helix," I hadn't a clue. I looked up at Jackie and shook my head.

"Okay, okay," Jackie responded impatiently, "forget the terminology for a moment. Let me just show you the diagrams of the double pyramids. They really say it all anyway."

Jackie stood up, put her knee on her chair, and positioned the diagrams so the three of us could see them.

"The current cycle of time began twenty-six thousand years ago—give or take a few thousand years—and allegedly ends in 2012," she began. "At the beginning of this cycle, the energetic configuration of the Earth was like this." She tapped the diamond. "In terms of consciousness, this is Earth's natural state. It represents an integrated

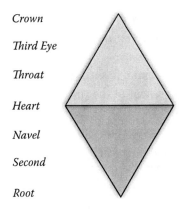

Crown

Third Eye

Throat

Heart

Navel

Second

Root

chakra alignment, with the root chakra at the base and the crown chakra at the top.

"The alignment, by the way, is fluid, not fixed. The Earth is actually pretty amorphous, I think—at least from her perspective. She can have earthquakes and morph easily. We perceive that as a big deal, but to her it is probably more like stretching or receiving a chiropractic adjustment. When I study pictures of other planets in our solar system, they seem fixed to me. They have a specific attention field. But when I look at the Earth, it appears fluid. That's probably why humans have incarnated here. It provides a malleable environment in which to change and evolve. Earth is like a laboratory, able to contain any experiment within her boundaries…which is actually very cool when you think about it.

"So, around the beginning of the ancient Egyptian culture, the global elite separated the two pyramids energetically. You could think of the two pyramids as above and below, Spirit and matter, heaven

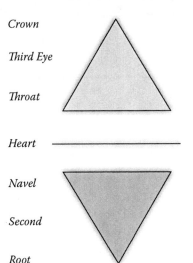

Crown

Third Eye

Throat

Heart

Navel

Second

Root

and earth. When they separated them energetically, suddenly the idea came into being that earth was not heaven, matter was not Spirit.

"This was the original split in consciousness, what some people call 'falling from grace.' It produced a major disconnect in everyone's psyche and was the first installation of *un*consciousness. When the two pyramids separated, the center of the resulting structure—the heart center—was emptied of love and devoid of flow. Without the integrated structure of consciousness, the heart became a wasteland, a desolate desert that no one wanted to venture into."

Our past life in the Egyptian mystery school flashed through my mind. Jackie was describing the exact moment of the turning point on the planet when our spiritual fall had taken place. My questions resurfaced. Had our fall created an opening through which the Patriarchy had entered? Had the snakes in my Egyptian life—the one wrapped around my heart and the other that bit my heart before I fell unconscious—been my own personal experience of the heart becoming a wasteland? I wanted to ask but held my tongue. I didn't want to interrupt, and I sensed that our work would ultimately reveal the answers.

"The second thing," Jackie was saying when I tuned back in, "happened later in Egypt, around the time of the pharaohs. The global elite changed the positions of the two separated pyramids. They reversed them. The pyramid on the top moved to the bottom position, and the one on the bottom moved to the top position. On an energetic level, they reversed their polarities. On the physical level, this was experienced as the Earth flipping her poles, the polar shift that geologists and physicists have documented.

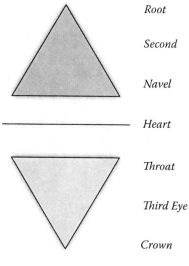

Root

Second

Navel

Heart

Throat

Third Eye

Crown

"At this point in time, the power of the feminine was truly *usurped*." She pointed at the lower half of the diagram. "Our teacher spent a lot of time telling us that women naturally orient to the three lower power chakras, that women are actually—despite appearances to the contrary—more powerful than men and better suited to wield power than men. So when they reversed the two pyramids, feminine energy—energy that expresses itself though all of the lower chakras—was taken out of its power position. And guess what moved into that place? Masculine power. The masculine took the reins of power on the planet. The reversal of the pyramids solidified the patriarchal base of power, and there was no turning back.

"In this new position, the pyramids had a tendency to move away from each other. Have you ever put two batteries in your flashlight not facing the proper direction? They don't conduct the energy the way they were configured to. They seem to fight each other and try to push apart. Energetically, in this position, the configuration was unstable, so one last step was necessary to create a stable configuration, something that would be usable by those who wanted to control it.

"The third and final change was that the two pyramids were inverted. At this stage, they repulsed one another energetically. This would be like putting two magnets together. But this configuration is actually energetically stable. The two pyramids are held in opposition by the *polarized force* of the patriarchal system. In other words, they had created the world of duality so often written about in ancient spiritual texts.

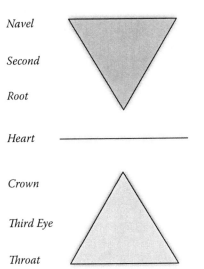

Navel

Second

Root

Heart

Crown

Third Eye

Throat

"Now we've reached the stage of *power over*, true domination. The alignment created by the global elite is held together by force. As we know, true power is the Love of the Divine. Force is the misuse of power, power as it is expressed in a dualistic world. Using force, rather than power, results in martial activity. So with the pyramids in this configuration, they had finally constructed a usable system."

She tapped the diagram one final time. "And right in the middle of the whole upside-down, inside-out bastardization, you have the heart center—the cosmic gateway for Divine Love and Light—holding out on itself, dominating itself into submission...something which is seemingly impossible but..." she smiled, "...*architecturally* brilliant."

Jackie sat down. "The bottom line," she concluded, "is that the patriarchal world is a reversed image of the original, and the planet needs to be returned to her rightful Diamond Body alignment." She paused and slumped back in her chair. "I rest my case."

"Wow," I murmured after a few moments, my eyes like saucers. "You've reverse-engineered the bloody Patriarchy!"

Jackie shrugged then folded her arms.

Alexandria nodded her head thoughtfully. "It's impressive work, Jackie. There's no question."

I had to confess that without the diagrams, I would have been lost. I really didn't comprehend all the details the way Jackie did, but I didn't have to. As our seer, that was her job. What was important was that the energetic configuration of the Diamond Body was of crucial importance, the end result that we needed to move toward.

I breathed a sign of relief. Our analysis was done. Now, in order to figure out how to proceed, we pooled our psychic skills.

13
A GLOBAL SEEING EXERCISE

Celeste always had a calm demeanor. Today her pastel blue caftan accentuated this. She had been absorbing everything Jackie had said, and now she drew a deep breath, exhaled slowly, then leaned forward, clasping her hands before her on the table.

"Here's what I think. One day, in meditation, I had a vision. I saw the inverted triangles with the points facing each other. My guides told me that the configuration represented the world and that it also represented me as I was then, in my unenlightened state. They said that the triangles inside of me were going to move down over each other...not all the way, but just until they formed a Star of David. Then the Diamond Body was to be a third stage. The Diamond Body formed as the two triangles moved completely over each other to unite at their bases. The imagery they presented to me was quite graphic."

"Like this?" Alexandria asked, showing us the quick sketches she had made.

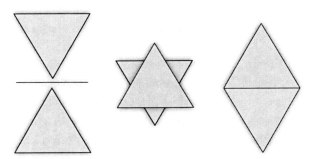

"Precisely," Celeste agreed. "At the time, I did some research on the Star of David. It looks exactly like the Jewish star and is historically linked to King David who had a Star of David in his astrological chart. But it is not limited to the Jewish faith and the Kabbalah. It also appears in Buddhist, Theosophical, and various other Eastern and Western traditions. It is a symbol of integration, linking heaven and earth, the masculine and feminine, yin and yang. In other words, as above so below." She paused, considering the diagrams for a moment. "So, I am wondering if this information is relevant now. Is the way to move the planet from where she is currently—the patriarchal inversion of the truth—to where she needs to be—the Diamond Body—to progress through the intermediate step of the Star of David?"

Jackie nodded vigorously.

"Okay," I said, "if you free the blocked-up heart energy of the planet, won't the two triangles automatically begin to move toward each another, form the Star of David, and eventually end up in the Diamond Body position? Isn't freeing the heart's energy the key to how we proceed with the project?"

"Yes," Celeste agreed, "but that may be a tough assignment right off the bat. You're talking about the imploded heart of the whole planet, the suffering of all humanity. There may be lynch pins that need to be pulled prior to working on the heart."

The Earth's Knot of Vishnu

"The first step," Celeste continued, "may be the Knot of Vishnu."

I was bewildered. "What is the Knot of Vishnu?"

"It's a point between the navel chakra and the heart chakra," Alexandria told me, "...the diaphragm, more or less."

"As an infant, it's the first place you contract when you cry," Celeste explained. "It's the place where people feel fear, the origin of the desire to control. I've noticed that my students hold a tremendous number of issues there, so when I start to work with a new student, I must initially help them free up their Knot of Vishnu." She pointed to the diagram. "It may be the same for Mother Earth. It's clear that her heart is being blocked. The heart is the Earth's strength, so it's obvious that the heart energy needs to be freed, but it seems to me that the first step is to help her untie her Knot of Vishnu. That would set her on the road to regaining her strength."

"So, if *people* feel fear and the desire to control at their Knots of Vishnu, what do you think *Mother Earth* experiences at hers?" I asked. "In other words, what does this mean in terms of collective consciousness?"

Celeste paused to gather her thoughts before answering. I knew that she had spent years explaining this to her students, but she now laid out the facts patiently.

"When a person meditates," she began, "kundalini rises from the base of the spine and passes through the higher chakras. After many lifetimes of spiritual practice, the kundalini stabilizes and naturally resides at one of the higher chakras. Someone may have pulled the kundalini up to the heart chakra in a given lifetime. In their next life, they may stabilize the kundalini at the level of the third eye. This is the ascension process. At each stage of ascension, the person's vibration speeds up.

"It is the same for the Earth. As she has evolved, her vibration has sped up, and successively higher chakras have gotten activated. During the Matrilineal Period—the era that preceded the current Patriarchal Period—the Earth resonated with the energy of the second chakra, and humanity learned lessons about birth and creativity. During the Patriarchy, the Earth's vibration sped up to the level of the navel chakra, so humanity has received schooling in both power and abuse of power. Because the navel chakra is the third chakra from the base of the spine, it makes sense that we refer to the world as the third dimension.

"Currently the planet is trying to move to a heart-chakra-based society centered at the fourth chakra—what I like to call the new fourth-dimensional world. The fourth dimension resonates with heart-based energy and is a place where one learns about unconditional love, where community, collaboration, and cooperation are the organizing principles. And as humanity struggles to move from the third to the fourth dimension, people get this discomfort in the area of the diaphragm. In terms of the collective consciousness of the planet, this is precisely where we are at. Under the surface, people are feeling like, 'Oh my God, if I don't follow the system, something terrible will happen. If I abandon the patriarchal model, I will become destitute and die.'

"The patriarchal system is predicated on the imbalance between masculine and feminine energies. Jackie has given us a technical explanation for how that imbalance came about. Now let me share the knowledge I've gained about the imbalance from years of processing it in the collective.

"To understand male dominance, we must first understand *chaos*. In the view of the masculine, the feminine is chaotic. By and large, when men encounter female chaos, their immediate response is to bring it under control, but this implies a misunderstanding of chaos. Chaos is actually the ability to surrender and let the Divine rule. Implicit in chaos is Divine Order, but that is not generally understood by men.

"This constant threat of chaos forces men into a dominant position. As authority figures, they cannot have any faults, cannot admit to having any faults. Men must not fail or, when they do fail, they must assume the stance 'That will never happen again.' They must remain superior, and that means holding women down. As long as this polarity of chaos and control reigns on the planet, equality isn't possible. If there were equality, men would lose control, and chaos would run rampant.

"The Bible states that man shall have dominion over the earth. When women submit to this dictate, they allow men to be in control, they project authority onto men. So, throughout the Patriarchal Age, women have operated with the mindset 'Obey or be killed,' 'Conform or be ostracized.'" Celeste paused and closed her eyes.

I was about to ask a question, then realized that she was meditating, feeling her way more deeply into the imbalance between the masculine/feminine. This was the issue that had captivated me for years. I held my breath, waiting.

After a minute, she drew a sharp intake of breath, opened her eyes, and placed her hand on her heart. "Women *agreed* to give away their feminine power! This is something new that I'm seeing only now. At the beginning of the Patriarchal Age, we all signed up for the same task, women and men alike. We all agreed to play out the third-chakra-based society, with its focus on power, for the evolution of the masculine and, therefore, humankind. Females have been repressed for thousands of years, and we have never understood why, but we actually *agreed* to help men learn about power so that all of us, men and women alike, could ascend into the heart."

I let this new information settle into my awareness field to see how it felt. I thought back to the beginning of the project. Initially I had looked on the global elite as the dark forces. Then, before my departure for Europe, I had put myself in their shoes, realized they didn't perceive themselves as dark forces, and stopped judging them. Now I tentatively investigated this new level of understanding. Did women really agree to give up the reins of power for the evolution of the planet? Yes. What Celeste had seen felt absolutely correct.

"So," Alexandria said softly, "that means that, truly, there is no good and bad in the world today. Men are not bad. Women are not bad. The man in the South Pacific and the global elite are not bad." A smile of resignation played across her face. "It also means that, regardless of the way things look on the surface, all of us—the global elite and light-workers across the globe—are working toward the same goal: to aid humanity in its ascension to a new level of consciousness. As light-workers, our job is to align ourselves with Spirit and to process patriarchal energies. The man in the South Pacific simply has a different job: to push humanity down so that it will finally rebel and ascend."

Silence fell on the group, the room grew very still, and we spontaneously lapsed into meditation. Then I became aware of a distinctly feminine energy. Slowly it filled the room, permeating and enlivening everything...so subtle...so refined.

What is this exquisite energy? I thought. Then I sensed Her—the all-encompassing presence of the Divine Feminine. Somewhere high above us, Mother Divine herself was gazing down on our tiny foursome. Her grace descended like infinitesimal raindrops, as if to bless our new depth of understanding. As it fell, it washed away any remaining illusion I might have held that women had been victimized during the Patriarchy.

Had I ever encountered the energy of the Divine Mother before? It was different from the rooted, unshakable energy of Mother Earth. It didn't have the caring, nourishing quality of Lakshmi. It certainly didn't resemble the fiery passion of Kali, nor did it feel like any of the aspects of the feminine I was familiar with. No, this energy was beyond all of them—pure presence, pure beingness, with the higher-octave vibration that is the trademark of feminine energy, that from which all aspects of the Divine Feminine issue forth. Perhaps I had experienced it before and just not recognized it. Perhaps it had been there all along but was too subtle to cognize. Until now.

The Earth's Assemblage Point

After we had taken a break and reassembled, I posed a question: "Do we need to shift the assemblage point of the Earth?"

"Refresh me on assemblage points," Celeste said.

"It's a mystical term," Alexandria told her. "When our teacher used to shift our assemblage points, he said that it changed the point in our awareness field at which awareness assembles. He explained that the universe is composed of luminous fibers. The position of your assemblage point determines your perception of those luminous fibers. It orders them, assembles them into a steady stream of perception, dictates the way you view the world around you. The assemblage point is the point in a person's subtle physical body around which their awareness is centered. When the assemblage point is shifted from one location in the subtle body to another, it results in a totally new perspective."

Celeste nodded.

"So," I told them, "I'm thinking that perhaps the Earth has an assemblage point, a point on the globe at which the attention of the collective consciousness is centered. If the assemblage point is shifted, perhaps humanity will suddenly have a new perspective. Everyone will be able to see the current patriarchal configuration of control more clearly. This would allow everyone to make a clear choice—either to continue in the world of control or to ascend to the new fourth-dimensional world."

Celeste excused herself from the table, left the room, and returned a few moments later with a world globe. "Since we agreed to work together," she told us, "the Isle de Sol has come to mind repeatedly. I don't know why." She pointed to a place off the coast of Africa. "These are the Cape Verde islands, and here's a little island in the chain called the Isle de Sol."

"Celeste," Alexandria interrupted, "do you remember the last time we flew to South Africa? We were on separate flights, but we both had to change planes at the airport on the Isle de Sol."

"That's right," Celeste said, continuing to look at the globe.

Alexandria smiled and shook her head. "When I project myself back to the Isle de Sol and remember its energy, it feels contracted, like the diaphragm feels just before you start to cry. Is it possible that the Isle de Sol is the Earth's Knot of Vishnu?"

Celeste nodded slowly, allowing time for feeling the concept, then said, "You're right. It *is* Mother Earth's Knot of Vishnu."

Jackie shook her head and chuckled. "This is amazing. Don't you see what has happened? All three of you are seeing the same thing!"

I stared at her in confusion.

"Look," she continued, "the Isle del Sol is Mother Earth's Knot of Vishnu. The Knot of Vishnu is the place where fear arises. The assemblage point for collective consciousness is located at the Isle de Sol. Get it? If humanity perceives the world via its assemblage point at the Knot of Vishnu at the Isle de Sol, that means that humanity perceives the world through the glasses of fear. So, in order for humanity to move out of its current configuration, humanity needs a new assemblage point." She grinned and opened her hands in a gesture of finality. "Therefore, the assemblage point needs to be shifted to a new location."

I nodded, stood up, moved to where Celeste was sitting, and asked to look at the globe. "The north and south poles are directly opposite each other, naturally. And look: Mount Kailas in Tibet, the Earth's crown chakra, and Machu Picchu in Peru, the root chakra, are directly opposite each other. So I wonder what is directly opposite the Isle de Sol?"

I rotated the globe and stopped short. "Give me a minute...." I quickly turned the globe back around and started over, carefully locating the latitude and longitude of the Isle de Sol, then finding the corresponding point on the other side of the globe. My finger was sitting on the islands of the South Pacific! I swallowed. "The assemblage point for the collective consciousness is directly opposite the man in the South Pacific. Do you suppose he lives in the South Pacific because he is actually holding the assemblage point in place? Is he holding humanity in a configuration of fear?"

I was answered by a stunned silence.

Jackie suddenly pointed to the globe excitedly. "What is halfway between the Isle de Sol and the man in the South Pacific? What if the assemblage point was shifted ninety degrees?"

I rotated the globe then drew a sharp intake of breath. "*We* are!" I slowly looked around the table at each of them. "Here in New Mexico, we are halfway."

Jackie whistled.

I paused to gather my thoughts, and my heart sped up. "I think I know where we are supposed to shift the assemblage point to: the Caldera above Los Alamos."

I walked briskly back to my chair and sat down. "I don't remember our teacher ever speaking to us as a group about the Caldera, but in a private conversation he said that the sinking of Atlantis was due to a giant explosion and that the land that comprises the Caldera was the spot where the explosion actually took place. When everything blew sky high, that's where the piece of land ended up. He explained how, during World War II, Oppenheimer developed the atomic bomb in Los Alamos. The scientists were able to construct the bomb in record time because they were drawing on the energy of the Caldera. So ultimately, what he said about the Caldera was"—I paused to assemble his exact words in my mind —"'Whenever it is time for the world to change, that's where it happens.'"

No one said anything. Celeste gazed at the globe. Jackie stared at her diagrams. Alexandria closed her eyes. Everyone reflected on the idea of shifting the assemblage point from the Isle de Sol to the Caldera, from the place of fear to the place of rapid world change.

"It all feels right to me," Celeste finally said.

Jackie and Alexandria nodded their assent.

I knew beyond the shadow of a doubt that the Caldera should be the new assemblage point.

The Game Plan

We put the diagrams away and finished our tea. Our seeing exercise was complete. That didn't mean that we knew precisely how the project would unfold; it only meant that we could identify the next few steps. As Jackie put it, we had assembled all the pieces of the seeing, given them a good shake, then thrown them out on the table to see how they fell.

So how should we proceed? We put our heads together and came up with a game plan for the initial stage of our energetic work.

First we would reclaim the seven Earth chakras. In their current state, under the control of the global elite, they were out of commission. If Mother Earth was to evolve, if her vibration was to speed up, if she was to ascend beyond her third-dimensional, navel-chakra-based configuration into a new fourth-dimensional level of unconditional love, then her chakras—and especially her heart chakra—needed to function optimally.

Afterwards we felt intuitively that we would be able to pull the lynch pin of the Knot of Vishnu, and that meant moving the assemblage point from the Isle de Sol to the Caldera, shifting perception, opening people's eyes to the Earth's spiritual transformation and, therefore, to their own ascended possibilities. We agreed that this should be done on the upcoming summer solstice. That felt like the right timing. It gave us more than three months to focus on the Earth chakras.

As for the Diamond Body, that would happen later. The Diamond Body was intimately tied to the nine rings of the New World Order. As Jackie had illustrated in her diagrams, the global elite had inverted the double pyramids energetically, created a perversion of the true alignment in consciousness of the planet, and manufactured an inverted version of the truth. The lynch pin here was the disconnected heart energy in the patriarchal system and, therefore, in collective consciousness. This piece of energetic work lay farther ahead and was harder for us to envision, but we guessed we would end up working on the nine rings. Perhaps we would work with all of the rings—the seven, the nine, the three, and the one.

"It sounds like you're set," Celeste said, "so I leave this project in your capable hands."

I grimaced. I hated to lose Celeste.

She smiled at me. "I've got my own projects. I have a whole spiritual organization to manage and lots of students. This is *your* project." She turned her head slowly, looking at each of us in turn. "This is your dharma, your life's work." Her eyes came back to me. "When you received your assignment, you were told to identify the mystical structure that underlies the Patriarchy, then take it apart. We've come to a deep understanding of the nine rings of the New World Order in our work sessions. Now it's time for the three of you—a seer, a sovereign, and a soldier—to dismantle them. It's time for you to use all the training our teacher gave you. It's time for you to become the mystical warriors you truly are."

Her words made me feel sad. Celeste had been such an asset, such a remarkable seer and facilitator. A wave of uneasiness crept through me as I thought about the uncharted territory that lay ahead. Would I be able to hold up my end as the team's soldier? Would we make mistakes without the benefit of Celeste's enlightened input? I took a deep breath and slowly exhaled. Only if I took the next step would I know.

PART THREE

DISMANTLING

THE UNDERLYING

STRUCTURE

OF THE

PATRIARCHY

14
THE MASCULINE VERSUS THE FEMININE—ROUND ONE

The following week I flew to Washington, DC, to investigate the notion that had taken root after our tea party at the Longevity Café: that I was supposed to live in the DC area in order to hold the Earth's fractured throat chakra. Intuitively, I felt I should move there in the spring, but moving halfway across the country was a major undertaking. What if my intuition were wrong? I needed to visit the area to be absolutely sure.

Anders had immediately jumped on the DC bandwagon. He felt he could get a superior education on the East Coast and had already started applying to universities.

My friend Robert invited me to stay with him and his wife, Elaine, in their Victorian home in Fairfax, Virginia. I was delighted. I had a soft spot in my heart for Robert, someone with a deep spiritual longing for truth and a highly cultivated aesthetic sense. He had a Master's degree in media from UCLA. He had also been a student of my teacher. Now he held down two jobs, one as a computer scientist and another as a writer, director, and producer of films—mostly films about Tibet, which had become his passion.

On my first evening there, as Robert poured chardonnay into two crystal glasses, I sat on the Italian silk couch in his living room and studied him: the finely chiseled features, the reading glasses halfway down his nose, his handsome cardigan sweater. He fused the formality of DC with the zest of Hollywood. He handed me my glass, then sat down in the easy chair adjacent to the couch, kicked off his loafers, and stretched out his legs on the ottoman. After we reminisced for a few minutes about the good old days with our teacher and the heretofore unrecognized brilliance of a stage play we had co-authored in Los Angeles, I described some of my energetic work in Europe.

Robert listened attentively but studied his wine glass for a long moment before responding. "You don't seriously think you changed the energy of the places you visited, do you?"

He lifted his head to look at me, and I bristled.

"What I mean," he continued evenly, "is that we all see our own minds projected out onto the world. We don't really see the world the way it is: a formless flux of energy. We see our own egoic structures, our own minds. There is nothing, really, but our own minds. What's out there," he gestured to the room then tapped his forehead, "is really a mirror for what's in here. To think that your energetic work is actually affecting places on the Earth..." He raised his eyebrows. "... that could be a dangerous stance for the ego to take, no?"

My body flushed with impatience. I had witnessed dramatic shifts in the energy of numerous Bilderberg hotels. Who did Robert think he was to cast doubt on my personal experiences? Yet I had to admit his logic was sound. My personal processing had certainly shown me that I viewed the world through my own mental constructs. I bit my lip and decided against arguing.

"I plan to drive into DC tomorrow," I said, changing the subject. "I'd like to see the Washington Monument. On my last visit, I noticed that its energy was pretty awful. Would you like to join me?"

He shook his head. "Thanks, but I have to work. Besides, if what you say is true, I'll be safer out here in the 'burbs." He winked. "But Elaine would probably agree with your assessment. She commutes into DC every day and complains constantly about the energy."

Washington's Giant Amplifier

The next morning I drove my rental car into the capital. It was a cold, clear March day. Rush hour was over, so I breezed along the

Curtis Memorial Parkway, then zipped across the Potomac River Bridge. The Washington Monument came into view, towering above the skyline. Its presence was riveting as I drove toward it, almost as though I was being pulled, a fish on a line getting reeled in, but I yanked my eyes away and made a left turn. I wanted to make a couple of stops first.

Standing in front of the World Bank/IMF, I could feel that Alexandria had been right. The World Bank was the One World Government ruse for commandeering natural resources. Again I sensed an energetic grid with lines running out in all directions. In Bretton Woods, I had wondered if they connected the World Bank with the countries it loaned money to. I could see now that they did: countries whose resources were being siphoned off.

From the World Bank, I drove south along Constitution Avenue to the Federal Reserve, parked the car in front, and studied it through the passenger window. With my visit to the Bank for International Settlements in Switzerland fresh in my mind, what did the Fed feel like? It felt like a stepped-down version of the Bank for International Settlements. That was easy, now that I knew it was all part of the Banking ring.

I waited for a break in the traffic, then made a U-turn and headed north toward the Washington Monument. As I parked the car, the heavy, drugged energy of DC began seeping into my awareness field. I wasn't going to let it get the best of me. I powered through it, walked purposely to the ticket booth, then joined the line of sightseers waiting for the elevator that takes visitors to the top.

I trembled as chilly gusts of wind shot past me. I zipped up my jacket and craned my neck to look at the monument: five hundred fifty-five feet of white marble, shaped like an Egyptian obelisk. All at once I had the unsettling feeling that something was about to happen. Then the line started to move, and I shook it off. I decided it was probably nothing.

Once at the observation deck, I joined the procession of tourists looking out the windows, marveling at the panoramic views of the capital far below, but my mind was so distorted that I couldn't see anything. I was alternately dizzy and nauseated. I stood to one side and closed my eyes, desperately trying to enter a more meditative state.

What would you like me to cognize here? I asked, hoping the Lineage would have some advice.

After a moment, I received an answer: *"You should...."*

My eyes snapped opened. The slowly intoned words had oozed degradation and manipulation. It had *not* been the voice of the Lineage!

I shouldered my way through the crowds, boarded the elevator, and felt it begin its descent. I knew exactly who it was. In Europe I had witnessed the man in the South Pacific arguing with Queen Elizabeth. Upon realizing that the Bilderberg web was coming unraveled, he had begun scanning, searching for the person responsible.

My stomach churned. The thing I had feared most in Europe had happened. He had located me! He knew who I was. My distorted state of mind on the observation deck had resulted from being steeped in the misaligned energy of the Washington Monument, but the spoken words had come from the man in the South Pacific. He wanted to throw me off, to prevent me from investigating.

When the elevator doors opened at ground level, I exited the monument, strode outside, and was immediately jolted out of my deliberations. Something lay on the stone pavement in front of me, and I jumped aside to avoid stepping on it. It was a long snake! Confusion flooded my mind. *A snake at the Washington Monument?* Cautiously, I bent over to examine it and released my breath. It was only a green, toy snake that some child had dropped.

I trudged back to my car. I was feeling shaken, but I was not giving up on my expedition to take a psychic reading of the Washington Monument. Perhaps gazing at it from a distance would prove more productive. I drove to the Thomas Jefferson Memorial on the opposite side of the Potomac River Tidal Basin.

When I arrived at the circular memorial, I devoted a few minutes to reading the inspirational inscriptions below the dome. That gave my consciousness a lift. Then I walked outside, sat on the marble steps, and gazed at the Washington Monument.

With the water basin in front of me to buffer the energy, I was able to have a clear psychic perception. The monument sat precisely on the Eastern Coastline—part of what I now knew was the planet's circular throat chakra, responsible for broadcasting the truth—and its job was to function as an amplifier. Had Mother Earth's chakra been free and clear, resonating with a higher frequency as it should have been, the monument would have been broadcasting beautiful energy. Instead, it was amplifying the dark energies of the bankers and the Bilderbergers who had commandeered it. The Washington Monument, whether or not it had been designed that way, was a giant, masculine symbol of power that amplified the oppressive energy of the global elite.

I sighed. More energetic work needed to be done to clear the throat chakra, but Alexandria, Jackie, and I would tackle it soon enough. Besides, I felt much too out of kilter to attempt it now.

I stood up and headed for the parking lot. As I passed two security guards walking along the sidewalk making their rounds, I overheard part of their conversation.

"...there were all these cars," the woman said to the man, "and each ran over this long snake in the road. It was like they went out of their way to run over it, but the snake somehow managed to keep slithering on."

I winced and hurried past. When I entered the sanctuary of my rental car, I locked the doors and took a couple of slow, deep breaths. Why did images of snakes keep coming up? Something about the two snakes seemed strangely familiar, but I couldn't quite place it.

The Soldier Finds her Base Camp

Over the next three days, I put hundreds of miles on my rental car driving around the DC metropolitan area—into Virginia, Maryland, Delaware—scouting out possible places to live. But none of them clicked. By the fourth day I was ready to throw in the towel. Maybe I wasn't supposed to move after all.

I decided to take a break and check out the school that topped

Anders' list, the College of William and Mary in Williamsburg, Virginia. It was a long way from DC—almost three hours south on Interstate 95—but as soon as I arrived, I felt like dropping to my knees. Williamsburg was where I was supposed to live! It sat directly on the throat chakra, and because it was connected to Jamestown—one of the first colonies—it possessed an aura of newness and change, the spirit of the founding fathers.

I found the college, parked on a side street, and passed beyond the gray stone walls that encircled the campus. Strolling along paths that Thomas Jefferson had used when he'd attended the school, I paused often to admire the ivy-covered buildings and stately trees. It was no mistake that I had come to William and Mary. Energetically, the campus was the heart and soul of Williamsburg, and Williamsburg was a circuit on the circuit board of the throat chakra. If I was supposed to shepherd this chakra, Williamsburg was the place to be.

I called Anders. "William and Mary is stellar. You would love it."

"Then go into the admissions office and do some magic," he insisted.

I hesitated. "What do you mean, 'Do some magic'?"

"You know, you know…some of that energetic work you do."

"Well, it may not be that simple. It needs to be in line with the dharma…"

"And remember," he interrupted, "it's an expensive school. So not only do you need to get me accepted, you need to get me a scholarship."

I shook my head. "Anders, if it's dharmic for you to come here, then you will." I sighed. "But I'll see what I can do."

I located the admissions building, sat down on the front steps, stilled my mind, and silently said a prayer to the Lineage: *If this is where Anders is supposed to go to school and if this is where I am supposed to live and if we are supposed to be together here in Williamsburg, then a full scholarship would be very much appreciated.*

Without hesitation, the response came: *"It's done."*

This time it really was the voice of the Lineage.

The Amplifier Gets Cleared

On my first morning back in New Mexico, I sat to meditate and turned my attention to the toxic Washington Monument, and instantly it was right in front of me.

Is it possible to clear its energy? I asked the Lineage.

As if in answer to my question, the white obelisk moved, ever so slowly, inside my awareness field. My body *became* the monument.

At first I was only aware of its sizzling toxicity. I held perfectly still. *Don't judge its energy,* I instructed myself. *Be neither attracted nor repulsed.* Gradually, I began to feel the strength of the monument's massive marble blocks. Its power engulfed me, and, as it did, the air became charged with the spirit of America's founding fathers.

I found myself making an announcement on the inner planes: *From this time forward, the Washington Monument stands as an obelisk of light, its energy extending out to all fifty states. May it broadcast life, liberty, and the pursuit of happiness.*

Little by little, it began to shed its distorted haze. After a few minutes, it stood pure and radiant in the morning light, like a diamond mounted on the ring of the throat chakra.

Suddenly I saw the man in the South Pacific in the distance, staring at the scene: another of his prize possessions taken, more of his handiwork destroyed, his attempts to block the energetic work thwarted. Cold eyes surveyed the scene, and a calculating mind assessed the damage. Slowly he looked from the monument to me, then locked his gaze on mine.

My balanced state of mind vanished. Panic stabbed at my gut, and fingers of fear tightened around my throat. Frozen, I tried to wrench my eyes away from his but failed.

Long moments passed. Then, ever so slightly, he bowed, a martial artist acknowledging his opponent at the start of a sparring match. As he turned his back on the scene, a faint smile flickered across his features. Then he was gone.

Getting Confirmation

The following week I wondered if the energy of the Washington Monument had really shifted. Was it possible to do this type of energetic work remotely? Perhaps Robert would be willing to visit the monument and check it out for me. I picked up the phone and dialed his number.

"Robert, do you have a moment?"

"Sure, but first I have a little matter to discuss with you."

"All right."

"When you were here in DC," he continued, "you told me that the Washington Monument was broadcasting dark energy, remember? Well, Elaine and I were in the capital yesterday, and after our lunch appointment we drove over to the monument because I wanted to check out your theory for myself. When we arrived I couldn't believe it. I've never felt anything like it. It wasn't broadcasting dark energy. It was pristine. The energy was unbelievably beautiful. We sat at the base of the monument and had a wonderful meditation." He paused. "Anyway, I just wanted to tell you that I disagree with your assessment. Now, what was your question?"

15

THE FEMININE COLLABORATES TO
RECLAIM THE EARTH

At the end of March, 2003, Jackie, Alexandria, and I began our collaborative effort to dismantle the underlying structure of the Patriarchy, a demanding journey that would change our lives forever. Following the game plan that had evolved out of our global seeing exercise, we began by meditating on the seven chakras of Mother Earth. As we did, we evolved a tried-and-true template for performing the energetic work.

To prepare, we researched locations, did sessions via phone, and placed pictures of the power places on our meditation tables. Then we scheduled virtual meditations, something like virtual conferencing. Each of us sat in her own home, and we began at a synchronized time: Jackie in California at 2:00 a.m., Alexandria and me on Mountain Time at 3:00. It was a pain having to set the alarm for the middle of the night, but it was the optimal hour for adventures in alternate dimensions. The world was still, people slept, and there was a minimum of psychic debris.

Our meditation model was always the same. At the beginning we performed an invocation. We asked the assistance of our teacher, the Lineage, Mother Earth, and other benevolent beings who wished to aid the Earth in her time of spiritual transition. We solicited Mother Divine to direct the work. Then we stated our intention to clear the work of the global elite, always adding a prayer: "If our seeing to transmute the energies of the ring is correct, if it is aligned with the will of Spirit, if it is dharmic for the Earth, for humanity, and for us, please use our bodies here on Earth in whatever way is appropriate."

After the assiduity of the invocation, a brief period of quiet always followed. We stilled our minds, moved our personal egos aside, and focused on the ring, our combined intention producing a stable, three-way mystical circuit. At this stage, our crown chakras opened. Light descended from some dimension high above us. The light was always blue-white in color.

At first we were puzzled. Why was the transformative light an ethereal blue?

Jackie found something interesting on the Internet that read as follows:

> "As [Earth] changes increase, outward signs occur, such as spiritual manifestations and signs in the heavens. One such heavenly sign is the Blue Star.... [T]his celestial object is pure spiritual energy, a star made manifest by spiritual forces.... It has visited the Earth many times, most recently 2,000 years ago...to announce the birth of [Christ] whose task was to remind man of his divine nature. This same star also visited Earth 12,000 years ago, to warn of the coming Flood—the sinking of Atlantis.... Each time the star came because it was called and its assistance was needed during [times of] transition. Once again, the Blue Star returns...."[141]

"This is where the blue-white energy is coming from," she determined. "We've been invoking its essence without even realizing we were doing it!"

Each time this luminous blue light of spiritual energy descended, it passed through the beings assembled in other dimensions, entered our crown chakras, and moved into our bodies. We would feel it collect in our heart chakras, then watch as it flowed out to the ring and began commingling with its patriarchal energies.

That always set off the fireworks! Then it was anything but quiet. From that point forward, it was anybody's guess as to what would happen next. The three of us would fasten our seatbelts for the wild clearing process that always ensued. Sometimes we simply bore witness to the fireworks. More often than not, we were given instructions for how to help. And because we were part of our teacher's Egyptian ring of power—a seer, a sovereign, and a soldier—the work always unfolded magically as the psychic baton was passed without verbal communication from one of us to another, at random but in perfect order, until the work was complete.

Afterwards, when we compared our experiences, we never ceased to be amazed at the synchronicity: We each meditated for precisely the same amount of time and had clocked the same shifts in energy, and our visions were so clear and vivid that we felt we had actually traveled to the place of power, felt its energies, and experienced its essence.

It was arduous work wrestling with the poisonous energies of the Patriarchy. Our physical bodies felt wasted, and we each often spent a day or two in bed recuperating, but the honor of being allowed to facilitate Mother Divine's magic more than made up for it.

Reclaiming the Three Intact Earth Chakras

Initially we focused on the three power places that still stood in their original forms: Mount Kailas, Machu Picchu, and Ayers Rock.

Mount Kailas—a great, symmetrical, domed mountain coated with shining ice and snow, and the crown chakra of the planet that serves as the gateway to higher knowledge—is located north of the Himalayan barrier in Tibet. During our meditation, we observed that millions of devotional prayers, prayers projected by spiritual seekers throughout the centuries, clung to the mountain like vines overburdening a trellis, but there was something behind the prayers: a dissonance, the hum of some contrivance that had been used to put Mount Kailas into bondage. Inside, a dark maze of energetic lines bound the core of the mountain. They had shackled Mother Earth's crown chakra with disease-ridden cords. They had taken the gateway to higher knowledge out of commission so it was no longer fully accessible to humanity!

As we meditated, a huge column of blue-white light descended and was anchored into the mountain. The lines snapped, one after another, making way for the light to enter the depths. When all of the cords were undone, light flooded in, the dissonance drained away, and Mount Kailas was free.

The mountain's vibration sped up, becoming more and more refined. Without warning, there was a tumultuous shift in the energy, and suddenly there were two Mount Kailases! The original Mount Kailas was still there in the physical world, but there was also a new Mount Kailas in the fourth dimension. The mountain had literally split into two parallel realities.

After our meditation, we had many questions. What had really been accomplished? My assignment had been to *disassemble* the underlying structure of the Patriarchy, so releasing Mount Kailas from bondage made sense, but why had the mountain split in two? What purpose did a new fourth-dimensional Mount Kailas serve?

We had no answers, but we didn't stop to ponder the questions long. Surely a deeper understanding would come as we continued. We moved ahead.

Machu Picchu stands deep in the heart of Peru, clinging majestically to a steep-sided mountain on the eastern slopes of the Andes. As the root chakra of the planet, it embodies the energy of survival. The truth about survival—the understanding that embodiments come and go but that the Universal Self within us is eternal—had eons ago been lost from the Machu Picchu root chakra and, therefore, from the collective consciousness. The global elite had given the mountain a lethal injection, pumping it full of its own notion of survival: kill or be killed.

As our session commenced, we saw clouds of mist surrounding the physical mountain, but also swirls of confused ideas about the nature of survival. Images of animal and human sacrifices hung in the air: raised arms, gleaming daggers, terrified victims.

Suddenly the earth began to shake, and flames of energy shot up. The flames came from a red-gold fire dragon.

The dragon preceded the snake as an ancient symbol of power. The classic image of the snake as kundalini, wrapped around the root chakra at the base of the spine, was apparently not just symbolic. Someone long ago must have seen the real creature in an alternate dimension. Now the dragon of Machu Picchu, the guardian of true power, uncoiled to its full length, unleashed its fiery breath, and fought to reclaim its home.

Somewhere in the distance, a bass drum was being hit slowly, repeatedly. It reverberated in the earth, activating something deep inside the mountain.

Machu Picchu was a giant combination lock! It held a secret code put in place a long time ago, a code set to go off at just this time in history. The drum pounded. The massive lock turned, grinding its way through the rock. When it reached the position it was seeking, immense tumblers fell into place, and the ground shook.

The lock was slow-moving. The mountain had been asleep for thousands of years. Again and again, with tremendous effort, it turned, found a position, and descended with a thud. When the sequence was finally complete, the lock clicked, the root chakra magically opened, and the true, reclaimed energy of survival erupted forth.

Blue light rained down. The realities split, forming two Machu Picchus. The light entered the fourth-dimensional mountain, lubricating the new configuration, oiling the parts of the lock. Little by little its vibration increased until it finally vibrated with exactly the same energy as the fourth-dimensional Mount Kailas. Then the fire dragon slowly and deliberately coiled itself around the root chakra, bedding down in its new home.

"But what are we actually *doing* in these meditations?" I wanted to know afterwards.

"No idea," Alexandria replied.

"Not a clue," Jackie said.

We emailed Celeste.

"You are beginning the process of constructing a separate reality," she wrote back to us, "an entirely new world that will be used by humanity for its ascension into the fourth dimension. The two parallel realities will look the same at first but will continue to develop differently over time. Years ago, this is exactly what the ascended masters told me was possible, but now I'm getting a clearer picture of what they meant. It's marvelous, isn't it? I have been working on aspects of this in South Africa, Egypt, and Jerusalem for years, and thousands of other light-workers have contributed."

Elated with this new insight, we pressed forward, zeroing in on the Earth's second chakra: Ayers Rock, stronghold of birth, creativity, and sexual energy. Located in the Northern Territory of central Australia, it rises as a solitary monolith higher than a thousand feet above the desert plain. It is more than five miles in circumference and extends one and a half miles deep into the ground. It is made of arkose, coarse-grained sandstone, and, depending on the time of day and the weather conditions, its surface changes colors dramatically from hues of red at sunrise and sunset to orange, yellow, blue, violet, or gray.

Long ago, sacred sexual techniques had utilized the second chakra to raise the kundalini in order to elevate consciousness, but these techniques had been forgotten. Members of the global elite who were initiated into this secret could channel their energy freely through the second chakra up into the third, but the rest of us, as their subjects, had been taught systematically that sex was inherently bad. The religions of the Patriarchy had made sure of that. The result had been a messy entanglement of sexual/non-sexual, good/bad, guilt-ridden mazes in the collective consciousness, and those mazes were anchored in Ayers Rock.

As we began, a bolt of blue-white energy sprang out of Machu Picchu in Peru and traveled across the surface of the Earth toward Australia. When it hit Ayers Rock, the power place awakened. Then, without warning, everything went mad. Massive bolts of lightning crashed down. Horrific torrents of rain were unleashed. Again, a dragon—the guardian of this place of power—lashed out at a maze of patriarchal lines that had defiled its rock.

At last things grew calm, and a new, fourth-dimensional Ayers Rock separated from the one in Australia. Then, without warning, thousands of shining lines—a beautiful, new image of sexuality— shot straight up and curved around the globe. The end of each line landed at a different location and locked into place as if to say, *"This second chakra energy will never be misused again."* With that, there was a huge wave of celebratory energy.

At the end of our meditation on Ayers Rock, I had the sense that I was suddenly whisked forward and upward. I found myself in the center of what looked like a perfectly formed tree. I turned slowly, taking in my surroundings. Glistening branches and grids extended out in all directions. The phrase *Tree of Life* came to mind. There were three rings encircling the tree—presumably the three Earth chakras we had worked on.

"This is the new fourth-dimensional world," I was told. *"Your body will still feel heavy and remain in the third dimension for the time being, but you'll really exist in these realms of light."*

All at once I realized that the being speaking to me was Mother Divine. I paused for a long moment, acclimating to Her rarefied vibration, adjusting my inner alignment so I was sure to reply with the proper degree of etiquette.

So I will hold myself in this dimension?

"You've been holding on for too long," She replied. *"Let me do the holding. That's my job. Just BE."*

I nodded, relaxed, and let go. It was sublime. I felt elated, but it was more subtle than that. There was bliss in every cell of my body, an ecstasy more refined than anything I had ever experienced. I drifted in the sensation for a long time, trying to memorize how it felt, wishing it could last forever.

Spiritual Teachings in the Desert

Our energetic work was not something we planned consciously. It evolved naturally out of our training with our teacher. Years before, on trips to the desert, he had transferred mystical skills to our subtle physical bodies, skills that we were now putting to use.

Throughout the 1980s and early 1990s, he took his students on nocturnal trips to the deserts of Southern California. We always met at twilight. After carpooling to the designated meeting place, the group—as few as twenty or sometimes as many as five hundred—would sit quietly meditating until my teacher arrived.

On one occasion, after climbing out of his four-wheeler, he told us, "I bring you to the desert, where the dimensions meet, so we can travel to other worlds. Here, you are in the world of the dream, the dream of the opposite self. As we go deeper into the desert, we go deeper into the heart of the dream. Here, you are the dark side and the light side. Here, there is no past and no future. Here, you are in the land of the other."

The desert was my teacher's mystical playground. In the city he broadcast the golden light of the supra-conscious, the highest-octave kundalini energy. In the desert he used the other primary form of kundalini, the mystical kundalini, a more intense, transformative energy which, when applied to his students, caused them to make tremendous spiritual leaps in a short period of time.

While his discourses in the meeting hall blended spiritual wisdom with instruction in mysticism, the desert was the pure magic of mystical experience, the place where he performed what most people would call miracles. We would sit in a semicircle around him and watch as he disappeared, walked above the sand, or painted astral pictures in the sky.

"They're not miracles, really," he told us. "They appear as miracles to humans. To me, they're simply the application of energy. All humans have the ability to evolve. We all potentially have the ability to perform miracles. In fact, from my perspective, *not* to perform miracles is not to understand your potential."

During these all-night mystical marathons, my teacher taught his students to see. He explained that it was easier to see if we could empty our minds of thoughts and expectations. "The trick is not to care whether you see or not," he said, grinning.

Of course we all wanted desperately to see, and, happily, as the evenings progressed, our chances increased. My teacher would throw open the doors of perception, our consciousness would lose its rigidity, and the desert would become liquescent.

He encouraged people to report their seeings.

"I saw your body lift up four feet in the air then return to its original position."

"I saw you bounce back and forth between the desert floor and the mountaintop, traveling along a band of light."

"When you meditated on the mountain, it began to shimmer, became transparent, then completely disappeared."

"Right," he responded, "and that's exactly what happens when I meditate on each of you."

One balmy summer night, in a gorge in the Anza Borrego Desert, my teacher called the wind. The air was perfectly still. He faced west, away from the entrance to the gorge at the highway, and looked into the distance. He was dressed in a T-shirt that said *Nirvana* and red satin jogging shorts. As I sat in the sand with my teacher towering above me, his legs looked very long.

"Watch," he told us. Lifting his hands out in front of him, he began making a low, whistling sound.

A chill moved through my body. After a few moments, from somewhere deep in the gorge, I heard the sound of the wind, rustling the desert bushes, whipping through the canyons, making its way toward us. Then suddenly, the wind was in my face, blasting through the group, careening past us toward the highway.

"Feel the wind," he said. "This wind blows from world to world and from lifetime to lifetime. This is the wind of dharma." He dropped his hands and, immediately, the wind ceased. Just like that. It stopped.

I felt sick to my stomach. I sat frozen, staring at my teacher's red jogging shorts, my mind a blank. Before I could conjure up some rational explanation, he raised his arms again.

"This is the wind of change."

As the process was repeated, I heard the whistling sound and then the wind. Again and again he called up different winds, then made them each stop. I sat in the sand, clutching my knees to my chest, my perception of reality shattered forever.

I was one of my teacher's psychically blocked students, and there were many things he did in the desert that I couldn't see. I would listen to others report their experiences and patiently try to learn, constantly hoping to release whatever caused me to remain locked in the third dimension. It would take me a long time to learn to see, but the experience of him calling the wind was a miracle that required no seeing.

"Once you've experienced a miracle, there's no going back," he told us. "I don't do it to impress you. I do it so you will think to yourself, 'Oh, I guess there's something to this meditation stuff after all. I guess I should work a little harder on myself.'"

His plan succeeded. Each trip to the desert dissolved our idea of reality a little further, inspired awe at the nature of existence, and kindled a desire to work on ourselves.

Later during the night, he would tell us, "I've just moved your assemblage point. Don't try to understand it with your mind. It's impossible. Just have fun with the experience. By shifting your assemblage point, I've changed the point in your awareness field at which awareness assembles."

He taught us about awareness by giving us guided tours. "In the past hour, I've taken you through a hundred levels of attention." It was purely experiential. He would open a dimension and everything was different: your thoughts, your emotions, your perceptions. Suddenly, you were immersed in a completely different world.

"If you've never been to Los Angeles," he explained, "but you have a friend who has, he can take you there and show you the sights. Then the next time you get the urge to go to Los Angeles, you can go on your own. You don't need your friend because you already know your way around. It's the same with dimensions. This is the way you teach someone to be multidimensional.

"In order to learn mysticism—which is all about entering into different dimensions—it is necessary to have a mystical teacher. The teacher, by bombarding his students with pure energy, forces them to let go of their descriptions of the world and brings them right out of their minds into alternate dimensions. Of course, the students will immediately rebel and want to run away and hide. Everyone clings to the physical structure of their being. So then the teacher must show the students how to integrate their experiences in alternate realities with their physical lives.

"Over the years, the student of mysticism takes the particles of her being and reorders them. The bonds that hold the personality and the egoic structure together get reformatted. It has nothing to do with the conscious mind. The conscious mind can't possibly do it. It has to do with the winds of Spirit. We allow the winds to reorder our beings, and by reordering the being time and time again, eventually the student becomes fluid. At that point, she begins to explore alternate realities on her own and, ultimately, that which creates all realities— Spirit itself.

"After many years, you'll suddenly develop powers and abilities. You won't know how or where they came from. They came from the teacher. The teacher has packed you with information, transferred mystical skills to your subtle physical body. Then, at some later time, you'll automatically execute a maneuver and be surprised to find that the conscious mind is completely uninvolved."

We would normally walk out of the desert at sunrise, if you could call it walking. Floating might be more accurate. The sand was luminous, reflecting the dissolved state of our minds. Always, as we neared the highway, we would stand in a circle with my teacher in the middle.

"Everything is made up of consciousness," he would remind us. "It's important to move through life, touching things lightly, without leaving a mark." Turning slowly, he would meditate on each of his students individually. It was his time to infuse our beings with one last blast of the mystical kundalini. It was our time to express our gratitude to the desert for the gifts she had given us and to our teacher for the instruction we had received.

Repairing the Four Fractured Earth Chakras

During the month of May, we continued our energetic work on the Earth chakras. I didn't say anything to Jackie or Alexandria, but I sensed the man in the South Pacific in an alternate dimension, a leopard eyeing its prey. Was he getting ready to attack? Was he already attacking, using some lower mystical strategy so subtle that we just weren't aware of it? I buried myself in our project. That way I didn't have to think about it.

As we turned our attention to the Earth chakras that had been fractured—the navel, heart, throat, and third eye—we gained a better understanding of their history. Attempting to master gravity, Atlantean scientists had blown up the continent, and it had sunk. After the explosion, the debris settled, and the pieces of the four originally intact chakras were spread out. During the age that followed, the global elite commandeered the fractured chakras, forcing their energies to run in a counterclockwise direction, grinding down into the planet like metal against metal. In these contorted configurations, they were out of commission. People didn't have access to their other-dimensional energies.

As our meditations continued, all of that changed. We invoked Mother Divine to direct the work and watched with awe as She reclaimed, cleared, and aligned each of them. Their direction changed from counterclockwise to clockwise, and each ring split into two; then the new ring separated from the third dimension and merged with the new fourth-dimensional world.

The circular throat chakra that ran up the East Coast and across to the European continent was healed as a spiral of blue light emanated from the core of the planet. The light spun, broke through the Earth's surface, and shot out into the universe, disseminating the pure expression of the truth. In the end, the energy of the throat chakra moved slowly and evenly, radiating balance, like a wide, sapphire-blue river.

The heart chakra appeared as a closed flower deep inside the Earth. It opened, then closed, then opened again as though it were testing its muscle. As each petal extended out, it touched a different point on the globe, creating a point of green light that broke through the surface—a glimmer here, a glimmer there. Then suddenly beacons of emerald shot out, carrying the energy of love's silent strength.

The third-eye chakra resembled the eye of Horus in Egyptian art, but initially the eye was closed. Repeatedly, blue-white light descended and passed through it. Repeatedly, the eye fluttered open, then shut again, like someone asleep and dreaming. Then without warning it opened completely and was fully awake, taking in the world around it for the first time in a very long while. It gazed without judgment, saw with clarity, and registered everything as the silent witness.

The navel chakra required no energetic work at all. The oblong ring encompassing Giza, Jerusalem, and South Africa looked like an impeccably tended garden. For fifteen years Celeste and her students had traveled back and forth to that part of the world. It was obvious that their work had been done with enormous care and expertise. They had transformed the chakra that dominated our times from one of patriarchal force to one that radiated the power of Divine Love.

I asked Alexandria, who had traveled to all the locations on the navel chakra with Celeste and done extensive energetic work there, what their trips had been like.

She laughed, her eyes sparkling. "Well, they weren't your average tourist trips! We visited the sites but spent most of our time inside the hotel, sitting together and processing polarities for the collective."

"How did you know what needed to be processed?"

"We generally had psychic perceptions about what was stored at the locations, but more often than not, all we needed to do was monitor what came up in our group."

I didn't understand and shook my head.

"Each of the power places resonated with the energy of certain frequencies held in the collective consciousness," she explained. "When we traveled there, those frequencies would trigger issues within our group.

"Maybe, for example, several people would be upset with Celeste for being domineering. Celeste, as you know, is anything but domineering. She's very egalitarian. When we looked more deeply into the issue by examining our personal experience, we would see that the energy of the place had really just amped up the egoistic programming we had been indoctrinated with about authority—that it is something outside of us, something to be projected onto someone else. So, we would process this collective issue as it was being expressed through our group. Each person would offer to dissolve that polarity in her own awareness field and be a conduit for dissolving it in the collective.

"We found that we could free up enormous blocks in the global psyche. Even if one person does the work of clearing a single aspect of her ego, the collective benefits. Suddenly there is a little bit more light on the planet."

Alexandria's experiences gave me hope that our energetic work on the rings would have a positive impact on the world, but the changes we were facilitating were taking place at such a subtle level of existence. How long would it take them to filter down into the physical world, and how would that play out?

I assumed that people might gradually become disenchanted with abuse of power and more inclined toward the heart, but what else? With Mount Kailas' gateway to higher knowledge open, would more and more people aspire to spiritual awakening? Because Machu Picchu's mandate of kill-or-be-killed had been abolished, would the warring nature of society decrease? When President Bush gave a press conference, would the refurbished throat chakra help people decipher whether or not he spoke the truth?**

The Trees Join the Collaboration

In the afternoons I often took walks along a hiking trail overlooking the mesa behind my house. When I was feeling fit, rather than turn around, walk back to the trailhead, and return along the sidewalk, I sometimes scaled the side of the mesa directly behind my house, weaving my way among the boulders and pine trees until I reached my back gate.

One day as I began my ascent, I noticed a dignified pine towering above the trail. Its massive trunk grew perfectly straight and then, about twenty feet up, took an unusual bend that dipped out over the canyon.

"Wow, what an incredible tree!" I said aloud, remembering my quest to find a tree in New Mexico to help us communicate with trees around the world. I inched my way up the side of the mesa to get a closer look.

What a perfect tree that would be! I thought to myself.

"*It's already taken care of,*" the tree said. Its voice was low and resonant and seemed distinctly masculine.

** In 2008, we would learn that when Oprah Winfrey and Eckhart Tolle offered an Internet seminar based on Tolle's best-selling book that affirms everyone is "being awakened", they had to schedule repeat broadcasts to accommodate the millions of people who signed up. After years of war in Iraq and Afghanistan, we would read the results of a poll in Great Britain showing that nearly half of British soldiers and officers were ready to quit the military. And as for President Bush, almost everyone would be rolling their eyes at his never-ending stream of lies about Iraq's weapons of mass destruction and waging war for peace. In 2008, it seemed clear that *something* had produced unprecedented change, but in the spring of 2003, we could only speculate and hope for the best.

I hesitated. *What do you mean?* I asked it tentatively.

"I stand directly below your office window," it told me in a matter-of-fact tone. *"I feel everything that happens with the three of you, every meditation you do, every realization you have. The information rolls off of the top of the mesa, and I catch it in my crook. This canyon connects to the Caldera. I use the currents of energy flowing down from the Caldera to disseminate updates to all the other trees around the world."* It paused, and then added nobly, *"We stand ready!"*

For a few moments I didn't say anything; I was too amazed. Finally I told it, *Thank you for your help. Is there anything that I can do for you in return?*

"A hug would be nice."

I laughed out loud. Often in the past, I had heard about people embracing trees, but I was a rugged soldier, hardly the type to indulge in such a thing. Now feeling shy, I made my way among the rocks and gave it a long hug.

From that time forward, in my invocations that began our meditations, I summoned Mother Earth, then called on all her trees. In addition to the pine behind my house, I could also sense the presence of a 350-year-old live oak on Jekyll Island and a tall, regal fir at the World Trade Organization. I would whisper to them, *Tell all the trees on all the continents. Ask them if they will help.*

All over the planet, trees would stir and rise to the task…and they always seemed to be delighted.

The Energetic Work Roles

By this time in our collaboration, Jackie, Alexandria, and I were not only employing mystical skills our teacher had packed into our subtle bodies in the desert but also our specialized mystery-school training as seer, sovereign, and soldier.

Jackie's seeings were remarkably technical and often abstract. She identified the problem—the way the energies had been bastardized by the patriarchal forces—then prudently carried out the instructions she was given for transmuting them. She operated in a calm, detached manner and seemed to have the uncanny ability simply to decide that the energies should be different.

In one session she became ensnared in a dense, tarry thicket of patriarchal energies and then became bored and decided it should change. Miraculously, as the tarry substance dissolved, it was transformed into glistening elementals of light. On another occasion she perceived the technical transmutation of lines of perception and bandings of attention, aspects that were so far beyond my understanding of how the universe worked that I could only guess at their meaning.

As our sovereign, Alexandria didn't contribute many seeings. Her way was to sit quietly and take everyone else's seeings through her heart, evaluating them for their level of truth, voicing her objection if they didn't have the proper resonance. Having incarnated in so many lifetimes as royalty, it was natural for her to consider every move we made in terms of its effect on humanity and the evolution of the Earth. But it went further than that. She continually asked herself how our work served the evolution of consciousness.

As Jackie once told me, "It takes a very special being to play that role, and there's no model for it in the Patriarchy, no template for steering from the heart. She has to be able to move completely out of the way and feel the answer. You and I move our egos out of the way, but some of our attention has to remain focused on what is transpiring—for me to see and for you to soldier. With Alexandria, it's different. She has to dissolve completely."

During our meditations, Alexandria was always given the job of holding an alignment. She might align herself with the power of love or the epicenter of the heart chakra flower. In one session, her alignment activated a star gate—a cosmic alignment of stars that amplified energy and opened a portal. By simultaneously holding different points around the globe in her awareness field, she allowed the energy flowing through the opened star gate to heal the fragmentation of the chakra.

As the soldier of the team, I was perplexed by this sovereign role. I was a doer, and Alexandria's job involved *non-doing.* At least Jackie was doing something when she saw things in other dimensions—that, I could appreciate—but Alexandria just dissolved and went away. More often than not, when we shared our experiences, she reported that the two-hour meditation, which for me had seemed interminable, had seemed to her to have lasted five minutes.

One day at her house, I teased Alexandria, with Jackie listening on the speaker phone. "Well, I suppose a meditation would seem like five minutes if your job is just to sit, align with love, and go away."

"Right," Jackie concurred. "Next time we'll let you take care of the black thicket of tarry thorns tearing into your skin."

"...or coping with a fire dragon," I added.

Alexandria fingered the gold necklace at her throat. "During my meditations I'm completely uninvolved with the events on Planet Earth and am working on another plane. That's my job: simply to sit in the stillness and hold the intent. Time becomes timelessness, and it is always over in the blink of an eye."

"How did you get this job?" Jackie asked.

"Good question." I turned to look directly at Alexandria. "What's your secret? How did you manage to get dealt a hand of one lifetime after another as royalty?"

"Please," Alexandria begged us. "Holding the alignment is very difficult...and important! It requires tremendous concentration."

"I know, I know," I replied. "Your back must be killing you by the end of each meditation from having to sit so straight on your throne."

"Right!" Jackie said. "I've always wanted to ask that, by the way. What *do* you sit on when you meditate?"

"Enough!" Alexandria said, raising her hand in a regal gesture that brought the conversation to a halt.

I acquiesced. "All right. We're just giving you a hard time."

My contribution was quite different than that of either Alexandria or Jackie. As the soldier, I projected my mystical body—using my lower power chakras—into the mystical dimensions, where I gathered knowledge, transmuted energies, and effected change. I often found myself working alongside Mother Earth on the front lines, attention sharp as a bayonet, caught in the crossfire of patriarchal energies. I was the one who, at the end of each meditation, could detect the instant to strike and bring the noxious configuration to its knees. Merging with such abrasive energies took a heavy toll on my physical body, but I wouldn't have wanted any other job.

As a former military officer, Anders always wanted to hear about my soldiering, but I sensed he was feeling left out.

"So," he said one evening, taking a break from his studies at the kitchen table, "you're going to continue meditating on all of these rings of power around the globe?"

"Yes," I answered.

"And you're going to do all of these meditations at home?" he asked. "All of you are just going to sit at home and do synchronized meditations?"

"Yes."

"You're not going to travel to any of these places?"

"No."

He sighed heavily and looked down at his textbook. "Well, all I can say is that you've become a pretty boring girlfriend since you figured out how to do everything remotely."

Everything Is Keyed to the Heart

The summer solstice was approaching and, with it, our trip to the Caldera to move the assemblage point. In early June we decided to err on the side of caution by meditating on all seven Earth chakras, just in case there was any cleanup work we needed to do; but as soon as we began, we knew something far more significant was about to happen.

Immediately the vibrational frequency of the planet began to increase—notch by notch, ten or twelve times. As we viewed the globe of Earth, our perception became sharper and sharper, like camera lenses being clicked into focus. The vibrational frequencies of our own awareness fields increased, too, until they were whirring so fast that we wondered how much more we could stand. Finally, when the energy climaxed, a massive column of blue-white light descended from the center of the universe and extended all the way down to the core of the planet.

For a little while, everything was still.

Then, like the first actor to step onstage, the new fourth-dimensional Machu Picchu appeared in the blue spotlight. She looked radiant, wrapped in vibrant, red-brown light. Without warning, her energy dropped down and connected to the core of the Earth. Machu Picchu had gotten anchored! The same thing occurred with Ayers Rock. Next came the navel chakra. There was a loud *whoosh!* and the whole planet shook.

We were stunned. The chakras were getting tethered to the core of the Earth! In a sense, they now felt more grounded but at the same time unhinged, like balloons tied with string so they wouldn't float away.

The heart chakra came next, with her elegant flower petals of green light. The procession paused for a long moment as a feeling of infinite love permeated everything. Then words echoed through the universe—*"Everything keys to this!"*—and the heart chakra floated gracefully into place.

Next, the vast blue river of the throat chakra slowly descended and followed suit. Then came the third eye, practically weightless, like light passing through crystalline raindrops that fell gently in slow motion.

The last was Mount Kailas, Mother Earth's crown chakra. It exuded no feeling: nothing and everything at the same time. There was no color, not even clear. Energy rose from the core of the Earth through the column of blue-white light, flowed out through the fully opened crown chakra, then curved slowly downward in a graceful arc and returned to the core of the planet, where it collected. The process repeated. The energy rose, curved, fell, and collected again and again—a slow-motion fountain of otherworldly light.

Celeste had said that the new world was a fourth-dimensional structure of unconditional love, but watching the energy rise and fall in what almost appeared to be a ritual cleansing, we wondered if it had the potential to become something even more remarkable.

16
THE MASCULINE VERSUS
THE FEMININE—ROUND TWO

I was just pouring my cooked oatmeal into a bowl for breakfast when Anders burst through the back door and into the kitchen. Waving a letter, he shouted, "I got it!" and then grabbed me and swung me around.

"Got what?" I asked.

He set me down.

"A full scholarship at the College of William and Mary!"

I laughed. "Well, did you doubt the Lineage? They said they would take care of it."

He held me at arms' length, looked me over, then narrowed his eyes. "It's pretty handy having a girlfriend who's a witch."

"Anders!" I disentangled myself, moved back, and studied him a moment. "What exactly are you implying? I mean, I have no problem admitting that I've been a witch in more than one past life, and, for that matter, there's nothing *wrong* with being a witch. The word is derived from *Wicca*, which means…"

"I know, I know!" He scowled. "*To bend or shape consciousness.* You've told me."

"Yes, I remember telling you. Several times. But that's not the way you're using the word." I scrutinized him. "Is labeling me a witch your way of cubby-holing the energetic work I'm doing? Are you trivializing it?"

He fingered the letter in his hands, and all the enthusiasm drained from his face. "I know I sometimes tease you, and I guess that means I'm making light of the energetic work you do." He glanced down at the letter and back to my face. "But this project you're working on is hard for me to understand. I was with you in Europe and felt the energy shift in places after you worked on them. And now this scholarship…." He thrust the letter forward, then pulled it back. "I guess I don't know how to think about these things. My only point of reference is *Hansel and Gretel*, all the children's stories they used to read to me." He looked up again and studied me. "I'm sorry. I'll try to be more respectful."

I held my ground, staring at him.

He grinned sheepishly. "Really, I will."

The Masculine Voice of Reason

The following week, I flew to Virginia to finalize plans for moving. I had been feeling increasingly tired from the energetic work. Now I was grumpy on the plane.

Why did I have to move? Why me? Jackie, who had lived in the Bay area for years, had been asked to hold the third-eye chakra right outside her back door. Alexandria had been handed the heart chakra on a silver platter and had the luxury of shepherding it from the comfort of her adobe home in Santa Fe. Why did I have to uproot myself and move two thousand miles to baby-sit the throat chakra? And what did I know about the expression of truth anyway? I was a lower-chakra soldier. Why had the throat chakra been assigned to me?

I bit my tongue when I arrived in Williamsburg. Only that morning, an ideal house had been advertised for rent. I was the first person to look it at, I struck a deal immediately, and the timing for the previous tenants to vacate was flawless. It seemed the Lineage was handling everything.

The next morning I woke up in a much better mood. Beyond the window of my room at a historic bed-and-breakfast, it was a perfect June day. I drove into DC to meet Robert for lunch, and afterwards we ventured over to the Washington Monument.

As we sauntered up the incline toward the obelisk, I paused to study it. It looked fabulous, gleaming in the sun. I felt like I was visiting an old friend. My adoration flowed out toward it, and, for a moment, I thought the monument acknowledged me.

At the top of the hill, we sat on the grass facing east. I closed my eyes and merged with the Earth's throat chakra. I was flabbergasted. All of the patriarchal energies had vanished. What was left was the luminous energy of the throat chakra, the pure expression of the truth. I turned to Robert with excitement. "The energy on my last visit was radically distorted. Now it's radically pristine!"

He paused for a moment fingering a blade of grass. "Please don't take this the wrong way. I hate to always be the masculine voice of reason, but surely you don't think that you are *doing* these things."

I turned to look at him. "Okay, explain again exactly what your point is."

"My point is that you are seeing your own mind projected onto this place. What you are feeling here may have nothing to do with the throat chakra of the planet. If you have cleared your own throat chakra energy, then what you are perceiving may be your own 'pristine energy' not that of the chakra. Don't you see? You are perceiving your own awareness field. It's just your ego that wants to believe you've changed the energy here."

This time Robert's comment triggered no agitation. "The way I see it, both of the things you're referencing are real: the place in the third-dimensional world is real, and my mind projected onto this place is also real." I hesitated in order to collect my thoughts. "I agree that it would be egotistical to think I alone had changed the vibration of this place. That would be incorrect. But it would be equally incorrect to deny that I had *facilitated* it. To do that would be to deny my own power as a human, as a mystic, and—to be more to the point at this particular time in history—as a woman."

I studied him. "Feel the energy of this place, Robert. Back in March you told me Elaine had complained constantly about the energy in DC, and then, on the phone after I had done the energetic work, you said that you both came here, and it was unbelievably beautiful." I made a sweeping gesture. "It feels very good here, and that wasn't the case three months ago, so please don't ask me to deny the reality of what I'm experiencing."

Robert sighed, then flicked his piece of grass onto the lawn. "Point taken." He hesitated, then looked at me. "But please," he said, stressing each word, "*be careful.*"

I nodded. I did need to be careful. If I had learned anything during the project, it was that power needed to be wielded carefully.

Power during the Matrilineal Age, the Patriarchal Age, and Beyond

I looked out over the lush carpet of grass stretching down the incline. A young family hurried passed with a picnic basket. A group down the hill played Frisbee. Looking south, I could just make out the Jefferson Memorial in the distance. All at once, my visit to the Washington Monument the previous March came to mind. The two snakes—it was so obvious to me now. Two snakes in Washington DC. Two snakes in ancient Egypt. The symbolism was identical....or was it?

I assembled the facts in my mind: In Egypt, inside the underground chamber where sacred grain was kept, I found the first snake coiled up inside of a basket. In an underground room where sacred snakes were housed, I found a second snake, this one dead. Following these two omens, an old beggar woman—actually a male mystic in disguise—wrapped a snake around my heart, then turned into a cobra and bit my heart.

In DC, at the Washington Monument, a long toy snake lay on the pavement stones. After visiting the Jefferson Memorial, I learned of a maimed snake who, despite repeated battering, continued across the road.

The snake symbolized power. A very long time ago, in matrilineal cultures, the snake was one of the symbols for the Mother Goddess, the power of the Sacred Feminine. More recently, in spiritual texts written during patriarchal times, the snake symbolized the kundalini life force coiled up at the base of the spine.

True power is alignment with Divine Will—power balanced by the heart—but the global elite had inverted the concept of power. For them, power equaled force. And what was symbolized by the various settings: an underground chamber of sacred grain; an underground room for sacred snakes; the Washington Monument, a giant phallic symbol of power; and the round, womblike rotunda of the Jefferson Memorial?

Suddenly, like a child examining a hidden picture puzzle who finally sees the concealed image, I saw in my mind's eye a caduceus, the medical symbol of two intertwining snakes. *Of course!*

The first snake symbolized masculine power. In Egypt it had been coiled up (masculine power ready to strike, ready to move into action) in an underground storage chamber (not yet in plain view) in a basket for sacred grain (somewhere it should not have been). The omen had meant that men were preparing to take the reins of power in the world, that we were entering an era when men and women would learn lessons about power by way of the abuse of power by men. Later, the male mystic had wrapped a snake around my heart. Wielding power in a balanced way—channeling the power of the lower chakras up through the heart—was about to become a thing of the past. Force was on the rise, and the heart's energy would be shut down for the duration of the Patriarchy.

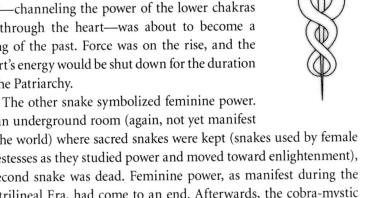

The other snake symbolized feminine power. In an underground room (again, not yet manifest in the world) where sacred snakes were kept (snakes used by female priestesses as they studied power and moved toward enlightenment), a second snake was dead. Feminine power, as manifest during the Matrilineal Era, had come to an end. Afterwards, the cobra-mystic bit my heart.

Venom from the king cobra acts as a painkiller. My heart had been anesthetized! It was Spirit's way of helping me bear the pain of incarnating repeatedly in a world destined to grow more and more out of balance over the next five thousand years.

But what about the snakes in this lifetime? There were some differences.

The first snake at the Washington Monument wasn't coiled, but elongated. The Patriarchy had run its course. And, more important, the snake was a toy...an illusion! In this lifetime I had succeeded in recognizing masculine power—force as it manifests in the world today—as something having no real substance!

The second snake at the feminine Jefferson Memorial was not dead. It was moving across the road. No matter how many cars ran over her, she still managed to keep going. The power of the Divine Feminine from the Matrilineal Age, power that had appeared dead in Egypt, had really survived. Despite massive propaganda campaigns by the Religion ring, Mother Divine was still on the move in the world.

The snake, once the symbol of the Goddess, had been demonized in the Bible's Garden of Eden. On the advice of the snake, Eve allegedly caused the downfall of humankind, and later, the poor snake was given legs and evolved into the devil himself.

But all of that was changing.

The dragons of Machu Picchu and Ayers Rock had been liberated by using Mother Divine's energy. The symbol of the snake had evolved from the dragon, the symbol of enlightenment, the integration of masculine and feminine, yin and yang. Now there were two dragons set free, two energies crisscrossing paths in a cosmic dance of divine masculine and feminine power.

Who Is the Man in the South Pacific?

I was still comparing the symbolism in ancient Egypt with that in this lifetime when I climbed into bed at the B and B in Williamsburg late that night. Something puzzled me: the masculine beggar woman in Egypt who turned into a cobra. Was there a relationship between the beggar woman and the man in the South Pacific? Was it possible that the beggar woman had actually been the man in the South Pacific in disguise? My blood ran cold and my pulse quickened at the thought.

I struggled to remain calm and think logically. What did I know about him? I knew that he had lived in ancient Egypt, that our group of priestesses had become sexually involved with a group of priests, and that after leaving my teacher's mystery school I had studied with someone who taught me lower mysticism. Had I known the man in the South Pacific previously in Egypt? Was the man in the South Pacific my lover? My instructor in the dark arts?

My pulse quickened another notch, and my heart pounded against my breastbone. Close to vomiting, I threw the covers back, stumbled out of bed, and made a dash for the bathroom.

Splashing cold water on my face helped. I dried my face, straightened to my full height, and studied my reflection in the mirror. *The man in the South Pacific was not your lover,* I assured the dazed eyes that looked back at me, *or your instructor of the dark arts! That is impossible!*

The reflection slumped a little as it asked, *Are you sure?*

17
THE FEMININE SHIFTS
THE ASSEMBLAGE POINT

Back in Los Alamos, a hot and sweaty Anders stood next to the moving van he had just loaded.

"You secured the plants in the back so the boxes won't fall on them?" I asked

"Roger that!"

"And you know you can't drive these big trucks fast, right?"

"For God's sake!" he sputtered.

"All right, all right...I know I'm being a control freak."

The plan was for Anders to set off for Virginia in the rented truck early the next morning, leaving me to drive the Mercedes there a few days later, after I finished the summer solstice meditation.

"Now," I told him, "there is one more thing I need help with before we're done. I need to water a tree in the canyon."

His eyes squinted as he scrutinized me, his shoulders slumping with exhaustion. "A tree," he enunciated slowly, "in the canyon?"

I nodded. "It's my tree friend in back of the house, the one that helps us with the project. I want to water it before we leave. "

Anders took a deep breath, all the while looking at me and nodding slightly. "For God's sake!" he said again, exasperated. "Do you really need to do that? I'm dead tired!"

"Yes," I insisted. "We've been in a drought. I think it needs water."

He stamped his feet a few times to relieve the tension. "Tell me what to do! Tell me what to do!"

I took a deep breath. "Well, we've got to collect all the water hoses," I began deliberately, "hook them together, and run them down the side of the mesa...."

"You're impossible, do you know that? Who would put up with you but me?" he complained, heading toward the side of the house. As he walked away, I could hear him muttering under his breath, "Now I know why witches are always depicted as living alone in the woods...."

"Okay, *Hansel*," I called after him. "I heard that."

Moving the Assemblage Point of the Planet

As we approached our long-awaited excursion to the Caldera, my excitement grew. I prayed daily that moving the assemblage point would be a success. I truly hoped that, afterwards, humanity would have a new perspective, that people would be able to discern the con game of the New World Order.

Finally the summer solstice arrived. That morning I scanned the newspaper headlines. Americans felt grumpy because President Bush might have misled them about Iraq. Exxon closed its cash drawer on another daily profit of $59 million. Children in South Africa were dying of AIDS. Those who had reserved copies of the fifth Harry Potter book rushed out to buy them.

For most humans, life that day seemed pretty normal. For Alexandria, Jackie, and me, the summer solstice on June 21, 2003, was about to unfold as a landmark event, although not one that would be covered in the mainstream media.

That evening as I drove us to the Caldera, Alexandria used her cell phone to call Jackie in San Francisco.

"Here's what I've been seeing," Jackie told her. "Not only will we be moving the Earth's assemblage point, we'll be facilitating a tremendous shift of energy, going well beyond the fourth dimension."

When we arrived I parked the car in a pullout alongside the Caldera. Alexandria and I held strands of barbed wire apart for each other and managed to scramble through the fence in the dark. Then, using our flashlights, we hiked for almost a mile, out into the center. It was still illegal to enter, but apparently the police had better things to do than track two tiny trespassers in the midst of the giant grassy bowl. We found a good spot, spread our meditation blankets, and settled in.

It was surprisingly cold for the end of June but, after all, we were at an elevation of eight thousand feet. I wrapped my down coat around me and put on my gloves. Then I took a moment to simply *feel* the Caldera. I had never been inside of it.

Phenomenal! We were truly in a power place where worlds met, dimensions intersected, and mystery prevailed. My teacher's words seemed more meaningful than ever: "When it's time for a world to change, this is where it happens."

I could also feel something high above the Caldera. It was almost as if there were cosmic bleachers, and they were filled to capacity! It appeared to be standing-room-only, as beings from countless dimensions assembled to witness Mother Divine perform Her magic.

This is going to be big! I thought. *Am I capable of facilitating what is about to happen?*

I didn't know the answer, but I had no choice except to try my best. I shook off my insecurity and closed my eyes.

Mother Divine's energy descended through the assembled beings, unleashing a blue-white avalanche of light. Then, for the next hour, it was impossible for either Alexandria or me to cognize what transpired. The event was so large, so otherworldly, and so completely holy that our conscious minds were barely able to grasp a handful of abstract images.

Dimensions opened, energy lines danced, and perception parted as the oars of the Good Ship Earth strained against the tide of collective consciousness. Worldly images moved aside. Knots of attention unraveled. Crystalline structures—visual tuning forks— appeared as moving mandalas of multidimensional forms. The lush, green heart of Mother Earth rose to link with the newly constructed fourth-dimension world of Mother Divine, perfection meeting perfection. The luminous light of the higher spheres rained down upon the planet. The world drew a long, deep breath, and the universe bowed to honor the flawlessness of existence.

Afterward, as we drove down the mountain, Alexandria poured hot tea from her thermos, and we passed the cup back and forth in stunned silence. Speaking about our experiences was inconceivable. Our beings were more dissolved than they had been on desert trips with our teacher. My awareness was so formless that I had trouble keeping the car on the road.

The following morning we staged a three-way call, hopeful that Jackie, from her vantage point on the West Coast, had seen what had actually happened.

"Starting at around ten o'clock your time, when I knew you were sitting in the Caldera," Jackie told us, "the energy began to build. It reached the point where the surges of kundalini energy through my body were so intense that I thought I might be leaving it! About forty minutes later, the Earth's third-dimensional assemblage point at the Isle de Sol started to dissolve. It was like film burning, when the black material melts into light. Then, like magic, it shifted. It shifted to the Caldera."

I sighed with relief. *Thank God!*

"From that point on," she continued, "there were just fields of light, energies forming and reforming and something that felt like the world turning inside out, then back again. Around midnight, I finally went to bed. Things were still moving but had evened out into a breathtaking field of grace."

Moving My Own Assemblage Point

Jackie suggested we take the months of July and August off. I hated to halt the forward march of progress, but my body had become increasingly fatigued and definitely needed the rest.

Anders and I used the time to settle into our new life in Williamsburg. Our house was very spacious. He took over the upstairs, which afforded him a bedroom and a meditation room, as well as a huge office, and began buying textbooks to fill the bookshelves in preparation for his school term. I commandeered the master bedroom downstairs, turned the dining room into my office, and installed my trusty whiteboard on the wall.

I had whined a lot about the move, but now I was elated. I felt like a different person. For one thing, our three-way mystical circuit felt more balanced. With Jackie in California, Alexandria in New Mexico, and me in Virginia, we now spanned the continent. Also, it was much easier for me to feel the throat chakra there!

Each day, I listened to the news on *Democracy Now*. Whistle-blowers stepped forward. Generals spoke out against the war. Politicians in DC squirmed. And somehow—although I couldn't say exactly how—my physical presence on the Earth's throat chakra was supporting that process.

My attitude about the man in the South Pacific changed, too. I decided that I had to investigate my aversion to him. I had to reconcile my fear.

In addition, the notion of writing a book about our mystical experiences—an idea that had been popping up for some time, but one about which I had been procrastinating—finally took root. I asked the Lineage if it was truly a dharmic task, and when they said that it was, I sat down at my desk in Williamsburg, on the Earth's throat chakra, and finally began to write.

18

THE FEMININE TAKES ON THE
NEW WORLD ORDER

In early September, Jackie, Alexandria, and I reconvened. A lot had happened since our Longevity Café tea party back in February. We had combined our skills to analyze the state of the world, then facilitated the reclamation of Mother Earth's chakras and the moving of the assemblage point. Now it was time to start our energetic work on the rings of the New World Order.

Freeing up the Resource Management ring—the inside-out, upside-down heart energy that held the patriarchal system in place— would set the Star of David in motion, and that would lead to the Diamond Body configuration we were after, the true alignment in consciousness for the Earth. The Royalty ring had been destroyed in Germany, so we planned eight synchronized sessions, during the months of September and October, on the eight remaining rings.

As we began the sessions, we were dumbfounded. They were so difficult! Meditations were supposed to be peaceful, but these were like being tortured!

The rings were entrenched. Their energies—the heavyweight energies of the planet—were almost impossible to move. And our third eyes were useless. Working with the seven rings of Mother Earth, our seeings had been crystal clear. Now we felt as through we were viewing a battlefield through heavy smoke cover. It was impossible to see what was happening or if, indeed, *anything* was happening. Even Jackie was at a loss.

There was only one strategy that worked. We had to *unplug* from each ring. This meant that we had to be ruthlessly honest about how we had bought into each ring, do tons of personal processing, and reconcile the energies of each ring within ourselves. Back in the spring, sitting around Celeste's dining room table, we had seen that the leaders of the nine rings were not essentially bad and that women had agreed to participate in the Patriarchy to assist in the evolution of humanity. Back then, it had sounded good. Now it was time to really *own* that theory.

My Very Own Patriarchy

The day before our meditation on the Government ring, Vice President Dick Cheney was reported to have said that we had invaded Iraq because Saddam Hussein had weapons of mass destruction. What propaganda! Who did he think he was kidding? I had done enough reading about Iraq to know that we had invaded to seize control of Iraq's oil fields and to protect the pre-eminence of the US dollar. I had seen the pictures of hospitalized Iraqi children after bombing raids. I knew that the US government had banned the media from showing the flag-draped coffins of soldiers. I had seen documentaries in which both American soldiers and Iraqi civilians were interviewed. The war was an unnecessary waste of human life. Cheney was arrogant and inhumane. He was acting like a conceited, testosterone-laden, teenaged boy rather than a mature, balanced political leader.

My meditation on the Government ring went badly. After half an hour I saw the problem. It was my own attitude. I had agendas about what was happening in the arena of politics. I had judgments about the way the world was being governed. I thought political leaders should be more humble and compassionate. As a result, I was unable to be a clear, unattached channel for the meditation.

I needed to investigate. Taking a deep breath, I looked into the mirror of current events to find my own reflection. How was *I* still arrogant? How was *I* lacking in compassion? To answer those questions, I had only to remember my most recent phone conversation with a customer service representative: *Why can't this person solve my problem? Is he stupid? And why can't he speak English properly? Do I really have to be subjected to this?*

My arrogance ebbed away. How could I possibly judge Cheney when I did the very same thing? The only reason Cheney's attitude triggered an emotional response in me was that, on some level, I *was* Dick Cheney and didn't want to admit it. I didn't want to own the arrogant, inhumane, teenaged boy inside of me.

My meditation started to flow. I focused on Cheney, holding his disagreeable vibration unwaveringly with my attention. My hands fidgeted in my lap. His image blurred in and out of focus as I struggled to overcome my apprehension. I bowed to him on the inner planes, honoring the vibration—as an aspect of him, as an aspect of me. Feeling more confident, I embraced it, letting the vibration take hold of me fully, letting it be present in every cell of my body. Finally I invited it into my heart, embodying it as one aspect of the universe, one vibratory form of consciousness in the cosmic dance of life. Arrogance and inhumanity, as expressed in the political arena, came to rest.

When we moved on to the Industry ring, it was Alexandria who captured its essence.

"The Industry ring affects every human who buys products. All across the world, people are addicted to material possessions and, if I'm honest, I'm as guilty as anyone else. My closet is a fine place to find evidence: Nike, Capezio, Eileen Fisher." She paused, and when she resumed, her voice was softer. "I suppose its time for me to examine why I always feel the need to appear at my best."

Prior to our meditation on the Military ring, it was Jackie who complained.

"It's Fleet Week here in San Francisco. The Blue Angels are terrorizing everyone with their fan trails. The naval fleet is in the Bay. There are military uniforms all over the place and a lot of jackbooted security. Welcome to our new police state! The scene truly captures the state of the union: our government has become the Pentagon and the CIA—a bunch of highly sophisticated assholes who think they have an understanding of the world—with a President who's a puppet and a Congress that has been reduced to a debating society! I don't know what the energy is like where you are, but here in San Francisco it sucks." She sighed. "But I guess Fleet Week makes it easier for me to process misuse of power—how I'm still arrogant to the effect my agendas have on others."

When we focused on the Arts ring, I had to grapple with my memories of arriving in New York, fine arts degree in hand, and finding not the art of theatre but the cutthroat attitudes of show business. With the Media ring, I wrestled with my resentment of media that spewed propaganda. By the time we addressed the Banking and the Resource Management rings, I found myself right back in the cesspool of arrogance and lack of compassion. *How can international bankers enslave the world through the hocus-pocus of fiat money and feel nothing as people suffer? How can the World Bank pillage the resources of underdeveloped countries and ignore the plight of indigenous peoples?*

In each meditation I reconciled the disagreeable energy of the ring—and often the man I viewed as the ringleader—by meeting, honoring, embracing, and bringing it into the heart. Each engendered fear. Each exacted a heavy toll. My body was so weary, my emotions so drained, but I told myself that it was practice for the man in the South Pacific, that reconciling the energies of each of these rings would prepare me for engaging my worthy opponent. It helped me drag myself forward, through session after session, for what seemed like two interminable months.

And it paid off. Unplugging from each ring changed me... significantly. My body may have felt brutalized, but my soul was more at peace. I accepted myself despite the ways I had bought into each ring. I accepted the world for what it was. The world really was in perfect order, a beautifully choreographed dance of ever-changing energies.

As we cleared ourselves, the smokescreen that obscured our psychic vision cleared as well. A distinct picture emerged of what was happening on an energetic level. Each ring separated from the Olympic-logo configuration. Then it split into two rings. The new fourth-dimensional ring broke into particles of energy, changed from a counterclockwise to a clockwise direction, and began to spin in an attempt to ascend.

Initially it would be too heavy. Some of them looked like newborn colts learning to stand on wobbly legs. But as the spinning continued, the vibration increased so that each shiny, new ring would begin to spiral up. As each came into its own, it looked celestial, like a graceful space station floating weightlessly. Each would glide through the air and come to rest in the fourth-dimensional world.

Our systems analysis had revealed that the rings of the New World Order were associated with *inverted* chakra energies, but in the new world, all of the fourth-dimensional rings docked in their rightful chakra positions. The Military ring came to rest at the root, the Industry ring at the second chakra, the Banking ring at the navel, and on and on up the Tree of Life.

Choosing Rings

But what did all of this mean for the average person? We glimpsed the answer during our session on the Media ring. After it split into two rings, we detected different psychic reactions from people employed in the media. Some were delighted. Some were confused. Others were angry.

"My hunch," I told Alexandria and Jackie, "is that people who have careers in media are now faced with a choice: either remain in the old patriarchal ring where it's business as usual or ascend along with the new ring into an entirely different configuration. Why don't journalists working under the patriarchal system excavate the truth and write about it? Part of it is because journalists are schooled by the global elite's educational system and, after learning to play the game, buy into the system. But it's more than that. Journalists have difficulty *perceiving* the truth because the global elite have used lower mystical methods to make the Media ring turn in a way that is contrary to nature and, as a result, is able to forcibly hold journalists in limited states of mind. But the new fourth-dimensional Media ring turns clockwise. A clockwise movement disseminates energy out into the universe, so the new Media ring—as the expression of the truth—will disseminate information freely. Journalistic stories that have been there all along will no longer be ignored by those who align with the new ring."

"These new fourth-dimensional rings function as dharmic paths, don't they?" Alexandria interjected.

"You're right!" Jackie agreed. "What you're saying ties perfectly into the diagrams Spirit showed me back in March, the way the global elite inverted the pyramids to create a perversion of the planet's true alignment in consciousness. A long time ago, the rings were dharmic paths. Then, over the course of the Patriarchal Age, these career paths were purposely bastardized by the global elite. Work within a given ring progressed from doing one's dharma—something that fostered evolution—to doing forced labor—something that restricted consciousness, a concentration-camp system where inmates help maintain one component of the führer's massive, self-serving war machine."

"But now," Alexandria interjected, "people have a choice. The new fourth-dimensional rings vibrate in a more refined way. Journalists who begin to disseminate the truth during their day-to-day routine will align more and more with the new Media ring. As they do, their beings will begin to vibrate in a more refined way. Their evolution will speed up, and, as a result, they'll begin to live more and more in a fourth-dimensional consciousness."

My Teacher's View of the Patriarchy

My teacher once told his students that if they were involved in a political system that was very bad, where all of their freedoms were being taken away, it became their duty to overthrow it.

"If the boat is going in the right direction, then you leave it to the captain and the crew to run the boat. If it's headed for the rocks and if you can't talk the captain and the crew into turning it around, then you have to have a mutiny."

I wondered what my teacher would have said about the state of the world in October of 2003. Having incarnated in the East—Tibet, India, Japan—for most of his previous lifetimes, he sometimes railed against the patriarchal mindset of the Western world when he was alive. I always liked it when he got on his soapbox. Combining the power of an enlightened mystic with a PhD in English literature made for riveting oratory. The gold light would intensify, surge through the room, and pin us against the backs of our chairs.

"I think democracy is a good thing," he told us one evening. "It's the best government going, the one that gives a person the most freedom. Hopefully someday all countries will live under a democracy. But as spiritual seekers in the West, we find ourselves in a society that doesn't care for enlightenment, a society that doesn't even acknowledge the divinity of existence, a society of beings gone mad. They tout their structures and their technologies but are completely oblivious to the spiritual experience of every given moment. It's a society where everything is backwards, where good is called bad and enlightenment is called abnormal behavior and abnormal behavior is applauded as reason, where people use technology to find faster and more efficient ways to kill each other, where love is just a four-letter word for desire, where beauty is laughed at, purity stained, humility ignored. In this prison-camp, Gestapo-state, brain-police society, what is normal is insane and what is insane is normal. Of course, it doesn't pay you to complain to the local politicians or structural organizations that run the place. They clearly didn't crucify Christ because they liked what he said!"

He took a deep breath. "Don't get me wrong," he continued after a moment. "There are some very good things about the West." He paused, staring into space, then looked back at his audience. "I'll think of them in a minute."

The Roman Catholic Church

We saved the Religion ring for last. I fortified myself with a cup of strong tea and got in my car to drive to the library, intent on studying the history of religion. Did the man in the South Pacific plan to bring everything under control by manipulating the rings of the New World Order, establishing the One World Government, then ruling via the uppermost ring of religion? Did he fancy himself the ultimate godhead, the Second Coming?

Once at the library, I found myself drawn to books about the Roman Catholic Church. Of course, there are many powerful religions in the world. I sensed that the underlying mechanics of all religions were similar and that all participated in the Religion ring, but having grown up in the West and raised as a Methodist, I felt pulled to understand the history of Christianity. I also suspected the Roman Catholic Church dominated the ring of religion.

I recalled my teacher talking about Christianity and The Church.

"The way of humanity is to turn everything into a marketable product, but when you turn a thing into a marketable product, it loses something. Christianity is a marketable product. It has very little to do with Jesus Christ. In fact, it has nothing to do with what the experience was like to be around him. Jesus Christ was a simple, enlightened man who walked around, glowed with the light of the supra-conscious, and said that we're all free if we pursue God. He spoke about self-discovery in terms of love, forgiveness, and self-giving. Like most enlightened teachers, that's basically all he said. He didn't say 'Let's form the Roman Catholic Church.'"

Once it was established, the Roman Catholic Church took a simple, enlightened teacher and cast him as a divine savior, spawned the concept of a church hierarchy through which one communicated with the Divine, sought to exterminate Gnostic practices that taught self-knowledge, sponsored numerous rewrites of the Bible, and preached the desecration of the feminine through tales of the disobedience of Lilith, the fall of Eve, and the whoredom of Mary Magdalene. As a potentially all-pervasive institution, it fashioned itself as the perfect instrument of the Patriarchy.

The Church's history read more like a lineage of power-hungry kings slaughtering everything that stood in their way than a church of priests spreading the word of God. In fact, the Catholic papacy is the oldest continuing absolute monarchy in the world. From the time Christianity gained legal status in 313, the Church has persecuted its enemies relentlessly in an effort to maintain and enhance its position. For almost two thousand years, it has remained a central presence in shaping and defining European life. For a thousand years, in alliance with despotic governments, it has wielded its sword over nearly one third of the Earth's population. Historians calculate that it has shed the blood of some sixty-eight million people in an effort to establish religious dominion.

As early as the third century, the Popes claimed primacy over other churches in matters of doctrine. By the fifth century this had evolved into complete legal jurisdiction over them. In the early Middle

Ages, the Popes became civil rulers—governing land and peoples as well as the Church—and, by "converting the barbarians," brought all of Western Europe into the Roman Church. In the seventh century, the Church's prestige was enhanced by its Muslim conquests in the Middle East.

In the eighth century, the Church's time of absolute power came when Emperor Charlemagne finally conquered most of pagan Europe. By the tenth century, Western Christendom had come into existence. Throughout all of Europe the state religion was Roman Catholicism, and the Holy Roman Empire ruled most of the known world. By the thirteenth century—after the divine right of the papacy prevailed over the divine right of kings—archbishops, bishops, and abbots were usually great feudal lords with rich possessions and military strength, and the Pope had more wealth and power than all the kings and nobles combined.

Then came the crusade waged against the Cathars, also known as the Albigensians. The Cathar culture promoted learning, philosophy, poetry, classical languages, and religious tolerance. The Cathars were a simple, devoted people. They practiced meditation, were strict vegetarians, believed in reincarnation, recognized the feminine principle in religion, and held their religious services out of doors or in any readily available building, rather than in a church. They rejected the clerical hierarchies of the orthodox Catholic Church established to intercede between God and human, preferring *gnosis*, or direct, personal, mystical knowledge. They upheld no fixed theology, but loosely defined attitudes subject to individual interpretation instead.

In the eyes of the Church, the Cathars posed a severe threat to Roman Catholic authority. By the beginning of the thirteenth century, the Church faced the prospect that this heretical religious philosophy might well displace Roman Catholicism as the dominant form of Christianity in the Languedoc region of southern France, and there was the additional prospect of its spread to other parts of Europe. Because the barons of Northern Europe coveted the rich lands of the South, the Church deemed they could be exploited to provide an army for the crusade. Pope Innocent III's opportunity arose when an official of the Church was murdered in Languedoc. He blamed the death on the Cathars, and the crusade began.

In 1209, an army of 30,000 soldiers, dispatched by the Pope, descended upon Languedoc. The territory was ravaged, towns were razed, and the entire population—men, women, and children—was slaughtered. As with earlier crusades in Palestine, the rewards for the soldiers included remission of all sins, an expiation of penances, an assured place in Heaven, and all the booty they could plunder.

When an officer asked the Pope's representative how he could distinguish heretics from true believers, his reply was the now famous quote: "Kill them all. God will recognize His own." The crusade continued for forty years, and the number of Cathars that perished is estimated as one to two million.

Then came the Inquisition.

The fires of the large-scale European extermination of so-called witches and heretics didn't really get lit until 1550. There were relatively few witchcraft cases during the fourteenth and fifteenth century because an extravagant papal court was preoccupied with other things, including numerous internal power struggles and, beginning in 1517, the Thirty Years' War spawned by Martin Luther's Reformation.

The Inquisition continued for another hundred years, primarily in Eastern France, Germany, and Switzerland. It was mainly concerned with exterminating religious heretics—in other words, anyone who did not conform to the orthodox doctrine of the Roman Catholic Church. Although the civil courts ordered the executions, the Church was responsible for the beliefs that justified the arrest, torture, and execution of religious minorities by those courts.

It was one thing to deny religious freedom to individuals who deviated from the doctrine of the Catholic Church. It was quite another to perpetrate the false belief that large numbers of people were committing evil, sometimes homicidal, acts in league with Satan.

Once witchcraft was brought into the equation, the Inquisition could charge almost anyone with heresy. Midwives were suspect, as they supported the act of childbirth, considered by the Church to be a defilement not only of the mother but also the child. Additionally, they administered herbal potions for the relief of pain and promoted methods of birth control. To the Church, this was unacceptable. It insisted that, because of Eve's Original Sin, all women were *intended* to suffer in childbirth. In addition, prohibiting birth control was a powerful way for the Church to control women's minds and bodies and to guarantee a continual increase in the ranks of the initiated, who were the Church's financial foundation.

Gypsies were regarded with suspicion, not only because anyone with no fixed place of residence might evade the Church's authority, but also because they engaged in the mystical arts of palmistry and fortune telling, the adverse of prayer through the auspices of the clergy. Older women past the age of reproduction—whose only supposed crimes were the knowledge of natural medicines and often a sixth sense that was perceived as a direct threat to Rome—were particularly vulnerable, especially as they were not useful to the Church either as child-bearers or as fillers of church coffers.

The Inquisition effectively purged Europe of its traditional beliefs, practices, and nature-based culture. Gnosticism was forced underground. Labeling Gnostic practices and nature-based philosophies as satanic, the Church continued its search-and-destroy mission to eliminate Satanism, paganism, and shamanism throughout Europe, Africa, the Americas, and the Polynesian Islands. In Europe alone, according to some historians, the ensuing witch hunts claimed as many as two million lives, and eighty percent of them were women. It was one of the largest holocausts the world had ever known—one which, even today, is almost completely unacknowledged.

Following the Inquisition, the Church's power began to wane. It gradually slipped into a diminished world role as all of its papal states were lost, leaving only Vatican City as the Pope's civil domain. Perhaps slaughtering sixty-eight million innocent victims had come with a karmic price tag.

The Religion Ring

When the time arrived for our meditation on the Religion ring, I tried to do an invocation but failed. The interruptions were constant:

scenes of crusaders marching, soldiers slaughtering, people running, children screaming, and, repeatedly, the self-righteous chant *"God is on our side,"* sung under the fluttering banners of religious reform. But they weren't just the standards of the Roman Catholic Church. The flags of many different religions flapped above their armies.

So many religions wove their way throughout the Patriarchy—so many belief systems, so many righteous attitudes. The mystical ring appeared like a charm bracelet with hundreds of charms hanging from it: the various religions, the networks between religions, the alliances among religious and political factions. It hovered at the top of the One World Government as the ultimate control mechanism, emitting an incessant babble of sermons that preached good-versus-evil duality, an eye for an eye, female repression, guilt, and the threat of hell.

Abruptly the thought arose in my mind: *My God, this ring is going to be destroyed!* Then the religious ornaments on the charm bracelet began to disintegrate. The bracelet broke apart into small particles that hung suspended in the air. I waited. I expected that it would behave like the Royalty ring in Germany—that it would slowly be blown apart—but nothing happened.

All at once, I knew why. I was partially responsible for holding the particles there. I had judgments about religion. I had my own controls, networks, and alliances. The morality I had been programmed with as a child still permeated my perception. I had abandoned religion but had transferred morality to my spiritual quest. I vacillated between being a good spiritual seeker and a bad one. I needed to let all of that go.

When I did, the particles of the shattered ring began moving out into space in an ever-widening circle. I knew that the man in the South Pacific would never reign as the ultimate godhead now.

It somehow made sense to me that Mother Divine would take out of commission the Royalty ring at the bottom of the structure and the Religion ring at the top, leaving only seven rings that aligned perfectly with the seven Earth chakras. Perhaps the energies of these two rings were so corrupt that they were beyond repair. Perhaps destroying them was the only option if humanity was to be set free. Perhaps that allowed a person to spiral up as far as she wished—or to spiral down, depending on the choices she made.

The Demise of the New World Order

Because our wrap-up meditation on the seven Earth chakras had proved to be so significant, we decided to do one on all nine rings. Alexandria suggested scheduling it on November 8, the day of a cosmic alignment called the Harmonic Concordance.

I did a search on the Internet. Astrological predictions for the Harmonic Concordance abounded. According to many sources, the planetary configuration would be a cosmic trigger that would create a harmonic vibration in the solar system, enabling global shifts in consciousness.

That all sounds promising. I continued to read.

Shortly after 8:00 P.M. on the East Coast, a total lunar eclipse would occur, and a grand trine (or triangle) would be formed by Saturn, the Sun, and Mars, as well as a second grand trine formed by Jupiter, the Moon, and Chiron, a comet with a 51-year orbit between Saturn and Uranus. The two triangles would form a perfect Star of David.

Unbelievable! I voted yes on meditating during the Harmonic Concordance.

As the day approached, however, my enthusiasm was overshadowed by an escalating sense of disorientation. I felt strange, almost off balance. It was as though my energy field had always spun counterclockwise, drilling down into the third-dimensional, patriarchal world, and I was now being urged to do a complete reversal, spin clockwise, and spiral out through the crown chakra into the fourth dimension.

Jackie's diagrams of the inverted pyramids flashed through my mind. The global elite had reversed the order of the nine rings in order to create a perversion of the true alignment in consciousness. Was this what it felt like to be free of that configuration? I was disoriented. Try as I might, I just couldn't seem to get the hang of it. It was like trying to start a cantankerous old car. I would turn the key, and the engine would sputter in an attempt to start, but when it wouldn't, I would have to release the key and let it rest.

On November 8th, Anders and I drove into Washington DC with the intention of meditating at the Washington Monument during the lunar eclipse. I took the opportunity to visit my holistic doctor.

"What have you done to yourself?" she asked after a few minutes examination. "Your body is filled with metallic energies! Are you still doing those meditations on the patriarchal energies you told me about?"

My doctor was very psychic, and I had kept her abreast of my energetic work. Now I nodded my head, feeling like a little girl.

She shook her head in dismay. "How has your energy level been?"

"Awful. I'm dead tired all the time."

"Well, it's no wonder!" She took a moment to scan the situation. "Don't you realize how lethal these energies are that you're taking through your body?" She hesitated. "Is this energetic work really necessary?"

I luxuriated briefly in the feeling of relief that would undoubtedly come from giving up the tortuous meditations. Then I remembered that I was part of the Lineage, a network of warriors who did battle with the forces that obstruct enlightenment. I couldn't expect the work to be a cake walk.

I nodded. "I'm committed to seeing this project through, I'm afraid."

She nodded slowly in response, then lifted her eyebrows. "I'll see what I can do."

After my treatment I glided out of her office and into the Mercedes, which Anders had waiting at the curb. I could have cried with joy. My body felt lighter and stronger than it had in a long time. Unfortunately my reverie was short-lived.

As Anders drove through the capital, I felt like I was hit by a ton of bricks as intense fatigue crashed down on me. I reclined the passenger seat and lay there, corpselike. Suddenly all I wanted to do was go home to bed. The thought of hanging around DC until 8:00 P.M. was unbearable. Why couldn't I just go home? Why did we need to mediate on all the rings of the New World Order anyway? We were never going to complete this project. It was too much, too big, too many metallic energies. I begged Anders to take me home.

"Home?" he exclaimed. "We've driven three hours to get here! We can't possibly go back home before the meditation. What's wrong with you?"

I didn't answer right away.

He was right. What was wrong with me? Where did the sudden fatigue come from? And why was I suddenly depressed? My teacher's often repeated warning echoed through my mind: "If you experience sudden fatigue, or your emotions suddenly spiral out of control, or you suddenly feel nauseated, you're under lower mystical attack."

I covered my eyes with my hand. It was the man in the South Pacific…again! He was tracking me, sensing pivotal moments in the project. Alexandria, Jackie, and I had made tremendous progress. We had disconnected all nine rings, and these wrap-up meditations were where the big breakthroughs came. We were getting close, and this evening's meditation must involve something significant. The lower mystical hit—the fatigue and the depression—were his way of trying to derail us. Besides, he never expected us to make it this far, to withstand the toxic energies. He anticipated we would quit.

I massaged my temples and turned to Anders. "Someone doesn't want me to do this meditation tonight. Do you think you could find a Starbucks?"

I waited in the car while Anders went in. With Herculean effort I fought off the fatigue, sat up, and drank the largest coffee he had been able to order.

As evening approached, the weather became cold and blustery, and I didn't want to meditate outside. We found a parking space on Constitution Avenue close to the monument so I could sit in the back seat of the car.

Anders wanted nothing to do with sitting in the car. He headed for the public park between the White House and the monument "to keep George Bush company."

Looking at the moon through the leafless trees outside the car window, I could see that the eclipse was beginning. Tourists passed on the sidewalk, returning to their hotels. A few locals walked their dogs. Traffic rumbled along Constitution Avenue, but as I settled into meditation, the sights and sounds of DC faded away.

The image of the Olympics logo appeared and hovered before me. I sat up straighter. I had the strange feeling I was about to be shown the big picture.

The Lineage began to speak to me: *"The man in the South Pacific is a brilliant strategist. He plays several men in each ring at all times. There is always one in each ring with whom he aligns himself, manipulating his ego, convincing him he is essential to the One World Government. The others are for contingencies."*

There was silence. Although the image remained, their pronouncement was over. I took a moment to absorb what they had said.

It's no wonder the man in the South Pacific hadn't wanted me to meditate tonight. I had just been given one of his key strategies. It explained his relationship with Queen Elizabeth. He had aligned himself with the Queen because she was the most powerful player in the Royalty ring. It also explained why he didn't attend the annual Bilderberg meetings but, rather, showed up at the end. As the man who wielded the most power on the planet, he had the right to an executive briefing, and he took the opportunity to check up on the Queen as his point person and those in the Royalty ring who covered contingencies.

He was using a tactic not unlike that of Adam Weishaupt. After forming the Bavarian Illuminati, he had two close associates into whom he could breathe his philosophies, they each had two below them, and so on. He believed he could rule over the most powerful men in the world without external force by activating his simple construct. The man in the South Pacific not only had two secretaries but breathed his philosophies into one person in each ring. The Illuminati was alive and well, constantly upgrading its methodology with the changing times.

I gazed at the nine ring configuration. In Germany, the Lineage had pointed out that the rings intersected and overlapped. Now they were calling attention to the ringleaders.

The intersection points.... The intersection points must be the mystical positions occupied by the leaders of the rings: well connected, utilizing revolving doors, sitting on each other's boards, sharing cigars and brandy.

All at once, the big picture crystallized. The nine-rings configuration was the One World Government!

The United Nations was not the One World Government, as I had read so many times during my research, nor was the WTO, as some people speculated. The One World Government was made up of the intersection points of the nine rings configuration—nine powerful men, aligned with the man in the South Pacific, networked together, manipulated by the lure of becoming the future rulers of the New World Order.

But wait.... That isn't the current configuration of the rings!

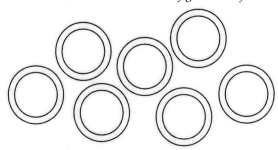

During our sessions, each ring had separated from the Olympic logo configuration. If the intersection points were the One World Government, we had effectively facilitated its deconstruction! That meant that the various point-men would no longer feel networked, wouldn't feel aligned with the man in the South Pacific, and wouldn't be able to agree on how to move the New World Order forward.

My heart pounded as my mind raced ahead.

Working independently, the seven rings that remained were relatively powerless. Like a company of soldiers scattered behind enemy lines, they would continue to fight, because that is what they were trained to do, but they would no longer have the power of a consolidated fighting unit.

The One World Government is gone!

I took a couple of deep breaths, trying to get used to the idea. It was really gone! It was only a matter of time before the cogs and the wheels of the patriarchal machine would cease to turn!

All at once, my mind came to a screeching halt. That was the *outer* Patriarchy. What about the *inner* Patriarchy?

We had facilitated the dismantling of the outer structures, but we had also dismantled the inner ones. By unplugging myself from each of the nine rings, I had disassembled my own rigid egoic structure. By unplugging myself, I had purged much of my patriarchal programming. That meant that my ego was now relatively powerless, that it would continue to function for awhile out of habit but that it would ultimately fall apart. I looked at my own awareness field. It was fluid in a way it had never been, more formless.

One part of me wanted to scream *"No!"* lock everything in place, and keep things as they were. Instead, something inside of me let go, and my energy began to spin. Again I experienced the feeling of trying to start an old car, but this time, when the key turned in the ignition, the engine fired right up. My energy spun clockwise, then it spiraled effortlessly out through my crown chakra, up into the fourth dimension.

When I looked down on myself, sitting in a car by the Washington Monument, I could see that my awareness field had an entirely new alignment. It looked remarkably like a Star of David.

Hitting Rock Bottom

Back in Williamsburg in the days following the Harmonic Concordance, things continued to spin. They spun, all right— completely out of control! My life went haywire. My emotions rampaged. I tried desperately to pull myself together, but it was impossible. Emotional chaos. Pure torment. I felt like dying would have been a gift.

Finally I caught a glimpse of what lay beneath my other emotions: *fear*—and lots of it.

So this is what it feels like to unplug from the nine rings. This is living hell!

Why couldn't I just have a good time with my life? I didn't need to save the world. I didn't need to drag myself from one meditation to the next. I didn't need to reconcile my aversion to the man in the South Pacific.

I decided to drop the entire Patriarchy project. I felt better. Then, an hour later, I was emotionally devastated all over again.

It went on for two weeks.

One evening, I appeared outside of Anders' office door.

"You're drunk!" he exclaimed, looking up from his desk.

"I am not," I said slowly, confident I was not slurring my words. "I've only drunk a half bottle of wine. I just had to take a break from the emotional pain."

Before I could stop myself, I burst into tears. He came over and took me in his arms.

"How can I go on like this?" I sobbed.

My knees buckled, and I sank to the floor. He knelt beside me.

"Where did all this pain come from? At times it feels like I'm not just crying for myself, but I'm taking on the pain of the whole planet. It's horrible. I can't stand it!"

Between bouts of hysterical screaming, I rocked back and forth on the floor or lay in a fetal position. Anders didn't say anything. He just held me, listened, and handed me one tissue after another.

After half an hour I calmed down and stopped crying. He studied my face.

"Do you think you're okay now?" he asked, brushing away my tears.

I nodded and blew my nose. He looked at me intently.

"I'm okay now," I said. "I just needed to cry."

"Jesus! You scared me!" He shook his head slowly from side to side. "You know, this will have to go into my book. I've got to be truthful about the inside story, and I'm changing the title. I'm going to call it *Sewers of the Enlightenment Process*."

I laughed for the first time in two weeks.

What Remains Is Love

The next day, the suffering continued, but something was different. My emotional body felt anger, but another part of me felt completely detached. My higher self stood back and observed, uninvolved.

For the next six hours, I spiraled farther and farther down through an emotional maelstrom: anger, doubt, confusion, fear, betrayal, loss, pain, guilt, shame, inadequacy, despair, worthlessness, hopelessness, desolation. Every emotion felt extremely real, including the desire to die that arose when I finally bottomed out; but, remarkably, I observed all of them from a place of absolute neutrality. From that detached state of mind, I could see things quite clearly.

Our energetic work on the nine rings—all the personal process-ing I had done—had accelerated my spiritual growth. I had taken a quantum leap forward in my evolution, an inner jump into unchart-ed territory. Who was I? My awareness field was different: freer, more expanded, more universal. I didn't know how to operate anymore, and that kicked up a tremendous amount of fear.

Fear. It always came back to that. What was this thing called fear? What if I investigated? What if I simply let go into the fear, *became* the fear? What then?

Magically, in my new detached state of mind, I was able to do just that. I let go. It burned through my body—heat in every cell. In the midst of the snap, crackle, and pop, I smiled. It was just a vibration… an unpleasant vibration, but just a vibration nonetheless.

I relaxed and let it consume me. I sacrificed myself to the fear. Then, all at once, nothing. The fear dissipated into light, peace, love. The fear *was* love…love disguised as fear.

Suddenly I laughed with the delight of a child. If I could merge with this fear, I could merge with my fear of the man in the South Pacific. *I am going to be able to do this. I am going to be able to reconcile my aversion to him!*

19
THE FEMININE UNITES
VIA SPIRITUAL KNOWLEDGE

When we had devised our game plan back in March, we knew we needed to do energetic work on the seven chakras of Mother Earth and on the nine rings of the New World Order. That work was complete. It had taken us eight months.

Now we knew we needed to work on *all* of the rings we had identified. Those that remained were the three of spiritual knowledge—Seeing, Power, and Love—and, finally, the One Ring of Power that ruled all the other rings.

We braced ourselves for another round.

We began with the three. What were these rings, really? They appeared as grids on the inner planes, like rings with netting that covered them. Each was composed of many smaller rings—Druid rings, Wiccan rings, Buddhist rings—groupings of likeminded individuals, *sanghas* sharing the same spiritual tradition.

Additionally, they were all interlinked. The three larger rings of Seeing, Power, and Love wove the common energies of the others together, so an individual who studied psychic development gained access to a larger psychic network, the ring of Seeing. Someone who trained in the mystical arts could garner support from other spiritual warriors in the ring of Power. Someone following a bhakti path was immediately a member of the larger heart space of the ring of Love.

But even though these three rings had been in the keeping of spiritual masters and their students throughout the Patriarchal Age, the inverted energies of the Patriarchy must have affected them. While enlightened masters may have been able to see into alternate worlds, wield power in a balanced way, and embody the expansiveness of the open heart, their students viewed the master and the teachings though the lens of patriarchal programming.

Would they be as difficult as the nine rings? They couldn't possibly be. We would sail through them, leaving behind the fatigue and pain of our earlier meditations. These rings had been cherished and protected, and we had clocked thousands of hours meditating on the third eye, the navel chakra, and the heart chakra, the energy centers that aligned with these three spiritual qualities. How difficult could they be?

We were caught completely off guard.

As we worked on the first two rings—Seeing and Power—we found ourselves recalling past lives where we had either misused the energy of the rings or used their energies correctly and had been punished for it. We relived being tortured, then dying horrible deaths. We were drowned, stoned to death, and burned at the stake. Jackie got migraines. I got nauseated.

Alexandria, on the other hand, reported that she relived being burned at the stake but that the experience evolved into gigantic surges of kundalini. "I remained poised, keeping the core of my being open, and entered into a timeless meditation."

What bullshit! I had reached the end of my patience. I had heard enough reports of timeless meditations. What was she doing when she meditated anyway? Was she really helping with the project? Jackie always contributed seeings and pitched in with the heavy lifting. I was constantly sliding on my belly through dark energies behind enemy lines. Where was Alexandria? Sitting on her throne, holding an alignment, having a timeless time of it!

I calmed myself down. I couldn't afford to get entangled in a judgmental state of mind. I needed to understand more fully what Alexandria was contributing. She was our sovereign, the guardian of the Earth's heart chakra. She provided balance. She held an alignment during our meditations. All of this I knew intellectually, but what did that really mean?

A Portal to the Fifth Dimension

"I asked Spirit to show me what is actually happening as we work on the three rings," Jackie told Alexandria and me a few days later.

I smiled to myself. *Jackie has had a seeing. Thank God! Perhaps she can shed some light on the situation.*

"Prior to incarnating on Earth," she began, "each soul, in conjunction with Spirit, creates a sort of quantum blueprint. That blueprint runs the incarnation from the unconscious mind. It gives the person certain talents and abilities. It drives them to undertake certain tasks. What the ego does or what the conscious mind is aware of during the lifespan is irrelevant. What matters is how we use our energies in service to this blueprint. As long as the soul learns the lessons it signed up for in a particular life, that is what's important.

"Most people are completely unaware of their blueprint. More evolved souls, however, often wake up to theirs. There are many evolved souls on the planet at this time that are aiding the Earth in her spiritual transition. Light-workers have incarnated into all areas of life—in business as conscious entrepreneurs, in technology, in the arts, in roles where they work with nature. There are visionaries, bridge builders, healers...lots of healers, because that's mostly what the planet needs.

"*Our* blueprints equip us to dismantle the underlying structure of the Patriarchy. In our past lives, each of us received specialized training: one of us for the ring of Power, one for the ring of Love, and me for the ring of Seeing. But as we do our energetic work on the three rings, we are learning to access their power in a different way. Once we've completed this phase, we will each be able to hold the energies of all three rings. As human beings, we are actually configured for holding power in a more complete way, so we are literally reconfiguring ourselves. This is an opportunity for the three of us to make a huge spiritual jump.

"I was shown a band of consciousness that ascends from the top of the new fourth-dimensional world into a whole new configuration. It spirals up. The three rings actually form an inter-dimensional portal that leads beyond the fourth dimension into even more expanded levels of awareness and truth—the fifth through the ninth.

"The fifth dimension is one of instant manifestation, a dimension of pure creativity, where energy becomes manifest as we think it. It has a heart-centered love vibration, the vibration of the Divine Mother.

"The sixth dimension has to do with sacred geometry: light, sacred structure, and perfection in form. It is the field of potentiality in form, the essence and integrity of structure. It holds the record bank of ideas and creations. The desire force draws structural information from the sixth dimension.

"The seventh dimension is all about galactic information highways of light: stars, planets, the photon band, cosmic communication spirals that connect cycles and systems. It's the source of thought-wave creation. It provides a connection with the galactic center.

"The eighth dimension is the birthplace of organizational systems, the lens of power, the guidance grid for the dimensions beneath it, so to speak...the organizational matrix for the universe as we know it, the origin of pattern and place.

"The ninth dimension is the realm of spiritual mastery, the monad or single-celled microorganism of mastery, the stellar self." She paused to breath.

"But getting back to the three rings.... The symbol for the power of three is the *triquetra*—trinity in unity. It has its roots in the Celtic tradition. Three looping lines called a *triskele* are linked in a sort of triangle formation that represents body-mind-Spirit, or, if you prefer the Celtic equivalent, maiden-mother-crone. Additionally, there is a circle intertwining and uniting all three loops. It represents the all-encompassing wholeness of divinity. It's basically a symbol of the embrace of Divine Mother,  but of course it's been labeled satanic by various religious types.

"So that is what we are currently facilitating: an inter-dimensional portal to the higher dimensions, the crown of the new world."

Wow! I thought. *This is much bigger than I imagined. My conscious mind hasn't been aware of any of this.*

"I did a little research," Jackie was saying, "and found out we can get a triquetra necklace. I've ordered one for each of us. You can watch for them in the mail."

The Ring of Love

Each day, for the next few days, I was given a spiritual test and managed to pass each one. Mostly the tests involved accepting different aspects of myself. Then, as we began our meditation on the ring of love, I heard the voice of the Lineage:

"Are you willing to return to the beginning of the Patriarchy and go through all of your human lives again?"

Their question loomed before me. My heart sank. That was asking a lot! I was so exhausted from the energetic work, so burnt out from endlessly processing aspects of my ego, so debilitated with all the emotional suffering that came with having a human body.

I closed my eyes. I thought about it for a long time, about all the suffering I had experienced in my lifetime. I thought of Alexandria and Jackie, how much processing they had done and how much they had suffered, of Anders' suffering as his final exams approached. I even thought of the man in the South Pacific and the suffering that results from obsession with power.

My awareness extended out, surveyed the human condition, touched the suffering of all humans on the planet. My heart expanded in compassion. Perhaps our project would make a difference for people; but, even so, could I really go through all the incarnations again? Would going through all the incarnations really help ease human suffering?

I suddenly sensed my new triquetra necklace around my neck. Maybe I didn't possess the strength to say yes, but I was not alone. With the combined strength of all three of us, perhaps I could find the courage to answer.

I reached out to Alexandria and Jackie in an alternate dimension. We came together to form a circle. We grabbed not each other's hands but each other's wrists in order to form a stronger unit. Then we each performed a forward somersault. The result was a triquetra.

The balance of our triquetra flowed into me. I breathed in a new sense of strength and announced my answer: *If that is your will, if that will facilitate bringing an end to the suffering inflicted by the Patriarchy, and if you will provide me with a new body and the needed energy, then, yes, I will go through all of the lives again.*

Dams began to break. All over the planet dams broke. A sea of golden light rolled in over parched lands. A wave of light rolled through my body, bathing it in infinitesimal bubbles of gold. It washed away the concern, the fatigue. My shoulders dropped. My body relaxed. My heart melted into the exquisite bubble bath of gold.

So this sea of golden light that I have experienced before, this is love? I asked.

It was Mother Divine who answered. *"What else could it possibly be?"*

I took a deep breath. *Then may my heart remain open throughout the eons of time.*

Gradually the experience intensified. Wave after wave of love swept through my being. The swells rose higher. They crashed on the shores of my being, obliterating all thought. They molded themselves into a tidal wave of strength.

How much more intense could they become? I aligned myself with the core of Mother Earth below and with Mother Divine at the center of the universe and prayed that my being would not explode with all the energy passing through it. The ecstasy was almost unbearable... so celestial, yet so intense.

I held perfectly still and surrendered. It was the only way, the only way to hold the volume of love passing through—total intensity held within total relaxation. I held the alignment and stabilized a sea of golden love with no boundaries. It was the hardest thing I had ever done.

"I also saw water everywhere in the form of liquid love." Alexandria said later. "All three rings are love, really. The ring of Power is love expressed as passion—all types, not just physical. The ring of Seeing is seeing through the eyes of love, and the ring of Love is, of course, the pure, uninterrupted flow of love. It is the divine dance, encompassing, creating, maintaining, and destroying all illusion. I held my alignment, took it all through my being, and dissolved in light, beyond time."

Now. Now I understood what it meant to be a sovereign. I understood what Alexandria had been contributing throughout the project. I understood what it meant to hold an alignment. *Wow!* I had been trained as a soldier, and my secondary skill was seeing. Now perhaps there was a budding sovereign inside of me, as well.

The Crown of the New World

To conclude our work on the three rings, we did a three-ring-calibration meditation. Once again it was time to consolidate, time to fine-tune the energies of the rings we had just worked on, time to facilitate their merger into the fourth-dimensional configuration.

After we formed our triquetra, the three rings were unplugged from the dark influence of the One Ring of Power, then aligned to form a crown for the new world. A spiral of consciousness formed. Slowly it ascended through the crown, through the inter-dimensional portal, then disappeared in the dimensions beyond.

At the end, Jackie was told, *"It has begun,"* Alexandria was told, *"The work of these rings will be ongoing,"* and I heard, *"Worlds turning...."*

Afterwards, we were surprised that the energetic work had been effortless. It seemed a relief after months of torture.

In the evening, as I sat writing at my computer, I suddenly became aware of the Lineage all around me. They formed a configuration, and they seemed to be waiting for me. It took me a while to figure out what was going on.

The first image to pop into my mind was that of a cattle chute used at slaughter houses—a device that forces a herd of cattle into a single-file line so that, one by one, each cow must move forward as cowboys on either side prod it and the cow hesitates, sensing what lies ahead. The Lineage held a formation—a sort of vertical cattle chute that extended up above my head. They were waiting for me to cognize the chute, move through it, and join them in another dimension.

Then, with a start, it dawned on me: *I am the cow! If I go through the chute, the personal self will die!* My heart raced. I was horror stricken. The work we had done in the morning, work that had seemed so effortless, had turned into a nightmare. I was trapped—trapped by the progression of our Patriarchy project! I had no where to go but up through my crown chakra, into the fourth-dimensional world, through the crown of the three rings, and on to the dimensions beyond.

I was rigid with fear as I scrutinized my formless awareness field. Then I heard words of the morning echoing all around me: *"It has begun...the work of the three rings is ongoing...worlds turning."*

20
THE FEMININE MAKES ITS PEACE
WITH THE PATRIARCHY

We scheduled our meditation on the One Ring of Power for the winter solstice, and in the days that preceded it, the cosmic bleachers began filling up. Not since our night in the Caldera on the summer solstice had I seen such an intense display of interest from alternate dimensions. Apparently, Mother Divine would be putting on quite a show.

On the eve of the winter solstice, we scheduled an all-ring-calibration session. We wanted to make absolutely sure the entire multidimensional structure was in perfect order before our meditation on the One Ring.

As we began, the three of us locked wrists as we had grown accustomed to doing. But before commencing our energetic work, we paused…the beings assembled in other dimensions momentarily forgotten.

This was our moment, a moment outside of time and space, a moment for only the three of us. We acknowledged each other and simultaneously bowed. It was a long, deep bow, filled with tremendous gratitude—for the work of dismantling the Patriarchy, for our inner transformations, for the new fourth-dimensional world, but mostly for each other. We bowed to honor each other's suffering, courage, and perseverance. We bowed to honor, with deeper understanding, each other's spiritual roles as seer, sovereign, and soldier. We bowed to the perfection of the entire collaborative event.

Then we somersaulted, formed a triquetra, and split into three separate entities. But something was different. This time we each retained the three-sided configuration. We morphed into three self-reliant triquetras and floated out through space in an ever-widening circle.

The Diamond Body

In the center of our circle loomed the multidimensional world—all of the luminous rings, the tree of knowledge with glistening branches extending out through them, and the superimposed image of a Star of David that we had seen in November. It looked breathtakingly beautiful, ravishing in every detail.

Alexandria, Jackie, and I began to spin....faster and faster. My spinning became so fast, I got nauseated.

"Hang onto your cookies!" my teacher told me.

After a few minutes I became accustomed to the sensation and let go. I knew that our spinning was raising the vibration of the new world. And when it was calibrated just the way Mother Divine wanted it, the spinning ceased.

Ever so slowly, the Star of David began to move. The top pyramid glided down, the bottom one rose up, further and further, until finally a perfect diamond slid into place, enclosing the tree with all of its rings. Instantly, the universe was bathed in love...so soft and refined. The heart of the new world was fully open.

Then, to our utter astonishment, the entire diamond configuration began to descend toward the Earth. How could that be? Over the past nine months, rings had split off and had *risen up*. The evolving new world configuration had been suspended above the physical planet. In June it had been anchored to the core of the Earth, but even then it had hung in the air. Now, the new world *descended*. Was it because light-workers had spoken about the *ascension* of the Earth for so long that we found this descent hard to fathom? But what we were witnessing was undeniable. The multidimensional world was sinking down, down, down into the Earth!

Silently the two worlds merged into one. At that moment, the entire configuration lit up! It looked like an enormous Christmas tree ornament. Exquisite! Then, slowly, it began to rotate in a clockwise direction. Around and around. A masterpiece hanging silently in the void for the entire universe to admire.

We all relaxed. It actually made perfect sense. The multi-dimensional world was Mother Earth's Diamond Body, her true alignment in consciousness that Jackie had diagramed months before. And the design was pure genius. Now we could exist on the physical planet and in the multidimensional world simultaneously. Now we could have *both*!

The One Ring

The Solstice arrived: December 22, 2003. It was time to confront the One Ring—the ring that ruled all the other rings.

We spent the day preparing. We worked out. We fasted. We arranged and rearranged our meditation tables. Everything had to be right. Everything mattered. If we were ever going to use our training as impeccable warriors, now was the time.

At the last minute we staged a three-way conference call. We all felt a little confused, a little worried. What exactly were we about to do? What *was* the One Ring of Power?

Jackie suggested it was egoic shadow, the unconscious mind, the dark side of collective consciousness. Alexandria felt is was pure power, since power was common to every aspect of life and since the One Ring bound all the other rings together. I, on the other hand, thought of it as force, the misused power of the man in the South Pacific and his ringleaders, the force that animated the intersection points of the One World Government configuration.

Each of us was seeing correctly...from her own perspective. The combined energies of shadow, power, and force produced *dominance*—precisely the conclusion we had drawn during our systems analysis: the global elite had usurped feminine power, seized the reins, and achieved dominance over the planet by force.

"Let's go back," I suggested, "to the definition of a ring of power as a mystical configuration. We know that the mystics who compose a ring are networked energetically in another dimension, and the sum of their parts is exponentially greater than the whole. So the One Ring is the ultimate ring of power on the planet. Does it network all of the other rings—the seven, the nine, and the three? Is it a ring that networks individuals from all of the rings?"

"Something like that," Jackie said after a moment. "There are rings within rings, plans within plans. Everything is vibration, and we are all linked into whatever we resonate with. Some people resonate with the One Ring, some with the three. Some people have one talent, some have many. It's difficult to categorize any of this, except to say that there are rings of evolving consciousness that intertwine or interweave or vibrate together."

"It reminds me of the One Mind," Alexandria said, "the field of attention that spiritual seekers believe is manifesting as we evolve toward 2012. I think of it as a co-creative collaboration of consciousness, the field of our collective human intelligence. Like the phenomenon of an entire flock of birds changing course—the flock operates with one mind." She paused. "Only this would be the global elite's version of one mind."

"The *perversion* of one mind," I suggested.

"Precisely," Jackie added. "Power *over* instead of just power. Force instead of pure energy. Dominance instead of Divine Oneness. Dominance is the global elite's method of achieving their idea of one mind: the One World Government, global domination. It is *power over* in demonstrable form."

"This is big," Alexandria said softly. "This is important. I wonder if I'm really ready for this." There was silence on the phone for a long moment. I didn't know about Jackie, but I was feeling exactly the same way. Alexandria finally took a deep breath. "I guess in our meditation, we just need to surrender and pray to be shown what to do."

In the wee hours of the morning, our alarms went off. Three women in their own homes took showers, drank tea, assumed a cross-legged position, and prayed to be shown what to do. Normally we saw and experienced similar things, but this was different. Each of us met the ultimate power of the One Ring and unhooked from patriarchal dominance in her own special way.

The Eye of the Buddha

For me, patriarchal dominance and the man in the South Pacific were inseparable. He who wielded the ring of power had been my

worthy opponent for the past year and a half. He had stalked me continuously and interfered continuously, and I had failed continuously
to reconcile my fear of him.

My physical body sagged with exhaustion as I entered the mystical
planes. The man in the South Pacific appeared. He towered before
me, an armored giant, holding up the ring defiantly for me to see.
I struggled to keep my breathing even. What was I supposed to do?
Did I possess the strength to go through with this? I tried to fortify
myself.

Without warning, something inside me snapped. My awareness
expanded through the universe to a place far beyond the vibration of
fear. My heart merged with the heart of Mother Divine.

The Divine Feminine is returning to the Earth, I whispered to him
on the inner planes. *Will you come and rest in Her heart?*

All of a sudden, the gargantuan man from the South Pacific
collapsed into the form of a child, a little boy who had slaved to build
a sand castle on the beach only to find that the tide had washed it
away. He screamed at a world that was too big for him. He wailed
at a universe in which he was powerless. He whimpered, afraid and
insecure.

I was stunned. He was a human being just like me, arrogant
and insecure at the same time. Suddenly it didn't matter that he was
trying to control the world. His job was an unsavory one, but that
didn't mean that he didn't have feelings, that he didn't suffer like any
other human being.

My heart opened wide. Again I invited him to come and rest,
and this time he did…like a child running to his mother. My arms
encircled him and, little by little, he came to rest. His form dissolved,
melting into my heart, and the world grew remarkably still.

My being began to expand again, growing larger and larger.

"There has never been anything outside of you," I heard. *"It's all a
dream in the eye of the Buddha."*

My mind clouded with confusion. What had we been doing all
this time? What was real? While we dismantled the Patriarchy, had
we only been dismantling its energies inside of ourselves? When the

new world's Diamond Body slipped into position, was it a purely personal experience...or had our work affected the Earth?

I expanded further and further. I expanded so far that I *became* the eye of the Buddha. I could feel the faint outline of a Diamond Body, but had no idea whose it was.

Then, I *collapsed into* the eye of the Buddha. I became one tiny cell in the eye, a cell capable of reflecting everything in the universe. Questions and answers didn't matter. The man in the South Pacific didn't matter. I sat in perfect peace.

The Dawn of a New Age

Jackie took her One Ring of egoic shadow to the blue-white volcano of Mother Divine and, without hesitation, leapt in. She saw organic miasms being healed. Structures moved and turned as they were mended, realigned, and rearranged. Dimension after dimension throughout the universe reformatted itself to accommodate the new multidimensional world and, all the while, she heard, "*...end of an age, end of an age.*"

"After the meditation," she told us later, "I put on a kettle of mulled apple juice and sweet wine. It's a Celtic tradition. You raise a cup to the dawn then keep the kettle on all day. So, taking my cup, I walked out onto the deck in back of my house and looked out over the garden. Pre-dawn light...perfect stillness. 'What a sacred space' I thought. And the garden replied, 'All space is sacred. It is all a garden. Most have just forgotten.'

"The sun rose behind the hills. How amazing it was to see the dawn of a new age. I remembered our meditation, and suddenly there was a huge down-pouring of blue-white light...so intense, so gentle. I knelt. I raised the cup. I drank. Then I bowed my head in gratitude for the grace I had received...for being given the honor to participate... for the dawn of a new age."

The New World

Alexandria was asked by Mother Divine if she was ready to "relinquish the illusion of power" and, when she assented, was given a royal tour of the new world, the abode for those who are choosing to move from the third dimension into the fourth and beyond.

Doorways opened to reveal alternate dimensions. Stairways ascended into crystalline structures. Portals spiraled into realms of light.

In the new world there were no boundaries. Everything was open. Unhinged. Free.

At the base of the tree of life—a machine room for the new world—crystalline devices hummed, all synchronized and clean.

She ascended through the lower chakras. Level after level. Each with different tree branches. Avenues of mind. Frequencies to be explored.

She unhooked from the third dimension. She surrendered to the Divine.

Each level spun. And Alexandria spun, too.

She spun through the super-fluid realm of the heart. She danced through the upper chakras. She spiraled through the three-ring crown.

Spinning. Spiraling. Beyond thought. Beyond time.

A chant arose.

Only love. Only love.

Alexandria spun

and dissolved

into

Light.

PART FOUR

THE
RINGS OF
SPIRITUALITY
AND
ENLIGHTENMENT

21

THE FINAL PUZZLE PIECES

"You're going to be in South Africa for how long?" I asked Alexandria during our three-way conference call at the beginning of January, 2004.

"Two months," she replied.

I gasped. "That's a long time!"

"Well," she said, "I'm helping Celeste with her month-long South African tour this year, and then I want to spend some weeks at my house there."

"Didn't you tell me," Jackie asked, "that your house sits on the Nilotic Meridian?"

"Precisely on it."

"Must be interesting to meditate there," Jackie ventured.

"It's incredible. Why do you think I want to spend an extra month?"

"What's the Nilotic Meridian?" I interjected.

"It's the longest land-contact meridian on the planet," Alexandria answered, "and the geographical center of the Earth's land masses. It used to be the prime meridian to the ancients."

"Longitudinal lines are arbitrary," Jackie explained. "Technically, you could begin measuring longitude at any longitudinal meridian on the globe. The Nilotic Meridian was zero degrees during the Sumerian civilizations, but other places have been used through the centuries—Rome, Paris, Oslo. Finally, they settled on Greenwich, outside of London."

I felt like a carnivore scenting big game. *The meridians....*

"So when do you leave for South Africa?" Jackie asked.

"Oh, not until the beginning of April," Alexandria replied.

I was only half-listening. I was still thinking about the meridians. "Why don't we use Alexandria's trip as an excuse to go to London at the end of March? You've got to have a stopover on your way to Africa somewhere, right?"

"I do," Alexandria said ponderously, "but Celeste has already purchased the tickets. I think we're going through Paris."

"London," Jackie mused. "Interesting. I definitely get a hit on going to London."

"Ever since my six-month research project," I told them, "I've felt I needed to go there. It probably has something to do with that fact that London is operations central for the global elite, don't you think?"

"Absolutely," Jackie said. "London," she repeated thoughtfully. "I have to admit that London sounds *really* interesting."

As it turned out, Alexandria was not able to change her flight plans. She was disappointed. We all sensed, however, that not only London but South Africa would prove to be important as the project reached its conclusion.

The Prime Meridians

Once again I put on my research hat and hit the books, focusing this time on the prime meridians. I studied all the meridians down through history, but the Nilotic Meridian had mystical connotations that the others didn't.

To ancient civilizations, the Nilotic Meridian was associated with the beginning of time on Earth, a golden age when the gods ruled the world, what the Egyptians referred to it as Zep Tepi or First Time. Zep Tepi occurred 450,000 years ago.

The story goes, according to researchers like Zecharia Sitchin,[142] that a group of beings called the Anunnaki—literally translated as *Those who from Heaven to Earth came*—traveled from their home planet of Nibiru in the Draco star system, landed on Earth, and created a civilization in Sumer, what today is the Iraq-Iran region.

Their global empire, with its great cities, temples and monuments, was the birthplace of agriculture, architecture, astronomy, language, mathematics, metallurgy, navigation, religion, and writing. It was also the first government on Earth—a monarchy—and the first rulers were the Anunnaki. Their rule over Egypt, Mesopotamia, and the Indus Valley is recorded in the histories of all three civilizations.

Their mission was to mine the Earth for gold and other minerals. Their mining operations eventually centered along the Nilotic Meridian, which had a channel of gold running underneath it. It became the gold-producing center of the ancient world.

At one point the Anunnaki workers assigned to be gold miners rebelled against their backbreaking labor. The decision was made to genetically engineer a slave race to take over the work. After numerous laboratory experiments, the *mixtured* worker, Homo sapiens, was created by combining Anunnaki genes with those of the ape man, Homo erectus. The first perfected model was later called *LU.LU* in Sumerian which means *man*, or *Adama* in Hebrew which, means *earthling*. Some researchers believe the ratio was one part Anunnaki to three parts Homo erectus, a ration that produced a physically strong, not overly intelligent, easily dominated work force.

Initially the new human workers were a subject of hot debate. One camp of Anunnaki believed that humans should remain an ignorant slave race—that, in order to keep the class structure in place, it should be taboo for the Anunnaki to share any of their sacred knowledge, even such things as writing and mathematics. The opposing camp felt humans should be allowed to "eat of the tree of knowledge" and evolve.

At some later point, Anunnaki males mated with earthling females, and the rigid class structure broke down. As time went on and this indiscretion was forgiven, these Anunnaki/human hybrids were trained as kings and queens. The larger ration of Anunnaki blood made them perfectly suited to the task. They were granted the "divine right" to rule various regions. When the Anunnaki finally went home, the royal bloodlines they left behind continued to govern.

Down through the ages, the royals have struggled to maintain the purity of their bloodlines by not breeding outside of their families. The ancient texts are filled with examples of brother/sister and brother/half-sister unions, and contemporary researchers claim that brothers and sisters, or fathers and daughters, can interbreed throughout as many as ten generations—some three hundred years—before genetic abnormalities occur.

Over time, some of these bloodlines moved into Western Europe, establishing new centers of power. Because one can begin measuring longitude at any longitudinal meridian on the globe, they simply proclaimed their new base of power as the new prime meridian. The Nilotic Meridian in Sumer/Babylon was made obsolete by the meridian of Mount Mario in Rome. This transfer of power manifested as the Roman Empire, the Roman Catholic Church, and Christianity. Later on, the Paris Meridian—sometimes referred to as the Rose Line— was heralded as the new prime meridian. It cut vertically across the ancient Celtic kingdom, which included Scotland, Cumbria, Wales, the southwest tip of England, and Brittany in France. Finally, in 1884, the Greenwich Meridian—the Greenwich Mean Line—became the international standard for the modern world.

The Greenwich Mean Line, together with the 180th meridian at 180° longitude, which the International Date Line generally follows, forms a great circle around the Earth, separating the Eastern and Western Hemispheres.

"Makes sense," Jackie told me. "If you split the planet down the middle with the GMT, it's easier to rule everything on both sides."

My study of the Greenwich Meridian led me to researchers who speculated that Great Britain was the center of the Earth's energy grid, and London was the primary site within that vortex. Whether or not these things were so, Jackie and I psychically perceived that the City of London, the historic one-square-mile area at the heart of Greater London that is governed by the City of London Corporation, served as operations central for the global elite.

We began looking forward to our trip in March, when we would be able to confirm our seeing and visit the Greenwich Meridian. Then, in April, Alexandria would travel to South Africa, and we would have firsthand knowledge of the Nilotic Meridian. My hunch was that the meridians were connected to the transmutation of the two final rings of the multidimensional world—the Religion ring and the Royalty ring—but so far, no one of importance on the higher planes was downloading information.

Egypt Revisited

At the beginning of March, I shelved my meridian books next to my One World Government research books, which had been collecting dust, and phoned Jackie.

"Egypt has been coming up for the past few days...and fear. I keep waking up in the middle of the night in a state of panic. What do you think this London trip is about?"

"It has something to do with taking back our power," she answered, "power that is rightfully ours as women, power that we lost in Egypt. In order to do our energetic work in London—whatever we end up being shown to do—we'll have to go against all the female programming we received during the Patriarchy."

My body trembled. It was time to remember the entire saga surrounding the Egyptian mystery school.

Years before, my teacher had said something in the desert: "We always form a circle at the end of desert trips because a long time ago, at the end of the Atlantean cycle, we made a circle and tried to change our field of attention. We attempted to go home, to jump to another world. You don't have to die to leave this world. This world is a dream, and there are other dreams. We tried to change dreams. But some people in the circle saw that not everyone would be able to make the jump, so they stepped back. They volunteered to wait until this lifetime, so everyone could."

At the time, my teacher's words had made me feel strange, as though someone was telling me something I already knew. I knew I was one who had stepped back from the circle. Alexandria and Jackie felt the same.

So what had really happened at the end of Atlantis? What exactly had we volunteered for? I plumbed the depths of my psyche. I had to remember.

I remembered the circle. I remembered stepping back. I traced the feeling of that event through time. Over the next few weeks, I painstakingly followed it forward and back until the key moments emerged.

It began in my past life that predated my incarnations on Earth. It began in that long line I stood in with seventy others, members of my lineage. We had volunteered to travel to Earth and use our spiritual skills to orchestrate an experiment in consciousness. We had done it in exchange for evolution. We had been told it was a difficult assignment, that many would fall by the wayside but that, in the end, everyone would come home.

We had planned to return home—wherever home was in the galaxy—at the end of Atlantis, but our exit strategy had failed. Some had been able to make the jump and had gone ahead, but some were unable to...and some had volunteered to stay on and help my teacher, an army general who refused to leave troops behind.

In Atlantis my teacher met with those who had volunteered. The remaining members of the Lineage on Earth would now have their contracts extended, so to speak. We would stay on Earth for another age. Then, at the end of the age, everyone would congregate.

In the late Kali Yuga, we would incarnate as a soul group. My teacher would find everyone and give them additional mystical training. At that point we would be moving from a global configuration based on power to one based on the heart. Changing dreams would be easier. Everyone would be able to make the jump. That was the plan, and those who had volunteered to help implement it would receive the gift of additional evolution.

But what were the specifics of this plan? What was supposed to happen between Atlantis and the Kali Yuga? How had Egypt figured into it? I forced myself to go deeper.

In Atlantis we had strategy meetings. We did seeing exercises. We mapped the course we would take. We knew that, at the beginning of the age, light would prevail on the planet then gradually give way to darkness. We saw the pivotal moment when the shift from light to dark would occur. It would happen in ancient Egypt. The volunteers would incarnate as a soul group. My teacher would give us specific mystical training. Then, at some point, we would take a spiritual fall.

My heart throbbed in my chest. We had seen our spiritual fall in advance. No, that wasn't quite right. We had *planned* our spiritual fall! The group of volunteers—those who had stepped back from the circle in Atlantis, the group of women who had incarnated in Egypt—had agreed to take a fall in consciousness. At that pivotal moment in history, we had aligned with the darkness and facilitated the shift—on purpose!

It had all been part of the plan! The Patriarchy was supposed to take birth…and we had provided the birth canal. Celeste had nailed it during our global seeing exercise when she said that women signed up to play out the third-chakra-based society, with its focus on power, for the evolution of the masculine and, thus, humankind. This was the part we signed up for.

Relief flooded my being, washing away the guilt I had carried for years. *I didn't take the fall in Egypt because I made a spiritual mistake. I agreed, in advance, to take it.*

The beggar woman…. *Oh, my God!* The beggar woman hadn't been the man in the South Pacific. It had been my teacher! My teacher had pulled me aside, said he wanted my help with something, then left on business the next morning. My teacher, the master mystic, had changed his form and appeared as a beggar woman. My teacher, the embodiment of the dragon energy of enlightenment, had reared up as a giant cobra of male power and wrapped a snake around my heart, shutting down my ability to wield feminine power in a balanced way. He had anesthetized my heart so I wouldn't feel the pain of the coming incarnations. Out of compassion. He had done it to help me. And he had given me a dream of one hundred incarnations—a reminder of the plan we had agreed to. He had been trying to tell me, "This is what will transpire. These are your future lives. This is the lifetime at the end of the cycle where we will meet again. Don't forget! It's all a dream. We will meet at the end and wake up from the dream. We will change realities. We will make the jump. And then we will finally be able to go home." *What a plan! What a revelation!*

But what of the hundred lifetimes after Egypt? What role had we played as the Patriarchy unfolded? I refocused my attention. We had planned everything in detail. We must have planned the other incarnations. What had we been doing all that time?

I froze. Suddenly, the phrase *taking a fall in consciousness* loomed before me. I had never really thought about what it implied. Now the ramifications petrified me. We had been living in enlightened states of mind in Atlantis and Egypt. We had assumed we would retain our level of consciousness during those hundred lifetimes. But that had not been the case. We had dropped all the way back down in the evolutionary cycle then spent a hundred lifetimes climbing back up! We had forgotten who we were!

The suffering of a hundred incarnations in ignorance flooded my awareness. I gasped for air. *A hundred lifetimes of pain and suffering!* Had we really understood what we were signing up for when we extended our contracts? Had it been in the fine print at the bottom that we failed to read? It must have been an oversight, an oversight with horrendous consequences.

I took a couple of deep breaths to stabilize myself. Finally I felt quieter.

But wasn't dropping down in the evolutionary cycle the only way it could have worked? Didn't it have to be done that way? Had we not gone through the evolutionary process, had we not suffered alongside humanity during the Patriarchy, our hearts would never have opened in compassion. We would never have taken on the Patriarchy project in this lifetime.

My experience during the three rings, the ring of love…the Lineage asking me if I was willing to go back to the beginning of the Patriarchy and do all of the incarnations again…. All at once, it made sense. It had been an instant replay. When I had agreed, dams had broken, and liquid love had flowed over the planet. It had all been done for love! Love of my teacher, love of the Lineage, love of the Earth. It had all been done for the evolution of consciousness.

Again I stopped. The evolution of consciousness? What was the evolution of consciousness throughout the Patriarchy? It was learning about power—specifically abuse of power. I suddenly felt uneasy, like I was skating on thin ice.

What did we do for all those lifetimes? Well, what do we always do? We assist the Earth and her peoples in their evolution. So....

My mind was trying to shut down. I didn't want to see what was next. I willed the distortion aside. I pushed my mind forward.

The evolution of consciousness...the abuse of power.... Our contract must have been to come back lifetime after lifetime to help humanity learn about abuse of power.

I shook my head. It was the global elite who had abused power throughout recent history. Had we worked with them? Had we gone undercover?

Without warning, an avalanche of horror descended on me. We hadn't *worked with* the global elite. We had *been* the global elite! Our job during those hundred lifetimes had been to *construct* the inverted patriarchal system! We architected the entire thing, in preparation for this lifetime when we would take it apart! How else would we be able to see the intricate details of its structure and know how to dismantle it?

No! It can't be true! I couldn't have been one of them!

We had worked to limit consciousness? We had repressed the feminine?

A doorway in my mind started to close. I caught it and slammed it open.

I AM going to see this. I am too close to give up now!

I closed my eyes. I prayed to the Lineage for strength. I let the feelings of horror burn through my body and felt them rise up through my crown chakra.

After a moment, grace descended. My heart opened. Gradually my equilibrium returned.

I was trying to be moral. I was trying to group all the beings who had taken part in this enormous experiment in conscious here on Earth into good guys and bad guys. But that wasn't how it worked. I contained the universe within myself. I contained both light and dark. Throughout the hundred lifetimes, I had played roles on both sides. I had chosen bodies and taken incarnation to do whatever needed to be done…and the task in this lifetime of dismantling the underlying structure of the Patriarchy, a project that fostered the expansion of consciousness, was no more important than what I had done in the past.

Suddenly the man in the South Pacific came into focus. In Egypt I'd had an affair with a priest from another temple. After leaving my teacher's mystery school, I had studied the dark arts. That had laid the groundwork for the incarnations in which I had worked to limit consciousness. The man in the South Pacific had been my instructor of the dark arts—my instructor *and* my lover. That's why I had been shown a vision of him at the beginning of the project. That's why I had been pitted against him. I'd had intimate knowledge of the man who was poised to rule the world.

22

STALKING THE MERIDIANS OF POWER

On the eve of the spring equinox, I loaded my bags into the car for the London trip. Anders sulked as he drove me to the airport. He wanted to go, but this trip wasn't appropriate for Anders. It was about reclaiming our power as women. I felt bad that he was sullen, but nothing I could think of to say seemed to reassure him.

I departed a few days before Jackie because I wanted to visit the meridians. The first was Mount Mario, the stronghold of the Roman Catholic Church.

By the time I arrived in Rome, took a nap, and walked to the Vatican, it was closing for the evening. Leaving the Via Della Concillazioni and the sounds of the traffic, I entered the repose of the plaza and seated myself on the ledge of one of its two massive fountains.

With its pillars arranged in a semicircle, the plaza was like a giant womb that enticed visitors to come and rest, drawing the eye toward the dome of the Basilica of St. Peter in the distance. People who had attended the last mass of the day streamed down the stairs into the plaza. Tourists consulted their guidebooks. An Italian family passed, on their evening stroll.

In the center of the courtyard was a regal Egyptian obelisk. I gazed it for a long time but couldn't read its energy. It seemed vacant, devoid of any kind of feeling. Perhaps it had served some energetic purpose in the past but was now dormant. A little girl of about four stood alone in the midst of the hustle and bustle, looking up, studying it, too. I wondered what she perceived on this warm spring equinox evening, standing in front of the most powerful church on the planet.

At the top of the stairs near St. Peter's' main entrance, a canopied platform had been erected, perhaps in preparation for Easter. The tidy rows of folding chairs looked cheap before the backdrop of Vatican wealth. I walked toward it, a tiny figure among hundreds of other tiny figures, slowly making her way across the enormous open space.

When I arrived I positioned myself under the window where the Pope appeared on special occasions. Then I turned and looked down on the plaza from this new perspective.

Vatican City. The Pope's civil domain.

I tried to imagine what it was like to be John Paul II, the Vicar of Christ, the infallible interpreter of divine revelation. What would he be feeling when he took his place at Easter and raised his hand in blessing to the thousands of people below, sandwiched between his God and those who vied for political control of the Church? A surge of patriarchal power coursed through the Vatican, passed through me, and broke across the plaza. It drained the energy out of my jet-lagged body. It made me feel old.

I took a very deep breath and exhaled. It was his role in this lifetime, not mine. I felt a shiver rising up my spine, and I let go. I let go of the Pope…let go of religion…let go of the memories of being burned at the stake.

Dusk descended. Gradually the crowds thinned, and a hush fell on the plaza. A janitor swept a piece of refuse into his metal trash container, and it softly clapped shut.

I continued to stand there, in the middle of Rome, feeling one with everything, completely at peace. A wave of forgiveness enveloped me—forgiveness for myself. I forgave myself for all of the lives I had spent constructing the Patriarchy.

The elaborately carved wooden confessionals of St. Peter's stood nearby, locked away for the night. I didn't need one. Perhaps in some lives it would have been appropriate. But now, in this life, I could perform the roles of both the confessor and the priest—a sacrilege to the Church, perhaps; a pleasing revelation to me.

I sighed. What an extraordinary evening it was in the still plaza. I was not an opponent of the Church; I was one with it. It was almost as though I had helped to create the Church so I could, one day, move beyond it. There was nothing I needed to do, nothing I needed to understand. I only needed to open my heart and let the Divine Feminine take her course.

That evening, I *was* the Divine Feminine—traveling, searching, exploring, yearning for completion.

The Meridian of Power in Paris

After traveling by train to Paris, I made my way to the Hotel Talleyrand, the former mansion of the Rothschild's. Looking across the busy Place de la Concorde, I studied the gold-capped Egyptian obelisk in its center. It was like the one in Rome. I couldn't clock anything about its energy.

Walking through the Jardin des Tuileries and past the Louvre to the Palais Royal, I found a bronze Arago marker, one of the hundred and thirty-five medallions embedded in pavement and floors across Paris to mark the Paris Meridian. I placed my feet on either side of it and momentarily closed my eyes. It felt like visiting a house where the residents had moved out a long time ago.

Approaching the Meridian in London

The next day, queued up at the Eurostar window at the Paris Nord station and waiting to check in for the high-speed train under the English Channel, I watched a dignified British attendant make his way down the line of passengers and examine each ticket, monitoring carefully all who sought to gain entrance to his beloved homeland. Finally he approached me.

"May I see your ticket, please?"

I handed over my Eurostar paperwork.

After a thorough examination he nodded perfunctorily. "Seems to be in order," he told me without emotion. As I was the last person in line, he stood ceremoniously waiting to do his duty with the next person to arrive.

I smiled at him.

For a moment he didn't respond; then he cleared his throat. "First time on the Eurostar, madam?"

"Yes, it is," I answered, trying to be equally proper.

He eyed me as if to assess my sensitivity to his next statement. Pulling himself up to his full height and raising his chin slightly, he told me in a proud but confidential tone, "The Queen traveled back to London on the Eurostar last week, you know."

I fixed him with my eyes. "No! I am *very* impressed."

He nodded gravely, momentarily closing his eyes.

"That must have been quite a day for you," I said, placing my hand over my heart.

"Oh," he sighed, "quite a day, it was. Quite a day, madam."

I refrained from mentioning that I expected to witness the dissolution of some of the Queen's mystical handiwork in London.

Later, when he gave the sign, I boarded and found a seat. With a lurch, the train then began its journey, picked up speed, and entered the dimly lit tunnel under the English Channel.

I was racing toward the heart of the Patriarchy.

23

OPERATIONS CENTRAL IN LONDON

The Waverley House Hotel in London was a disappointment—a veritable Holiday Inn, by American standards—but Jackie and I agreed not to expend precious time looking for another. We liked the location, only a block from the British Museum. Jackie had seen before leaving that the museum was going to provide an important clue.

On our first evening, sitting in meditation on my twin bed in the hotel room, I flinched involuntarily. I was sitting right in the middle of the global elite's base of operations, the vortex of ultimate power on the planet. It was like having an enormous blueprint inside of me. I could feel the Earth in a different way. I could feel all the patriarchal systems, and I could feel how they were controlled from the City at the heart of London.

My awareness was pulled down into a dimension just below the physical level of the City of London. I was puzzled. I looked around, attempting to make sense out of what I was being shown.

It looked like a machine. It was black and dark brown…. It had moving parts….

I forced myself to relax and drop my judgments. My vision cleared a bit more.

It *was* a machine, a very complex piece of machinery; but there was something strange about it, something sinister. I stopped my thoughts, and as it gradually came into focus, I froze in horror.

It was a giant squid! It was a complex piece of machinery, but it was organic!

My flesh crawled. I shook my head clear of the vision and opened my eyes, then glanced over at Jackie sitting on her bed. She had finished meditating, so I described what I had seen.

"What in God's name is it?" I asked.

She sat still, her eyes went out of focus for a few moments, and then she answered, "Frankly, I'm not sure...but I bet we find out by the end of the week."

She lay down and stretched out with her hands behind her head, her long red-brown curls spilling over the pillow. "What *I* saw is that, during our week in London, we will create an energetic corridor to the core of the universe through which Mother Divine will do the next piece of work. When we worked on the nine rings, new fourth-dimensional ones split off and became part of the new world. But seven of the nine old rings are still intact. They have been recalibrated and laced with Divine Love, but they are still part of the third dimension, and they still function in the world."

She paused for a moment, reviewing her seeings, then continued. "While we're here, powerful cosmic alignments will occur. Each day will involve a slightly different configuration. These configurations in the cosmos will create openings that will affect things on Earth: they will align the old rings in the third dimension, as well as the new fourth-dimensional rings within us. As each day passes, some new energy will click into place.

"I was shown what it looked like from the outside. It resembled a combination lock. Each ring has a code. All of them have to click into place for the combination to work, so as we move through our experiences in London, we will be deciphering the codes of the various rings. Then I was shown what it looks like from the inside. It reminded me of the arches inside a gothic cathedral. It's the path we will take through the combination lock.

"By the end of the week, all of the energies will line up and create a sort of access corridor. When we do our meditation with Alexandria at the end, Mother Divine's energy will be able to come through the corridor so the energetic work can happen. The corridor will align with the core of the universe and be used to harness Her energy like a fourth-dimensional generator. The fascinating thing is that I don't think its normal for these arches to line up. This is a rarified moment in time, a time when the patriarchal system—predicated on the imbalance between masculine and feminine energies—can get completely reconfigured. I think that's why we've come at the end of March."

"So our physical presence in London—and the way we are holding the new rings within ourselves—will facilitate that?"

She rolled onto her side and looked at me. "Exactly. In order to do the work at the end of the week, we need to shred the last remnants of female conditioning programmed into us during the Patriarchy. This week will be like an initiation. Each day we are here, we will pass through another arch or initiation. Each day will help us realign ourselves, process our fears, and clear our conditioning. We've come to London to take back our power as women."

Spiritual Teachings on Women

In the seventeen years I studied with him, my teacher's number one priority was the empowerment of his women students. During the eighties, he lectured on the topic nonstop. He said, "When an enlightened being finds himself in the physical world, in a specific time and place, he looks around and asks, 'What is the greatest need?' When I ask myself that question, the answer is obvious: the enlightenment of women."

One evening in the winter of 1983, he strode onstage, took his seat and, immediately and without ceremony, began to speak with enormous seriousness.

"In addressing the topic of women's enlightenment tonight, you could say I'm addressing all topics. I feel if we can correctly understand this one subject, we will understand all subjects. If we fail to understand this one subject, we will fail to understand any subject. All subjects in our world are predicated upon this subject. I feel it is that important.

"It is much easier for women to become enlightened than it is for men," he told us. "A woman's subtle physical body accepts light, in this world, much more readily than does a man's. It seems a curious fact, therefore, that throughout the history of spirituality on this planet, there have been very few enlightened women. There are a number of reasons for this, and whether you are a man or a woman, it's essential that you understand them.

"On the deepest level there is no difference between men and women. Each individual has a soul. Each individual contains Spirit within itself. The soul is neither masculine nor feminine. It is both. Yet in a particular lifetime, we manifest as one or the other gender.

"The physical bodies of men and women are different, and so are the subtle physical bodies. As a woman, it is vital that you understand the differences, because it affects you more than you realize. All subtle physical bodies are composed of luminous fibers of light. The subtle physical body of a man is denser, more fixed, more tightly packed. The subtle physical body of a woman is more pliant. It conducts light or vibrates with light at a different rate. Women are essentially much more powerful than men. The kundalini flows through them more readily, so, in my estimation, it is easier for a woman to absorb light, change, and evolve."

He sighed and shook his head. "The problems are really very few...but in order for you to understand the importance of the subtle physical body, you need to understand that a woman's essence is power." He paused to regroup.

"The primary reason so few women attain enlightenment is that they have a misunderstanding of their purpose as women. Women think of themselves as being," he paused, searching for the right word, "well, women." He made a gesture of helplessness. "And you are not. You have a preconceived notion of what it means to be a woman. This notion is incorrect. It has been given to you by society, history, men, and other women.

"Everything is reversed in this age. Men appear to be more powerful than women, but in reality the opposite is true. As a woman, you must realize that you have everything you need within you. Women have become dependent upon men. They feel that they have to draw power from a man. They build their identities around men or around their children and, in doing so, they do themselves, all other women, and all men an injustice. You must realize that your true aspect is power. If you think of yourself as being feminine—in the sense of being weak, genteel, constantly self-effacing, always cleaning up after others—then you misunderstand your power and your purpose.

"While a woman's subtle physical body being pliant is her strength, it is also her biggest problem. In this age, destructive energies are very powerful. If the energy is good, a spiritually oriented woman will progress swiftly. If the energy is bad, it will be just the opposite. Men are not as affected by the vibratory forces of this world. For women, these destructive energies are a huge problem.

"The damage that occurs to the subtle physical body of a woman occurs in several ways. Most of it is sexual. Most women lose their power in sexual relationships or by being exposed to the lower sexual energies of men. Sexuality is neither good nor bad. It depends on how you approach it. But for most men, sexuality is filled with violence. During the act of sex, many men become angry. They often hate the women they are having sex with. There's this need to conquer, to assert your identity, and it is because men are afraid of the power of women. They sense this tremendous power and, rather than fostering it or accessing it, they want to control it. They're afraid of their own impotence, afraid of the womb that bore them.

"This sort of unrefined masculine energy enters easily into a woman when there is a sexual relationship because women readily affix themselves to men. When a woman falls in love, she thinks constantly about the man she is in love with. And when she does, she affixes herself to his consciousness psychically. Whatever is in his consciousness will enter into her consciousness. If there are a number of destructive or, let's say, high-velocity forces in a man's consciousness—forces which perhaps a man's subtle physical body can handle—then the woman draws those forces into herself. And while they may not destroy the man's spiritual potential, they will destroy hers."

He scanned his audience, filled with an equal number of men and women. A couple of people coughed. A quiet rustling filled the hall as people shifted in their seats. I heard one woman behind me whisper to her neighbor, "Who does he think he is? A man telling us about the role of women." The men around me seemed even less pleased with the subject.

"You must understand," he continued after a few moments, "that there is no good or bad. Men are not better. Women are not better. We are all children of God, and we are all following the path to Light. There is no fault here. I don't see that men are more to blame than women. Both have allowed this to happen. But we have to understand the operative conditions of the universe. It is men who make the wars. It is men who are interested—by and large—in hatred and killing. And these types of unstable energies manifest because men are afraid of their feminine side. If they could accept their feminine side, their own femaleness, then there would be balance.

"On the other hand, women allow this to happen. They foster an image of being weaker. They want to be taken care of to a certain extent. They want a daddy. They want someone to make decisions for them. They don't want to claim their own power and intensity. They *choose* attachment to the family instead of the pursuit of enlightenment. And women don't support other women—they're jealous, they're vindictive, simply because they don't realize that they have enough power within themselves. If they did, they could enjoy other women. They would understand that it's not necessary to compete with other women for a male."

He shifted gears and began explaining what women needed to do in order to attain enlightenment. I leaned forward in my seat.

First he explained that it was important to break up patterns. For this, meditation was a key factor. By meditating each day, we became stronger, clearer, and purer. Next he said there were two types of yoga that work best for women. The first was karma yoga. The second was mysticism.

"In karma yoga, through selfless giving, a woman accesses her power. Then as her power increases, the path of mysticism opens itself to her. For men, bhakti yoga, the yoga of love and devotion, is best. It stabilizes their energy and is the natural choice for their earlier years. Then men graduate to jyanna yoga, the yoga of discrimination, where they learn that it is necessary to give up even love, to move into the Void. Learn all four yogas, but understand that there are certain pathways that are easier for men and women.

"As women, you also need to get beyond the feeling that you have to be nice, that it's okay to let people walk all over you. You don't help men by allowing them to do that. It actually fixates them in a bad state of consciousness. Whenever you allow someone to abuse you, you're not their friend, because you're allowing them to incur bad karma.

"Also, women are conditioned to manipulate men. And it's understandable in a world where women have been denied the right to education, to spiritual advancement, the right to vote, to own property… In a world where women *are* property, everything is contingent on winning the best possible husband. Her well-being and safety depends upon the husband. The well-being of her children depends upon the husband. So through the years, women have been systematically programmed to manipulate men, using the mystical side of their being. They psychically *wrap* the man they are interested in.

"This skill is passed down from one generation to another. The little girl is taught early on how to dress, how to walk, how to move her eyes so she can ensnare the best possible man. And, from my perspective, this is not a problem. In a world where women are dependent on men, that's a good use of a woman's energy."

He paused for a moment to let this sink in. "But it is not a good use of energy for women who are interested in enlightenment. Why? Because the energy of enlightenment precludes the energy of manipulation. If you expend your energy on manipulating men, you will not have the prerequisite energy to wake up. It takes a tremendous amount of power to become enlightened, so it's necessary for you to examine this tendency in yourself and eradicate it.

"Women also need to learn to be more unattached. There's this idea that women are more emotional than men—and that's how they act—but they are not. It's actually quite the opposite. Men are much more emotional. They love more quickly than women do. They feel more devastated when a relationship falls apart.

"All and all, what I'm suggesting is that the way we see men and women outwardly, the way they act in society, is not the way they really are inwardly. Everything in this age is reversed, and that's why not that many people in this world attain enlightenment."

He paused, studying the floor in front of him, then looked back at his audience.

"As a man, you should find enlightenment in this age quite easy. This is still the age of men. But the age of women is just around the corner."

I straightened in my seat. He was seeing the future. He was seeing an age of women. I closed my eyes and savored the feeling of what that might be like.

"Don't be afraid to change," he concluded. "And the most basic change each of you must make in this incarnation has to do with your sexual identity."

Starting with these controversial lectures during the early eighties, my teacher worked tirelessly throughout his teaching career for the enlightenment of women. He spent an enormous amount of time with his female students, coaching them on all aspects of their lives, everything from how to dress in order to empower themselves to how to break through the glass ceiling in their careers. Not a single detail was left to chance. He was determined to help them take back their power.

Many years later, Celeste and others would refer to this brand of woman—the embodiment of strength, passion, creativity, and action—as the *solar feminine*. While many courageous women have bucked their patriarchal conditioning in the *lunar feminine*—pure yin energy which is gentle, receptive, and nurturing—to express the solar feminine in all walks of life, it has been all but lost as a spiritual archetype. One must go back to Kali, the Hindu Goddess of destruction, Pele, the Hawaiian fire Goddess, or Sekmet, the Egyptian Lioness Goddess, to find its remnants.

My teacher hoisted his modern banner of the solar feminine earlier than most spiritual teachers, something that evoked tremendous criticism from people attending his public lectures, the press, and even his own students. "Following my convictions has come at a personal price," he told a small group of women students on one occasion, "but they are important enough that I have been willing to endure the abuse."

He smiled broadly and sighed. "Besides...fuck 'em if they can't take a joke."

Why Was the Religion Ring Destroyed?

The following day Jackie and I headed for St. Paul's Cathedral in the City. Jackie navigated. Years before, she had gotten her music degree from Oxford and spent a lot of time in London. She knew its streets and Underground subway system like the back of her hand.

I smiled to myself as we rocked along in the Underground, standing amid throngs of Londoners, hanging onto the overhead hand grips. If anyone could get to the bottom of the Religion ring, it was Jackie, seer extraordinaire. I felt certain that the Vatican had been the main charm on the religion bracelet. In Rome, I had experienced the Pope's energy and picked up a few clues during my visit to the Vatican, but I was eager to get Jackie psychic reading of St. Paul's.

Once inside the church, we walked slowly through the nave, scanning our surroundings, until we arrived at the dome. Directly underneath it was a gold seal, embedded in a star design formed by the floor tiles. We both had the same experience: heavy distortion, dizziness, and nausea.

Jackie laughed. "Lower mystical energy, anyone?"

After moving to one side, we examined the artwork of the dome.

"Well, that's interesting." She grinned. "We've got the first level, at the base of the dome, that is all mosaic. Lots of gold leaf. Lots of angels. Very beautiful. Uplifting to look at. Then the actual dome above the whispering gallery, the next layer, is paintings of epic battle scenes. All done in gray. The military. Totally intimidating."

"So," I said, closing my eyes for a moment, "what is happening to our energy as we stand here under the dome? The crown chakra opens ever so slightly, but then the energy doesn't fully ascend."

"Correct. It's because they have designed the architecture to *hold down* the uplifted energy. It causes people to assume that this distorted energy is divine alignment. Just the artwork alone says it all." She pointed upward. "Look at those military battle scenes. The message is: 'Don't go there. It's dangerous to aspire to the higher dimensions. Stay down here with the angels where it's safe.'"

I nodded.

"Come on," she said, tugging at my sleeve. "Let's go up into the dome. Let's see what the energy feels like in the whispering gallery."

About halfway up the circular stairwell that numbered, according to the sign, 259 steps, I called ahead. "For God's sake, Jackie, slow down. I've got ten years on you."

"Sorry," she said, settling herself on a stone window seat and patting the space beside her. "Well, there's one thing we can be glad about," she said between deep breaths, "we've already gotten our cardio for the day."

"Yeah," I huffed, mounting the last step before the window seat, "St. Paul's Stairmaster." I sat down to catch my breath.

"Do you believe that?" Jackie asked, pointing at the wall opposite us. "You've got to love the British. They've got an arrow pointing up the stairs and a sign under it that says, 'Way Up.'"

I laughed between gulps of air.

In the whispering gallery, Jackie stopped suddenly, frowning. "This distortion is familiar somehow." She paused. "Ah," she said a little too loudly, "my mother! This is the way her energy used to feel when I was growing up, this distorted buzz. This was the religious energy she communicated to me. It caused me to misinterpret spirituality for a long time. Jesus, the indoctrination they give you as a child! They feed you this designed consciousness that you then misinterpret for the Clear Light."

After circumnavigating the whispering gallery, we continued to follow the Way Up signs an additional 119 steps to the Stone Gallery, the outdoor balcony at the top of the dome. Outside, there was no distortion, and we took a few minutes to let our heads clear. Leaning over the railing, we gazed at the streets far below.

"Ingenious!" Jackie said. "It's clear they understood the energetic lines in the area. The streets follow lines that move out from the dome, and all of the various sectors they create feel different. The very streets were laid out to hold different meridians of segmentation and control." She whistled softly. "It was designed that way from the time they rebuilt after the Great Fire in the seventeenth century when the City was destroyed."

"So, what are you seeing, Jackie?" I asked. "You see this stuff so easily, and I have to work so hard at it. What are the mechanics you're using to see these things?"

"I just feel my way back into it. Look," she told me, pointing downward. "Look at that square in front of the office building."

"You mean the one with the pillar in the middle?" I asked.

"Right," she said, "the distortion blaster. They've erected those things all over London. See the layout of the square, the way the tiles create a design that looks like the spokes of a wheel? See how they all lead to the distortion blaster? It energetically pulls people in. Look at all the people sitting at the base of the pillar, eating their lunch, basking in the distortion. Just let go of your mind for a moment and feel your way into it."

I did as she instructed.

"Now," she continued, "pull back a little and look at the overall street design. See how all of the streets lead to the cathedral, pulling people into its vortex of distortion?"

"Yes, I can feel that." I looked at her and smiled. "This trip is going to be an education. Maybe I'll improve my seeing while we're here."

"Your seeing is fine," Jackie assured me. "You see power structures. You're a soldier, and your job is to take power structures apart, so that's what you are skilled at seeing. It's all a power structure on one level. Just look at it that way if it makes more sense to you."

We walked back inside, stopping in the little room that preceded the descent to study the church's original architectural floor plans by

Sir Christopher Wren.

Jackie laughed. "Well, here it is! Their mystical strategy on display for the whole world to see. Look at this central cone of brick they've built to hold in the domed energies. That's why we didn't feel the distortion standing on the outside balcony. This brick cone holds the distortion in and buffers it from the outside."

She looked at me, taking a moment to assemble her thoughts. "Cathedral domes are purposely designed to hold a specific type of consciousness. First, they cap the crown chakra, while making you feel uplifted and expanded. Second, they broadcast distorted energy that makes you feel dizzy or spacey. So this is what most people interpret as sacred energy. And that's just the architecture! Intellectually, these guys have designed a set of moral rules that keep people locked in duality, a polarized system of good and bad, right and wrong, savior and one who needs salvation. And I'm not even going to get started on Eve and the famous apple. What the Church has done to women is unspeakable!"

She pulled herself up to her full height. "It's all a manipulation of awareness, a forcing of the assemblage point into a location that limits consciousness, a blatant lie! And who does that lie serve? Only those who wish to perpetuate a specific version of reality. No wonder the damned ring was taken out."

I nodded in agreement, a student in an Oxford classroom at the conclusion of a lecture. "Well said."

Why Was the Royalty Ring Destroyed?

On our second day we took the bus to Windsor Castle, the oldest and largest inhabited castle in the world. The Queen's standard was flying high atop a turret, which meant, Jackie informed me, that Queen Elizabeth was in residence. It appeared it was time to pay our respects to what was left of the Royalty ring.

The gardens were in full bloom with daffodils, lilacs, and hyacinth. Entering the quadrangle, we passed a crowd of people watching the Changing of the Guard but didn't stop. We wanted to see the State Rooms inside the castle.

Making a quick detour, we entered St. George's Chapel to see how the energy of the Church of England compared with that of the Roman Catholic Church. It was slightly different from St. Paul's, but a restricted consciousness nonetheless. We emerged from the chapel, sauntered along the cobblestone street, and finally came to the castle entrance.

We showed our pass to the guard, then walked slowly through the magnificent rooms used by the royal family for ceremonial and state occasions, marveling at the exquisite care that had been taken with every detail—the silk rugs, the brocade fabric on the walls, the finely crafted furnishings, the beautifully carved wood, the delicate ivory accent pieces—and the unbelievable expense.

"Everything is incredibly refined," I whispered to Jackie. "It's obvious they've made every effort to create a refined vibratory field for themselves."

"Absolutely," she agreed, "they know that surrounding themselves with refinement elevates consciousness. And money is no object. They can buy literally anything they want."

I hung back to look at a large glass display case full of gold dinnerware—plates, bowls, eating utensils, serving vessels. I had never seen so much gold. With so much of it isolated in one place, it was easy to feel the vibration. It literally radiated power. And the cost of such luxuries was mind-boggling. Here was the Royalty ring's feudal system in plain sight. No wonder British taxpayers complained about paying the royal family's annual allowance.

I felt a tap on my shoulder.

"Like the vibration of the gold?" Jackie smiled.

I lifted my eyebrows and nodded. "And look at this case with china," I said, pointing to the adjacent one. "My God, everything they touch is ultra-refined. Too bad Alexandria isn't here to see this place."

"She doesn't need to see it," Jackie assured me. "She probably commissioned the interior design in her past life."

We passed through St. George's Hall, used for state banquets, and the chapel dedicated to the Order of the Garter. Something about the architecture capped off my energy at the level of the third-eye chakra. Proceeding further, we entered the resplendent Queen's reception room and, instantly, my crown chakra opened right up.

"What a contrast to the other rooms!" I exclaimed.

"It's the gold leaf they've used throughout the room," Jackie told me, glancing around. "How interesting that they use the metal to open the upper chakras and make you feel royal. They've thought of everything, haven't they? You enter the Queen's reception room when the Queen is seated on the throne, and suddenly you think you're in the presence of the original Anunnaki bloodline."

My mouth dropped open as a tumbler fell into place. Queen Elizabeth was not a direct descendant of the Anunnaki! The Royalty ring was not composed of bloodline families. It all went back to something I had read while researching the Catholic Church: The Donation of Constantine.

In the eighth century, the Church suddenly produced The Donation of Constantine, a document supposedly written in the fourth century by Emperor Constantine. Its authenticity has been hotly debated ever since. The writing style differs from that of Constantine's era, and it refers to the Latin Vulgate Bible translated by St. Jerome, who was born twenty-six years after Constantine supposedly signed the document.

It stated that Emperor Constantine's newly appointed "Bishop of Rome" was Christ's elected representative on Earth, the Vicar of the Son of God, and it gave him the unchallengeable power to create and depose kings. The Pope, in other words, reigned over all other earthly rulers as his subordinates.

Whether or not the document was authentic, the outcome was that the Pope became the supreme head of Christendom, and the nature of monarchy changed entirely. When the Vatican implemented the provisions of the document in 751, the bloodline kings, who upheld the ancient concept *To rule is to serve*, were deposed and supplanted by usurpers, those who had formerly acted as their palace mayors.

The Church devised the concept of the coronation and anointment. In the past, when practiced at all, a similar ceremony would simply have recognized a bloodline king or formed a pact with him. Now, the coronation *created* a king. The sacred oil of the anointment could magically sanctify the blood of a usurper or anyone sanctioned by the Church. Through the oil, the Pope bestowed divine grace upon a ruler. The outcome was that these new European kings were servants of the Church rather than servants of the people.

From that point forward, the Vatican sought to wipe out its competition, the ancient bloodline kings and anyone who openly supported them. They were perceived as a threat to the Vatican's quest for domination. The ancient bloodlines were systematically hunted down and persecuted throughout the Albigensian Crusade and the Inquisition.

So here was the inside story of the Royalty ring. It had been a ring spawned by the Religion ring. The usurpers, ruling with entitlement only—entitlement bestowed by the Church—had been more interested in power than people. *To rule is to serve* had been replaced by *To rule is to be served.*

I shared my revelation with Jackie. "Now I understand why I wanted to travel to Rome and Paris. I have been stalking the meridians, following the cold trail of the Royalty ring, the kingdom-usurpers who overthrew the bloodline families as they moved west across Europe.

"The Religion ring and the Royalty ring shared an unspoken agreement to work together. Both believed in their divine right. The Royalty ring at the bottom of the Patriarchy's inverted pyramid configuration held the out-of-sight feudal system in place. The Religion ring at the top held people down in limited states of consciousness. Working together, they formed a vice grip that trapped humans in a maze composed of the other seven rings, a maze from which there was no escape. That's why the two rings had to be destroyed."

Jackie nodded, smiled then patted my back. "Nice seeing!"

The Playing Rules for the Patriarchy

In my meditation the next morning, I found myself back at the machine room under the City. My awareness dropped to a deeper level. Beyond the squid-like machine, there were energetic lines. It was the center of the power vortex, where all of the lines intersected under London. It was quiet and expansive, as though there was vast space around me.

Where am I? I asked. *What am I supposed to see here?*

Then, like a camera lens that zooms in on its subject, I saw the lines up close. They were coated with the dark stuff of the Patriarchy.

I pondered the machine room while Jackie and I ate our British breakfast. Afterwards, we took the Underground to the Temple Bar, the area of London that houses the British legal system. It was completely surrounded by a high-walled enclosure. On a busy thoroughfare, between two shops, we found a stone archway and passed inside.

We were met by a hushed silence and an abrupt and total shift in energy. We had entered another world. Treading quietly along the narrow cobblestone avenues, occasionally passing a barrister in robes and powdered wig, we peered into windows that revealed highly polished offices adorned with stately bookshelves lined meticulously with law books. We sat down on a stone bench.

"There's a very precise architecture of energy here," Jackie commented, "like a designed reality that hasn't changed from the twelfth century. It's mathematical, isn't it? A square, flat, stratified consciousness."

I nodded, "Like we are sitting inside of a container. It's as though they are saying, 'Here are the parameters; operate inside of them.'"

"Exactly." She looked around with awe, shook her head, then whispered. "This is where they developed the playing rules for the nine rings."

Owning Our Own Power

The following day, we went to the British Museum. Jackie paused in the lobby to read the sign.

"The Enlightenment Exhibit. The vast world of knowledge gathered in the eighteenth century had to be classified and organized…" She laughed. "These guys are great! Imposing the age of reason and British acquisition on the concept of enlightenment!"

"Of course," I countered, "it could be a subtle hint from Spirit. It may be the sole purpose for coming to the museum."

"That would be convenient," Jackie said, laughing. "We could get what we came for in one exhibit and not have to walk through the whole bloody museum."

"I vote yes for less walking. My feet are killing me!" I said, sighing and followed Jackie through the Great Court toward the King's Library where the exhibit was housed.

As we entered, she put her hand to her forehead and stopped.

"Are you all right?" I asked.

She paused for a moment. "Just dizzy. I'll be fine."

She drifted off toward the exhibits.

Along all of the walls were tall glass cabinets, each having five shelves for displaying items. The collections were grouped by culture. In a given cabinet, for example, one could see religious and ritual objects, pottery, utensils, vases, and coins from China. The next cabinet contained similar objects from France. I could tell we were in the right place, and I studied each cabinet dutifully, but glancing over at Jackie, I knew she was tapping into something much deeper.

"What do you see?" I asked after a quarter of an hour.

"This is truly amazing," she said in a low voice. "Each vertical case is a grouping that represents the collective consciousness of a culture. The British explorers went out and collected icons representing the collective consciousness of a country, a region, or whatever...."

"Oh," I said, suddenly seeing where she was going. "If they could tap into the collective consciousness, they could see the culture's energetic openings and figure out how to control them."

"Precisely." She looked over at the case nearest her. "They collected, classified, codified, and controlled these areas through their indigenous iconology." Her eyes went slightly out of focus as she stared at one of the cases. "I think that they used to assemble all of the items from one country in a closed room, lock a seer in with them, and have her 'read the daily news.' Once they had a download from the seer about the internal architecture of the country, they could develop a strategy to manipulate and control the country's consciousness."

I shook my head in disbelief. Jackie's ability to see was amazing.

She pointed to case 207. "Look at this. This case is a perfect example of the patriarchal control mechanism. Start with the bottom shelf. They've put fern fossils here. So we've got earth energy in its natural state. Coming up to the next shelf, there's an open urn: collecting the energies. On the third shelf is a closed urn: captured energy. On the fourth shelf is a mosaic tile display: codified energies. And last but not least, on the top shelf, they've put mini pillars."

I laughed. "Distortion blasters!"

"Right," she agreed. "Broadcasting the codification for control." Jackie smiled, pleased with herself. "There you have it," she said, stepping back from the case and gesturing with an open palm. "The system of usurpation…in icons!"

We drifted apart again, and for awhile I had fun trying the read the cases like Jackie did. But the implication of what Jackie had said troubled me. How many control schemes had the global elite conceived? Fear consumed my body and, once again, for the hundredth time since arriving in London, the hair on the back of my neck stood on end.

Then something in a case in the center of the room caught my attention. The exhibit was labeled *Magic, Mystery, and Rites.* The case contained mystical objects. Among them was a wax seal called the Sigil of Ameth (Seal of Truth) that had been made by Dr. John Dee, a mathematician, astrologer, and magician during the reign of Queen Elizabeth I.

I looked for Jackie and spotted her sitting on a black marble bench. Walking toward her, I examined her more closely. She looked ill.

"Are you okay?" I asked, concerned.

She appeared to come out of a daze. "Oh," she sighed, "I was realizing that one of the reasons this is affecting me so much is that I used to be a reader. They would lock me in a room full of objects and expect me to interpret them. Now I know why I felt dizzy as we entered the hall." She smiled wearily.

I reached into her tote bag and pulled out her water bottle.

"Have a drink," I suggested.

Jackie was very private about her emotional processes. She didn't discuss them with anyone, to my knowledge. I supposed she didn't have to. She was incredibly skilled at dissecting them. I didn't want to pry, so I just sat there and kept her company, but I wondered if she was feeling a sense of fear...the type of fear that kept coming up for me.

She took a sip of water. "In Atlantis, we did this by sitting in a room of programmed crystals. Can you remember that?"

I shook my head.

"Back then, it was bidirectional," she continued, "Not only could we read the consciousness, we could broadcast consciousness to the area. We used our minds to work with the people and the energies. As the density on the planet increased, the crystal technology was forgotten, and symbolism took its place. This collection and the ones they used to make me read are all about symbols, codified vibration."

"Well," I said, patting her softly on the back, "the good news is that Spirit led us to exactly the right exhibit."

Jackie nodded and took another drink of water.

"Are you feeling better now?" I asked.

"Yeah."

"Then let's walk over here."

I led Jackie to the display case with mystical objects and pointed at the seal.

She bent down close to the glass to look, then gasped.

"That's our combination lock!"

She moved even closer to study it.

The seal was round, about five inches in diameter. The center contained the symbol for the four elements, surrounded by a pentagram. This was then enclosed in a larger symbol, the Merkaba. Along the outside rim was a seven-sided figure with seven divisions on each side. All of the designs were engraved with symbols and signs and magical names in Latin,.

"It's a star map," Jackie whispered to me. "Remember before the trip I said we needed to go to the British Museum because there was a clue there?" She tapped her finger against the glass case. "It's a

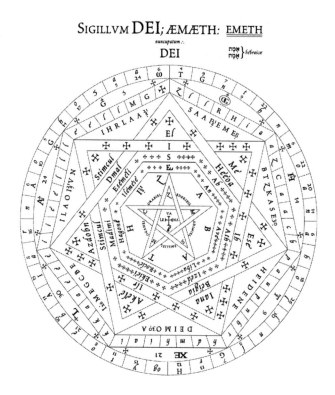

star map. The figures are flattened down onto a seal, but it's actually multidimensional. Can you see that?"

I scrutinized it...to no avail.

"They've just collapsed the dimensions down." She studied it more closely. "It may contain a clue to the combination lock I saw earlier." She hesitated, then stepped abruptly back from the case and looked at me. "I've got it! You can either *use* it or you can *own* it."

I stared blankly.

"This guy...." She glanced briefly at the display. "This Dr. John Dee, conceived this magical seal so he could use it. The display says he used it for incantations, but that's bullshit. He used it to astral travel. He *used* it. We, on the other hand, have come to London to *own* it."

The implications of what she was saying began to wash over me. Taking a deep breath, I nodded for her to continue.

"If someone *owns* the knowledge represented on that seal, if they live in multidimensional states of mind, if they function from that universal place—and especially if that someone is a woman—that person has a major problem. The problem is that you've broken free of the system they've created, and they come after you."

I quivered, understanding at a deeper level what we were up against. "So, we're here in London looking at all of these designed realities that compose their system—the held-down higher knowledge of the church, the feudal foundation of the royals, the stratified playing field of the legal system, the codification of world control through icons.... Nothing has been overlooked. The man in the South Pacific and his Illuminati predecessors have worked for hundreds of years to construct an elaborate system, a system which makes people afraid of evolving to their highest potential..."

"...and we are here to finish the work of taking it apart," Jackie interrupted. "That machine you keep seeing? It's a fear generator! It pumps fear throughout their One World Government with its nine rings, throughout their sprawling concentration camp, with its nine functional areas that sustain their system of exploitation and war. If people are afraid, they won't question the system, it won't even occur to them to try to break free of the system. The One Ring was dominance. *Fear* is the vibration used to achieve dominance. The fear generator is the broadcast mechanism they use to make dominance take hold in people's minds, their ultimate strategy."

"So in order to move from a fear-based world into a fourth-dimensional, love-based world, the fear generator has to be...." I bit my lip. When I continued, it was with a weak voice. "Do you think we're going to be asked to unplug the fear generator?"

Jackie lifted her eyebrows. "We've spent the whole project unplugging things. It wouldn't surprise me."

Ice ran through my veins. The implications were huge. "That will...that will take down..."

Jackie nodded. "...the whole system."

We were both silent for a long time.

Suddenly Jackie broke out laughing. "That actually puts us in a rather precarious position, doesn't it? The patriarchal system is the system in which we live. When the whole thing collapses, it will be our own lives, our lifestyles, our livelihoods that are collapsing. It's not an easy thing to demolish the system you've been conditioned to believe supports you. It's like dismantling the floor you're standing on."

I stared blankly at her for a moment. "This is going to sound weird, but I think in this stage of the project we're processing our *attraction* to the Patriarchy."

Jackie cocked her head.

I continued. "The system of duality is filled with polar opposites, right?"

"Ah, attraction and aversion."

"Right. So, during the initial phases of the project, we reconciled our *aversion* to the Patriarchy—which, for me, expressed itself through my fear of the man in the South Pacific—and now we're reconciling our *attraction* to it, our attachment to keeping the system the way it is. Because if the system as we know it goes away...."

"Uncharted territory. A complete unknown." Jackie laughed again.

I grabbed her elbow and guided her toward the exit. "I'm glad you're finding this so amusing. As the soldier of the team and the one who will be asked to yank the plug on the damned thing, all of my female, obey-or-be-killed conditioning is up in my face."

The Obelisk Download Device

The following morning it happened again. I was pulled down into the machine room under the City, only now I knew it was a fear generator.

There was fear all right. Mine.

I heard the voice of the Lineage: "*You must expand your awareness further so you contain it within you. Then the Patriarchy becomes a tiny spec in the midst of the universe you encompass.*"

Later that day we strolled along the River Thames to Cleopatra's Needle, the Egyptian obelisk erected during the reign of Queen Victoria.

Jackie gasped. "Wow! There she is. Look at that."

We approached the obelisk, stopping a short distance away to study it. Its energy felt exactly like the similar ones I had seen earlier in the trip. "What do you think its purpose is?"

"Not sure," she answered. "It's a little hard to read, isn't it? Either it channels something or it broadcasts fear."

"Well," I mused, "it's more powerful and quite a bit more elaborate than the obelisks in Rome and Paris. Look at these two metal sphinxes that flank it and the way they've designed a metal base for it."

"Right," Jackie nodded, "it grounds it, makes its energy more stable."

"Come on," I told her, "let's go to the Savoy."

I had read that the Savoy Hotel, a block from the obelisk, was the meeting place of the English branch of the global elite, and I wanted to see it. We made our way through Victoria Embankment Gardens, strolling along the foliage-lined avenue and inhaling the hyacinth fragrance. But when we walked into the Savoy, its energy was unbearably heavy, and we walked right back out.

"Why don't we go to that tea shop we passed near Cleopatra's Needle," Jackie suggested.

As we walked back through the gardens, she suddenly stopped and pointed to a small circular pool with a modest fountain in the center. Directly beyond the fountain was a large granite memorial dedicated to Major General Lord Cheylesmore. Jackie turned first in one direction, then another, looking around.

"There is Cleopatra's Needle," she said, pointing, "and there's the Savoy. This sits exactly between them."

"So?" I asked.

She hesitated. "Oh! Cleopatra's Needle is a receiving device. The reason it's hard to read is because it's dormant right now. It's only active when they meet at the Savoy. During their meetings, they use it to pull down higher-dimensional energy from the center of the universe and formulate strategies for running the planet. They channel the data through Lord Cheylesmore's pool of water, right into the hotel."

"Do you think they're conscious of what they're doing?" I asked her.

"You bet! They're mystics. They've passed the knowledge of mysticism along from generation to generation. They know *exactly* what they're doing. That's why they built the bloody pool there. I mean, think of how the obelisk is positioned. You've got the River Thames down below it to buffer the energy. You've got the obelisk anchored in iron at its base. There are two sphinxes guarding it. And when the energy gets channeled through it, you've got the pool in a direct line to the hotel to transmit and reflect the information. It's brilliant."

I nodded, smiled, and, as we meandered back to the tea shop, thought about the obelisks standing in front of the Vatican and the Rothschild mansion in Paris. Was someone using those in a similar way?

As we approached the tea shop, we saw small, white wrought-iron tables and chairs, each with a different color umbrella. It made a pretty picture, nestled in the midst of the gardens. We choose a table with a red umbrella and ordered tea.

I looked over at Jackie. "Maybe we should meditate on the obelisk. Maybe this is a little warm-up exercise for our big meditation with Alexandria at the end of the week."

"Like Save a Tree; Free a Pillar?" She smiled.

After a few minutes, our tea arrived.

"I have to confess," I told Jackie after our waitress left, "that I don't feel much like doing this. That's strange, don't you think?"

"Well," she answered, "I don't know about that. Let's just take our time. We're in no rush."

"I feel…." I examined my awareness field. "I don't know. I feel bored. But that seems completely out of context. That has to be an emotional cover-up. I guess the question is, what's underneath the boredom?"

"Exactly," she agreed quietly, focusing discriminately on her teacup.

"If I feel down below the boredom," I said slowly, "there is frustration." I took a few moments to close my eyes. "Oh," I said suddenly, "underneath that I feel sadness and grief. And it appears to be tied to ancient Egypt. Something to do with contracts."

I looked at Jackie, and we both laughed.

"Do you think it's time to put that contract in the shredder?" she asked.

I nodded. "I'm seeing it more clearly now. The feelings go back to the contract with the Lineage in Atlantis, the mishaps of Egypt, and the fear of giving up the identity I've carried for a hundred lifetimes. I didn't read the fine print, and look what happened: I had to come back for a hundred lifetimes. Of course, those lifetimes—chocked full of female conditioning—are all I have. If I let go of that, where will that leave me? Who will support me? I'll be completely alone, on my own. I'll be a woman who has disconnected from the Patriarchy but is still stranded inside of it."

"Precisely what we saw at the British Museum."

We sat for a few more minutes, sipping our tea in silence. I worked with my feelings until I felt calm.

"I'm okay now," I said. "Do you want to meditate on the obelisk?"

Jackie nodded, placed her teacup in her saucer, and positioned her chair.

As we began, Cleopatra's Needle looked fuzzy and out of focus. Then she started to spin. Energies scattered. Dark crusty places— patriarchal programming—cracked off. Abruptly the spinning motion increased and, at the same instant, the obelisk uncoiled, like a spring coming unwound very fast.

Gold light descended, passed through the obelisk, and connected with the core of the Earth. As the light continued to flow down, it spread out, trickled into the machinery underneath the City and loosened things up. Next, the top of the obelisk blazed with light. Five beams shot out. They connected to other obelisks: Rome, Paris, and three others somewhere. Then she shivered a few times, settled into pure light, and finally nestled down. She seemed so happy to be free.

"I had the strange sense," I told Jackie afterwards, "that the obelisk *knew* us."

"Yes, yes," she said excitedly, "I got that too. She definitely knew us...from Egypt! And she became our ally. She offered to help with the big meditation the day after tomorrow."

Finding the Fear Generator

The City is the square mile on the north bank of the Thames River that was the original walled town of London. Within a few years of its establishment in 43 A.D. by the Roman General Aulus Plautius, it had become a great trading center. After the Norman Conquest, it was named the capital of England. The area then continued to develop as the financial center of the world. Today it enjoys the accolade of The Wealthiest Square Mile on Earth.

The Rothschilds operate out of an area in the heart of the City. All major British banks have their main offices there, alongside branch offices for almost four hundred foreign banks. It is home to the London Stock Exchange, the Bank of England, the London Commodity Exchange, the Royal Exchange (originally a center for commerce but now a high-class shopping complex), the Baltic Exchange (for shipping contracts), the London Metal Exchange, Fleet Street (for publishing and newspaper interests), and Lloyd's of London (the insurance giant).

The next day I told Jackie I wanted to find the fear generator. We took the Underground then made our way to the small plaza off of Threadneedle Street at the heart of the City. I walked over to the tourist plaque. It had a diagram of the buildings surrounding the plaza. Just to our left was the Bank of England—Britain's central bank, the Old Lady of Threadneedle Street—and directly in front of us was the Royal Exchange. The energy was the worst I had ever felt anywhere in my life: dark and heavy and distorted.

Jackie turned to leave.

"Where are you going?" I asked.

"I can't do this today."

"Do what?"

Jackie took a deep breath and seemed to be collecting her thoughts. "We've been running around, seeing places all over London, and much of it has been helpful. But you and I work in different ways.

You evidently need to visit these places and walk through their dark energies. I do better when I just station myself in one place, sit, let my energy pool out, and feel what is going on in the other dimensions."

I was stunned…and I felt guilty for not being a better seer.

"I'm sorry," she said more quietly. "Maybe I should just go back to the hotel and have some tea in the park, where I can meditate quietly by myself for awhile."

"All right," I croaked, fighting back tears.

She nodded and walked off. Then she stopped, turned, and called back. "May the gods be with you." She smiled and waved.

That made me feel better. I watched her scurry down the street. We were both feeling pressured about our big meditation the next morning and what we might encounter. Perhaps time alone would do us good. I walked across the plaza, sat on a bench, closed my eyes, and took a few deep breaths to steady myself. Gradually my body calmed down, and my mind grew quiet.

I let my awareness drop down below the City. From this position, it was effortless to feel the device I had been shown in meditation, with its long squid-like tentacles, a monstrosity that was half organic and half machine. Did the man in the South Pacific create this abomination? No. His style was more straightforward than this. This was elaborate, complex, a little showy. The man in the South Pacific used it, but it had been crafted by one of his Illuminati predecessors.

I passed through the machine room to the energetic lines below. I could see where they all intersected. What was below that? I dropped down even further. A single, large energetic line covered with black, tarry stuff descended deep into the Earth. I half expected it to be connected to a rock, which had been the Bilderberg method, but that was not the case.

As my awareness kept descending, I was amazed, then horrified. It was connected to the very core of the Earth! They had harnessed the core to drive their fear machine. It was the complete subjugation, not just of a power spot, but of Mother Earth's energy!

I opened my eyes, stupefied, and stared into space for a few moments while I allowed the feelings of disgust to subside. Gradually,

I focused on the buildings around me, taking in the Bank of England, the Royal Exchange, and the Palladian facade of the Mansion House, the official residence of the Lord Mayor. It was amazing, really. Here I was, sitting in the heart of the Patriarchy, perched on top of the mechanism that controlled the planet.

I glanced at the tourists, the people coming and going from work. Could they feel it? I took a deep breath and let my awareness pool out, trying to see as Jackie did.

The energies of the City were very old. Its mechanisms were well oiled. They moved efficiently. No friction. No noise. It was almost undetectable. Unless you knew what you were looking for, you would never feel it. It wasn't like Wall Street. In New York, the financial district had a hum. This was more silent. New money in New York. Old money here. Lots of it.

Old money flowing into the City, then out through the nine rings. The Stock Exchange. The Commodity Exchange. It was all about exchanging one thing for another, moving power around. It was about the man in the South Pacific doing a business deal on one side of the globe and bringing an underdeveloped country to its knees on the other. The money flowed through the City, and the Temple Bar flattened it out onto a level playing field. The rules, the judgments, the yeses, the no's…a carefully constructed design set up to protect the opulent.

The mechanism ran fear through all nine rings. It was especially easy to feel with the Banking ring that had so many offices in this square mile. As money circuited through the City, it got laced with fear. On some level it passed through the fear generator. As the most basic building block of the Patriarchy, money was the fundamental form of control. Money laced with fear caused people to hold onto it, to feel there would never be enough. And that sense of scarcity led to fear of destitution and, ultimately, fear of death.

These guys were good…*very* good. And tomorrow morning the mystical planes under the City would become a battlefield.

I stood up and headed for the Underground with my teacher's words replaying in my mind: "Never underestimate your opponent."

Unplugging Fear

Jackie and I reconnected in the late afternoon, had a Theakston beer with our fish and chips dinner, and sorted out our feelings. There wasn't much to sort out really. The time apart had been good. She had sat in the park, meditated on London, and felt that we had covered everything, that we were ready for the big meditation the next morning.

I told her my experience in the City. "Let me lay out what I'm sensing. See if you think I'm right."

She nodded.

"The global elite have enslaved the core of the Earth to drive their fear generator. So our beautiful feminine planet is subservient to male forces that have dominated her. But, as a female, her true aspect is power. Men are afraid of female power. They sense this tremendous power and, rather than fostering it or accessing it, they want to control it. If their generator gets unplugged, their mechanism for striking fear into the heart of humanity grinds to a halt. Then Mother Earth can take back her power, power that is stored at her core.

"Now...." I traced the project back in my mind. "On the summer solstice in 2003, the assemblage point of the Earth was shifted to the Caldera. The multidimensional world was constructed. Then it was anchored out there in New Mexico with a line that connected it to the core of the Earth. On the winter solstice, the Diamond Body slid into place, and the whole thing was activated.

"But when we did our systems analysis, you said that the Earth is fluid. Doesn't that imply that her assemblage point shouldn't be fixed? Maybe tomorrow will be the moment for the new world to be released from her assemblage point. If the new world is untethered, Mother Earth will be completely fluid, free to change and evolve as much as she wants."

I paused to collect my thoughts. "So, at the moment, there are two lines connected to the core of the Earth—one to the fear generator and one to the new world. What if we do our meditation tomorrow morning here in London and we ask Alexandria to station herself at the Caldera? What if, in our invocation, we offer to unplug the fear generator and to release the core of the Earth from bondage. Theoretically, that should facilitate a transfer of power from the old construct to the new, multidimensional world. Then if we offer to untether the new world...." I opened the palms of my hands.

"Ooh," Jackie whispered, "that gives me chills."

I nodded. "Me, too."

After dinner we phoned Alexandria and recapitulated our week. After calculating the time difference, we agreed that our meditation would begin in London at 3:00 A.M. the next morning, April 5th. For Alexandria, it would be 8:00 P.M. on April 4th in the Caldera. Then Jackie and I turned in early to get some sleep.

During the night, I had a dream. I was in a castle. The window by my bed in the dream was ajar, just like the hotel window by my bed overlooking Southampton Row. I somehow knew that an assassin had plotted to kill me.

I must get up and close the window, I thought in the dream. *No, this is my fear. I must meet it.*

I tried. I tried to drop down into the fear, but it was like being boiled alive. Again and again I tried, but I couldn't. It was too painful.

In the dream, I got out of bed, stumbled to the bed next to mine, and tried to awaken my mother. "We have to leave," I pleaded.

Then I went to the window. Someone had apprised me that the assassin, after killing me, would escape through the window. Flinging it open, I saw that he had hammered a metal cleat into the windowsill and hung some clothing on it.

He knows he will have to change out of his bloody clothes! I panicked. *This is real. There really is someone trying to kill me!*

The alarm went off. Jackie showered first while I closed the window. After I showered, I told her my dream.

"But what if all the characters were merely aspects of you? What if your mother was your female conditioning? What if the assassin was your alignment with the Patriarchy or, as you said in the British Museum, your attraction to the Patriarchy? Then all you have to do is bring it through your heart and reconcile it."

I nodded. She was right. I could reconcile it.

We positioned our pillows on our beds and got ready to meditate. The city was quiet. A car passed in the street below, but for the most part, London slept.

As we began, a shaft of golden light descended from the center of the universe, passed through the City in London, and traveled to the Caldera, linking the two locations.

Without warning, Jackie and I were swept up in a punishing series of experiences. It was like a movie, only we were *in* the movie. Fleeting images of things we had seen in London appeared in rapid succession: the dome of St. Paul's, the Queen's standard, barristers, star maps, plazas, obelisks, pillars.... Scenes from history played out: a king being anointed, a priest giving communion, a man getting tortured, a woman being burned.... One scene would suddenly drop away, only to be replaced by some new ordeal. Each scene enveloped us as a comprehensive experience, filled with emotion. There was nothing for us to do but remain impassive and let them pass through.

Alexandria was at the other end of the line of light, where the Caldera acted a giant particle accelerator. The dark energies being released in London—the images and scenes—were drawn through the Earth, where they were absorbed by the Caldera, transmuted, then flung off into some other dimension. The giant grassy bowl eradicated the energies of the Patriarchal Age in order to birth the energies of the next. Once again, my teacher words echoed: "When it is time for a world to change, this is where it happens."

It lasted forty-five minutes. Then, when the avalanche of scenes and energies stopped, a hush fell.

As the soldier, I knew my moment had come. I asked what needed to be done.

"Unplug the old world. Untether the new."

I hesitated, frozen in time and space. Time passed. Was it a minute? An age? What was it the Lineage had instructed me to do? To expand my awareness so the Patriarchy became a tiny speck inside of me?

I prayed to Mother Divine, *Please help me expand my being so I can place this in the proper perspective. Please help me reconcile my alignment with the Patriarchy. Please give me strength.*

My awareness moved out beyond London, beyond the Earth, out into space. The machine room looked small, like a child's toy. I reached down. I unplugged the fear generator, then unhooked the new world. Easy. Like reading the last sentence in a book and closing the cover.

For a moment nothing happened.

Then it was as though huge factory switches were being thrown to the OFF position. Large systems of dark energy began shutting down—grid after grid of distorted energy. In a completely mechanical and technical way, the cogs and wheels of operations central ground to a halt, and the structures melted in place.

Everything became very still. We waited.

Somewhere a dam broke. Water in the form of love began to flow. It flowed everywhere. It rose into a flood. Love entered all the systems. The earlier images reappeared, but now love surged through all of them. Heart energy worked its way through the architectures of limitation and fear. The histories dissolved. The scenes were washed away.

Cleopatra's Needle came alive. She synced up to the other obelisks, and all of them began broadcasting pure heart energy across the globe.

Blue-white light rained down. The whole planet looked like Mother Divine's garden, a beautiful, alive vortex of pure energy. The Earth was her creation, her child, and she cherished each and every atom unconditionally.

When the meditation ended, I looked over at Jackie. She was crying.

The Greenwich Meridian

Afterwards we went back to bed. In fact, we slept in. Our energetic work was done, and it was our day off.

After a hearty English breakfast, we decided that a boat ride down the Thames to the Greenwich Mean Line would provide the perfect ending to our journey.

When we disembarked from the boat, we walked through the park in Greenwich. The crowds thinned as we headed up the hill to the Royal Observatory, so we had the path to ourselves.

My weary feet threatened to go on strike at any moment. I had blisters from all the walking we had done. Reaching out to grab onto the chain link fence, I pulled myself along for a little ways.

Jackie broke out laughing. "Look at us. Some spiritual warriors we are! The Lineage must be looking down at us and saying, 'Are you sure we did the right thing, sending those two to London?'"

At the top of the hill, we paused to look down at the Royal Navel Academy, the green wooded areas, and the river beyond, letting the April breeze sooth our souls.

"Take a picture of the Academy for Anders," Jackie suggested. "He's feeling left out these days. Maybe the picture would make him feel better."

Then we finished climbing the hill, took pictures of the dateline and, with great ceremony, set our watches.

All of a sudden, Jackie turned to me with panic on her face. "Our watches are off by an hour!" She looked up at the large Greenwich clock, and I could see her mind doing rapid calculations. "Do you think we meditated at the wrong time this morning?" she asked, horrified.

"Do you think so?" I asked, getting worried. "We calculated so carefully what time it would be in New Mexico. Surely we were all meditating at the same time."

"Excuse me," the attendant said behind us.

We turned.

Extending to his full height, he pulled his red jacket with a navy blue collar down to straighten it and took a discrete step toward us. "I overheard some of your discussion about time. I believe you may be forgetting to account for daylight savings time."

Jackie and I looked at each other.

"This," he said, with a stiff gesture toward the clock, "is Greenwich Mean Time." He enunciated each syllable slowly and distinctly. "One could hardly expect that we would change Greenwich Mean Time to reflect the season."

Neither Jackie nor I said anything for a few moments.

"Of course," Jackie said finally and released a big sigh.

"Thank for you clarifying this," I added, nodding respectfully.

I grabbed Jackie's arm and guided her to the path that led down the hill.

"So we meditated at the right time, didn't we?" I whispered, starting to get tickled.

She nodded.

"Wow! That could have been a real screw-up—Alexandria over there in the Caldera, and we unplug the damned thing at the wrong time!"

We both giggled like little girls.

"Yes, indeed!" Jackie smiled. "The Lineage has sent its best warriors to London." She skipped a little ahead.

"Oh," I moaned, "how can you do that? My feet are killing me."

We both howled with laughter, as the tension of the previous week bubbled off of us and rolled down the Greenwich Mean Line.

"Right!" She stopped and saluted. "Just call us the girls who unplugged the Patriarchy."

24

THE UNIVERSAL SELF

My first morning back in Williamsburg, I was unable to get out of bed. It wasn't just jet lag. I awoke in a state of abject terror. Fear coursed through every cell of my body.

What in God's name is going on? I need to get up and carry on! But it was impossible to carry on.

Each morning, I awakened in a state of fear. When it became unavoidable, I made hurried trips to the bathroom, then immediately reinstated myself under the safe, warm bedclothes until noon. In the afternoons I made a couple of calls or paid a few bills to keep my life running. In the evenings I drank wine or watched movies to escape. Repeatedly I sat up in bed and tried to meditate in order to meet the fear. It was hopeless.

"May I come in?" Anders asked, standing at my bedroom door.

I nodded.

He sat on the chair near the bed.

"What's wrong?"

"I don't know," I confessed. "I've been unable to figure it out."

"But it's been two whole weeks." He frowned. He studied me then shook his head. "I don't understand. You finish a phase of your energetic work, then you plummet into one of these dark-nights-of-the-soul. I thought you were a soldier."

I was determined not to cry. I fussed with the covers on the bed.

He sighed. "What are you feeling?"

I crossed my arms. "Anger, depression, terror..."

"Who are you angry with?"

"My teacher. The Lineage. I'm *livid* with my teacher. For all of those years, he led me on with his bullshit about evolution and enlightenment. And I soaked it in, did everything he said, tried to follow every suggestion. And then the Lineage came up with its ludicrous assignment: identify the underlying structure of the Patriarchy. Take it apart. It's your dharma, your way of evolving. And look at me. I'm not evolving. I'm a mess. You're right. I'm supposedly a soldier and I can't even get out of bed! How, after thirty-five years on a spiritual path, can I still be this un-evolved?"

He took a deep breath, exhaled, and stood up. "I hope you feel better." He patted my hand and walked from the room, shaking his head.

I would have liked Anders to be more supportive, but it was, after all, my process to work through. At least, after voicing my predicament to him, I managed to gain some perspective. The anger was a cover-up. The depression was a cover-up. The real issue was the fear.

What was I so afraid of?

Then, suddenly, my awareness ascended a notch and felt less hazy. Something bizarre occurred to me: What if the reality was just the opposite of my cover-up? What if, instead of being depressed because I was *not* evolving, I was terrified because I *was*?

That was it!

The problem was not my failure to progress towards more enlightened states of mind. The problem was that enlightenment was barreling down on me. I was on a freeway going ninety miles an hour with my accelerated evolution in hot pursuit. Hadn't we gone to London to take back our power as women? Hadn't we known, standing in front of the star map at the British Museum, there would be consequences if we did the work of reconciling our alignment with the Patriarchy? Hadn't I had a dream where a killer stalked me through a castle trying to kill me—the "me" that had been conditioned as a woman?

The energetic work we had done in London was huge! It had been a huge leap in my evolution. Of course the result was terror.

Now I could meditate. I sat in meditation for one week, for long hours every day, meeting my fear again and again.

The following week, I called Jackie. "I haven't phoned because I've been in the hell worlds since London."

"I've been in the hell worlds, too," she confessed. "The worst hell is my calculated projection about enlightenment. What does enlightenment mean? What does one *do* with it? Is it something that pays the bills? Couldn't we just stick to trees and rocks and increasing the park spaces?"

I chuckled. "It's good to talk to you, Jackie. It's good to laugh at the whole thing. I went through my journal last night and read the London entries. Then I thought, 'My God, no wonder I've had a reaction.' It's funny how the mind can instantly forget everything that happened, just block it out completely."

"Right," she agreed. "A major piece of work in London. I was in such a very different space when I got back. I feel so..." She paused, searching for words. "...ancient, in a weird way. Or alien. Maybe that's a better word. Like, it's time to find a new planet."

"Or, perhaps," I suggested, "just a new multidimensional world to live in."

After that three-week period, everything shifted. The change was striking. I was completely at peace. There was no longer a goal of evolving toward enlightenment. The concept of evolution had completely vanished, as though someone had taken a surgical knife and removed the part of my brain that had obsessed about it. I simply lived my life. Every morning I got up and luxuriated in the day. There was no future. I didn't think about it anymore.

My heart was completely open. I could view things from other people's perspective. I was more aware of how they felt, more patient, more compassionate. My mind was different, more expanded somehow. It was difficult to describe. It felt as though my mind was a vast space filled with an equanimity that was continually expanding and applying a slight pressure all the time. And my higher self—the Universal Self—that I had previously sensed only sporadically was more integrated and visceral. It was enormous...and it contained no feeling other than peace.

Spiritual Teachings on Selfless Giving

"Why aren't you at peace?" my teacher asked his students in 1982. "Why aren't you satisfied with your life?

"Deep down inside you know that you're not really happy or satisfied or free. You're entangled in a mass of emotions. You're bombarded by thoughts and desires. Why aren't you happy? The reason is very simple: you are not focused on being of service to others.

"Many people claim that they're beyond doing work or service. They're simply afraid of getting their hands dirty. They don't understand that getting their hands dirty washes their being. You advance yourself by advancing others. Don't judge others. Be of service to them. But as you do, beware of egotism. When you aid others in their evolution, be careful that you don't have a sense of self. You must act impeccably, with the sense of being a servant of existence or of being nothing at all. Observe your actions, but be so busy that you never contemplate their effects. Devoting your life to selfless giving, with this consciousness, leads to enlightenment. Everything else is illusion."

Often he reminded us that selfless giving should go hand in hand with meditation. The two balanced each other. He explained that someone could meditate perfectly and still not attain enlightenment because there might be selfish motives the person was not aware of. By engaging in selfless giving, those selfish motives got worn away. But, on the other hand, to concentrate on selfless giving without taking the time to meditate would result in burn-out. We needed to balance ourselves daily by returning to the wellspring of meditation. Meditation would renew us and allow us to see the proper way in which to give.

As his students, our selfless giving took various forms. In the early eighties, when he interfaced with the public, we staged his lectures. As our careers developed, we had substantial buying power as a group.

We pooled our money to publicize a new book he had written or to rent the San Francisco Asian Art Museum for a special occasion and, because an enlightened person's aura is sensitive, and dealing with the energies of the Kali Yuga are abrasive, we always ensured that he had everything he needed to buffer himself from the world.

In the early nineties, he gave us the task of teaching basic meditation classes. "Whether you achieve enlightenment in this lifetime or not," he told us, "you can still, after many years of study, reach levels of advancement that enable you to teach people and be of great help to them."

His task surprised me. For so many years I had been absorbed in working on myself, examining my ego, perfecting my meditation practice. Now he was asking me to shift gears, to consider someone else's well being.

Initially, I was concerned I might not be qualified, but as I began to teach, my heart opened, I fell in love with the process of helping people and longed to acquire the more advanced teaching skills that my teacher possessed.

He advised us to go beyond teaching a few meditation classes, to sacrifice our lives on the altar of selfless giving, to ask Spirit to act in and through us so that each moment of the day became an act of selflessness. "It is only when you become totally concerned for the welfare of others, with complete commitment and simplicity and humility and humor…it is only when you take on the task of selfless giving and do it perfectly that real evolution begins to occur."

As someone who loved mysticism, I always found the technical side of his teaching fascinating. He once gave a technical explanation for why selfless giving worked. He said that people fall into two categories: those who try to make themselves happy by fulfilling their desires and those who have figured out that happiness can only be obtained by devoting their life to making others happy.

"An individual contains everything. Each of us is an aggregate. We are composed not only of our own physical, emotional, and mental bodies, but we hold all people and all experiences as well as the universe within our awareness. When we are born into an individual life, we are trained to identify with the personal self. We are fixated on ourselves as limited personalities, and as long as we remain in the mode of trying to fulfill our personal desires, we reinforce the idea of ourselves as the personal self, and we imprint the limited self more deeply. When we engage in selfless giving, we affirm that our being is larger, that it contains the universe within it. In short, selfless giving is the pathway to freedom. It opens the doorway to the Universal Self."

25

THE FINAL RINGS

In April Alexandria traveled to South Africa. In May she emailed Jackie and me in the States, "In 1999, when I accompanied Celeste to Egypt, we realigned the Great Pyramid and opened a star gate at Giza. Now I've realized that a mountain within clear view of my house in South Africa is also a star gate and a counterpart to the one at Giza. They sit at opposite ends of the Nilotic Meridian. Somehow the star gates and the meridian are related to our project."

So that's why Alexandria went to South Africa rather than London!

Jackie and I pulled our meridian books off of our bookshelves and leafed through them, looking for clues in this new meridian/star gate puzzle. The first thing to spark our interest was the gold underlying the Nilotic Meridian.

The Anunnaki who colonized the planet had turned the meridian into the gold-producing center of the world. After their departure, their genetically engineered humans had continued to work the mines down through history. In the late nineteenth century, Cecil Rhodes, commissioned by Queen Victoria, prospected for gold and mined all up and down the meridian.

Gold is a spiritual metal. It has a profound metaphysical purpose. That massive line of gold running through the heart of Africa had been there for a reason. The metal acted as a balancer for the planet. From the mining of the gold, the energy of the meridian had been destabilized...on purpose. The global elite didn't *want* the planet in balance.

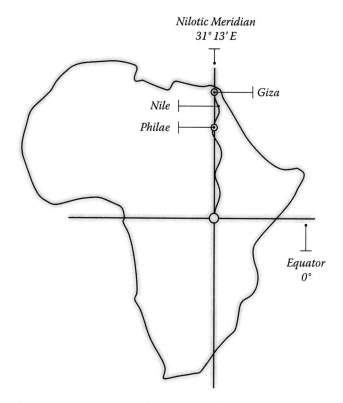

The three of us agreed that the meridian needed to be healed if the Earth was to evolve to her highest potential.

But what about the star gates? We finally stumbled across a clue. The Egyptian funerary texts describe an overarching shower of stars that run along the meridian. The ancient Egyptians believed that at death, the pharaoh's soul ascended through this star river to the sky-world.

Something clicked for Jackie. She saw that there were not just two star gates—one at Giza and one in South Africa—but a whole series of star gates overarching the meridian. In ancient times, stellar light—knowledge from the higher dimensions—had descended freely through these star gates and been caught by the meridian. The highly refined gold metal was able to stabilize and hold the vibration of the higher frequencies so it could be accessed by the Anunnaki. Together, the star gates and the meridian acted as a circuit.

We scheduled a send-in-the-probe meditation to confirm our seeings. Our seeings, we were told, were correct. Our job was to repair the damaged meridian by merging with it and holding it in our bodies. Once it was healed, we would be able to open the overarching shower of stars.

It should have been obvious to us that we were beginning the process of transmuting the energies of the two final rings of the new world. These were the only loose ends that needed to be tied up, and we had been dancing all around it for some time: the meridians in Rome and Paris, the Greenwich Mean Line, and now the synchronicity of Alexandria's travel to South Africa. But it actually took some time for the tumblers to fall into place.

Eventually we saw that the Religion ring—the topmost ring that had been destroyed, the ultimate control ring of the One World Government that capped spiritual aspiration—would be reborn as the Spirituality ring—a ring that fostered reverence for the Earth and opened humanity's way to divine oneness with all things, unity consciousness. If the Spirituality ring fostered reverence for the Earth, it must be *of* the Earth. It must be grounded *inside* of the Earth. So what more logical grounding place than the Nilotic Meridian, the meridian whose gold had once stabilized the planet?

And the Royalty ring—the bottom ring of the crowned heads of Europe bent on controlling the Earth through lower mystical means—would be transmuted into the Royalty ring of enlightened leaders—a group who would guide the Earth into the golden age by accessing information via their crown chakras. If all of the star gates were opened, enlightened knowledge from the higher dimensions would be free to rain down on the planet and utilized going forward into the new Aquarian Age.

We rolled up our sleeves to begin, feeling hopeful that the end was finally in sight. It had taken only a few moments for the Religion and the Royalty rings to disintegrate. If someone had told me it would take five months to transmute their energies, I'm not sure I could have forced my weary body forward. But how could we possibly have known that the Anunnaki, prior to leaving the Earth, had taken steps to prevent the very thing we were working for from happening?

The Final Piece of Opposition

In June we began a series of weekly synchronized meditations. Repeatedly we witnessed a searing blue-white laser light tracing the path of the meridian, performing surgery on the continent of Africa, with sparks flying in all directions. Repeatedly we held the meridian inside our own awareness fields, feeling the energetic upheaval inside our bodies...and repeatedly we spent the day recuperating in bed.

By July it didn't matter if we were sitting in formal meditation or going about our daily routines. The sensation of holding the meridian in our bodies went on continually. Each of us began reporting the same thing: "I wake up every day feeling I've been run over by a truck."

At the end of the summer, an email arrived from South Africa that held the portent of good news. "When we first arrived," Alexandria told us, "it was hard to walk directly on the meridian. It actually hurt the calves of my legs. Now walking feels great. I think we've succeeded in repairing the meridian."

Thank God! I honestly didn't know how much longer I could last. Why was it taking so long? Why was it so difficult? Something was very wrong with my body. My energy was slowly being siphoned off.

In September Jackie reported, "A couple of star gates have come back online: South Africa and one other. I don't think they're fully functional yet, but they've started to open."

Soon after, we began to catch glimpses of two star rivers. One flowed above the Nilotic Meridian, and the other ran under the planet, on the opposite side of the Earth. They were two-dimensional rivers of light. The upper, Milky Way river ran north to south. The river under the Earth ran south to north.

During the next month, we forged ahead, but my health declined seriously. I became increasingly fatigued. Some days I was too tired to sit up. Anders made jokes about wheel chairs and retirement homes, but to me it wasn't funny. Something was definitely wrong.

I could be dying!

At the end of October, I struggled out of bed, made a thermos of hot tea to fortify myself for the long drive into DC, and paid my holistic doctor a visit.

After examining my body, she scrutinized me. She looked particularly serious. "As a holistic practitioner, I always look at all the possibilities. What I'm about to say to you, I normally wouldn't say to one of my clients, but I know you've been working with patriarchal energies." She paused. "I think you've tapped into a curse."

My felt my jaw sag. I was speechless.

"The mystical hit is actually occurring on the level of your blood," she continued. "You're anemic."

After my treatment I drove home to Williamsburg and immediately emailed Alexandria and Jackie. For the rest of the day, I went through five months of journals, reviewing everything we had done in connection with the meridian and the star gates. That night, tossing and turning in my bed, I continued to work on the problem in my dreams, but I couldn't identify anything that resembled a curse. Then, the next morning, I replayed my doctor's words. I was being attacked on the level of my blood.

"Oh, my God," I said out loud. "Bloodlines! The Anunnaki!"

In order to keep the class structure in place, the Anunnaki camp that opposed human evolution made it taboo to share their sacred knowledge. Stellar knowledge was their exclusive privilege. Before they left the planet, they had shut down the star gates and had booby trapped the Nilotic Meridian. Any human who dared attempt to access the forbidden knowledge was cursed: "You may find a way to open the star gates, but without the royal Anunnaki blood, you'll never live to receive the downloads." Knowledge of the original Anunnaki curse had been jealously tucked away through the ages, handed down from generation to generation, right through to the Illuminati and the man in the South Pacific.

Jackie concurred. "We hot-wired them," she told Alexandria and me on the phone. "The ancient bloodlines are the keepers of the vibrational keys that open the star gates. They hold the vibrations in their bloodline bodies. From their point of view, we hot-wired them. In other words, we went around the Anunnaki bloodlines and reconnected the energetic openings along the Nilotic Meridian in a way that didn't require bloodline buy-in."

"Of course," Alexandria said quietly, "we are co-creators with

Mother Divine. Her blue-white light reconfigured the star gates so that the bloodline carriers were no longer the only ones who held the keys. We opened them with the energy of the heart. And as we move into a love-based world—a more godlike system—for the first time in the planet's history, humans will be able to eat freely of the forbidden tree of knowledge...whether the Anunnaki and their global elite descendents like it or not."

The Final Rings Are Born

Now we would be able to complete the work of the final two rings. Now that we knew what the blockage had been, we could overcome it. We had only to ask that the curse be nullified.

On November 7th we met on the inner planes for our final session. We were confident that this would be our last synchronized mediation. The enormous number of beings who looked on from other dimensions—more than had ever assembled in the past— seemed to confirm that this was indeed the project's finale.

It turned out to be the hardest energetic work any of us had ever done, and we each had precisely the same experience. For one solid hour, the session was sheer physical torture, and then, when the hour- hand hit twelve straight up, the energy shifted abruptly and totally.

My body had never felt so tormented. I shifted my sitting position constantly in an effort to ease the pain. I might have survived the curse, but this meditation felt as if it was definitely going to kill me.

No clear images would come. I wrestled with how to hold the meridian in my awareness field. Should I hold it vertically? Horizontally? I struggled with how to open the river of stars. Should I proceed? Wait? At one point I asked what to do and was told to simply feel the meridian, but it didn't make any difference. The session was still excruciating.

Maybe we were wrong to imagine that the two final rings would be transmuted today, I thought. *But no! During the entire project, our intuition has never been wrong.* But nothing was happening. Agonizing minutes crawled by with no end in sight.

Gradually a feeling of remorse shrouded me. Slowly the remorse deteriorated into wretchedness. I was doomed. I was hopeless. I had failed completely and utterly.

Then, after exactly one hour, my teacher appeared and insisted, *"Don't listen to your mind."*

I nodded. He was right. My warrior spirit arose. Straightening my body, resuming a half-lotus position, I squared off with the resistance I was feeling. I raised my voice across the mystical realms: *It's not over until it's over!*

I looked across what appeared to be a smoldering battlefield. My eyes scanned the terrain until they fell on someone standing in the distance.

"You're wrong!" he bellowed at me. *"The situation is hopeless. It is over!"*

I knew instantly that it was the man in the South Pacific. Heat flushed through my body. I focused my intent. My reply was quiet and very directed, a laser beam of red-hot light perfectly beaded on its target.

That is a lie. The aversion to your world has been reconciled. The attraction has been reconciled. It is your situation that is hopeless. Move out of my way!

With that, my crown chakra opened. In the next moment it felt as if the whole universe came unhinged. The heavens exploded. Both star rivers lit up to become one massively long star gate. They all opened simultaneously. Golden encoded information streamed down into the meridian. All the knowledge of the universe was flowing toward the Earth. The highest dimensional frequencies. Completely available. Constant and unremitting. Relief flooded my body as I surrendered to the downpour of light, and the downpour went on and on and on.

Now, I whispered. *Now, it is over.*

I could see the man in the South Pacific through a haze of gold. He was lying on the ground, motionless. Did I feel fear? Not the slightest trace. And yet I hesitated. Was he the man who wanted to rule the world, or was he merely my worthy opponent? Had the entire project been a personal journey of overcoming my fears, or had we staunched the flow of fear on the planet?

A tear trickled down my cheek. At that moment, it didn't matter. He was my worthy opponent, the man who had caused me to experience unprecedented spiritual growth, and there was only gratitude in my heart.

I crossed the battlefield and knelt down beside him. Tears began streaming down my face. Gathering his limp body in my arms, clutching him to my breast, I whispered, *Thank you*. I sat rocking him back and forth as the flood continued. Gold light everywhere. A mind full of gold light. The star gate and the meridian resplendent with gold light. The last two rings of the new world finally in place.

At last I bowed to end the meditation, but as my mind was the universe, it was the universe that bowed. The universe bowed to itself and all of its living creatures.

The crowd of inter-dimensional onlookers respectfully dispersed. It had the feeling of people in a theatre who had gathered repeatedly to watch successive acts of a play. Now the final curtain had fallen. Programs lay scattered on the floor. The bleachers had emptied out. A few remained behind, talking quietly in small groups.

I sat for awhile longer. It felt so good to sit there with the stellar light raining down.

It just felt so good to be done.

26

THE FINAL RECONCILIATIONS

On the morning of the winter solstice of 2004, I began my morning meditation. As a team, Jackie, Alexandria, and I had planned nothing special for the occasion. Our work was complete, and although we stayed in touch, we had gone our separate ways.

Jackie continued to do her own energetic work and offered her services as a seer. Alexandria worked on the South African AIDS project that she and Celeste had created and did energetic work to uplift that area of the planet.

It was just me, sitting alone, as I had done on the summer solstice of 2002 when I had received my spiritual assignment from the Lineage.

How much had transpired since that time! It seemed like lifetimes rather than two and a half years. I had been instructed to disassemble the Patriarchy, told that I had been trained for many incarnations to do the task. The woman who received that instruction had been hesitant, doubtful, and full of fear. Now she had reclaimed her place as a member of her Lineage, deepened her bond with the Earth, and accepted her role as a co-creator with Mother Divine. She had stood in her power as a woman, unplugged herself from the energies of the Patriarchy, and balanced her being, and all because she had asked for, accepted, and followed her dharma.

I had so much to be thankful for. Although I normally reserved the act of bowing for the end of meditation, I bowed at the beginning. Then, floating in and out of planes of light, I sat, absorbed.

Reconciling the Dark and the Light

I thought about my teacher, and he was instantly with me. I loved his presence, but I was a little weary at the same time—weary of holding him separate. I remembered my last encounter with the man in the South Pacific, the way I had cradled him in my arms. I yearned to do something like that with my teacher. I wanted to embrace him so he would become part of me.

My teacher appeared in my mind's eye. His being was pure golden light, just as it had been when he was alive. Beautiful. Pristine. The amount of gold light he radiated was equivalent to the amount of selfless giving he had performed. He had incarnated in order to find his students and complete their training. He had done it impeccably with a careful balance of power, light, and love. He had guided me, empowered me, helped me remember who I was, and he was doing it still from across the dimensions.

All at once I noticed there were two figures: my teacher on the left and the man in the South Pacific on the right. Both men stood there, resurrected.

Oddly enough, the man in the South Pacific also radiated light. He didn't appear dark or sinister. His aura was clear. His being was precise and directed—an incredible mystic, but without compassion. Whatever his role in the world, he had been my worthy opponent, the man who had pushed my back against the wall, forcing me through one spiritual transit after another. I couldn't love the man in the South Pacific, but I could respect him.

They stood there, the two most important beings in my life. I gazed at them across the dimensions—a moment suspended in time. I bowed to express my appreciation. I honored both of them.

As I watched, the two images began to move toward each other, ever so slowly. My body stiffened. A red flag was hoisted in my mind. *No. That can't be right!* I changed my sitting position, took a deep breath, and rebooted the system: my teacher on the left, the man in the South Pacific on the right.

My breathing slowed and I stabilized my mind, but just as I relaxed, they began to move toward one another again. Little by little, they were gliding through the dimensions, coming together. My breathing quickened. Heat flashed through my body. My mind clouded over. Then, from some recessed cavity in my intellect, I remembered: the man in the South Pacific was my instructor in a past life. He had been my…teacher.

Oh, no! I swallowed hard. *No!* I froze the scene of the two of them. I had to be rational. There had to be a perfectly good explanation for this.

They cannot be the same person. That's impossible. That makes no sense at all.

I felt like an animal backed into a corner. I had to think this through. *Could my teacher be the man in the South Pacific? Could my teacher have projected the image of a worthy opponent into my mind purely for the sake of speeding up my evolution?* My mind raced. *Could this be the complete reconciliation of dark and light in my own awareness field? My teacher was an incarnation of love. Pure. Luminous. The man in the South Pacific was…he was….*

I sobbed involuntarily.

Desperately I fought to relegate them firmly back into place. I willed them back. My teacher: left. Man in the South Pacific: right. *Freeze.* But as hard as I tried to hold onto them, the two figures began to move again. Slowly, ever so slowly, their beings slid toward one another.

My face contorted. I clasped my hands in my lap. Then, for some reason beyond my own will, I let go. My mind stopped struggling to understand. I raised the white flag of surrender.

It's going to happen whether I want it or not.

Gradually the two figures merged into one. As they came together, there was an explosion, an explosion of effulgent golden light. The two beings dissolved and, in one giant movement, a tidal wave of gold rose high above the scene and crashed down over me, engulfing my being, obliterating my mind.

Gold everywhere. Ecstasy flooding my being. My teacher was gone. The man in the South Pacific was gone. The woman who had unplugged the Patriarchy was gone. There was no one left, no one to witness the sea of gold.

Reconciling Anders' Karmic Debt

A few nights later, Anders and I made love, very gently and sweetly...the most perfect lovemaking we had ever shared. As my body climaxed, emotion welled up and burst forth in tears. Some hidden knowing rose from the depths of consciousness and spilled into my mind. I knew, beyond the shadow of a doubt, that he would be leaving me.

I had felt it coming, a restlessness in him, a wandering of his attention. Now I saw it clearly, and I cried and cried. I knew that everything was in order, that it was right for him to go. I knew that other experiences awaited him, that other women needed to enfold him in their arms. I knew that everything was perfect. But still, I cried.

Anders held me. He didn't ask why I was crying, and I didn't tell him.

Gradually I calmed down. I turned over, reached for a tissue on the nightstand, and dried my eyes. When I turned back to Anders, he had fallen asleep.

Amazing! Amazing how, after such upheaval, he can fall asleep. Instantly.

I lay there watching him for a long time. We had been on quite a journey together, and it was a journey I couldn't have made as easily without him. He had supported me. He had counteracted my experiences with the dark energies of the Patriarchy with his lightheartedness. How many times had he made me laugh?

I had seen at the beginning of our relationship that we had been samurai together, that he owed me a karmic debt from that lifetime. It had certainly been paid in full, and then some.

Anders always looked like a little boy when he slept...so peaceful. I studied his face, fixing his features in my memory for future reference. Then I rolled onto my back and stared up at the ceiling.

Reconciling the Inner and Outer

I could feel my teacher and the Lineage all around me. They were always there now. I supposed they always had been, had I cared to notice.

Our project is complete? I asked

"*Your project—this phase of it—is indeed complete. You have unplugged the Patriarchy. Next you must unplug the Patriarchy's female conditioning. We're approaching an Age of Women. It's imperative that women throw off their conditioning and begin to stand in their own power.*"

I sighed and closed my eyes. If there was to be another project, I would think about that later. Now, I wanted to rest.

I listened to Anders breathing, slow and even. Outside, the December wind prowled around the house, rustling hedges, making them scratch the window screens. Somewhere on the roof it caught a loose air vent. Tap. Tap. Tap-tap.

But there was another sound. I listened intently.

It sounded a little like all of the beings who had assisted our project over the past two and a half years—Mother Divine, my teacher, my Lineage, ascended masters, bodhisattvas, angels, Mother Earth, dragons, trees—were chanting "*Om.*" But not exactly. I couldn't quite identify the sound, only that the universe seemed to be singing one song. The phrase arose in my mind: *Song of the Spheres.*

In my mind's eye, my teacher stepped center stage.

"*Throughout my teaching career,*" he told me, "*I disseminated a wealth of knowledge. That body of knowledge is like a matrix, a very bright and shiny matrix. Anyone who follows my teachings can use the matrix to navigate the world and have an uncommonly fine life. But a matrix, no matter how high, is still a limitation. A matrix is still a description of the world, a way of perceiving reality. One must shatter the matrix in order to move beyond it. One must completely dismantle the personal ego and merge with Spirit again and again. In doing so, you* become *that body of knowledge.*

"*You've done well in terms of dismantling your ego. Now, if you chose, you can move beyond the matrix, beyond the Patriarchy, into the uncharted territory of the next age.*"

There was a long pause while I digested this information.

"*It's time to say goodbye,*" he told me.

I was stunned. *To you?* I asked.

"To me and to the Lineage."

My heart stopped. They had supported me for hundreds of lifetimes. I lay there, not breathing, my mind a blank.

Then he whispered, *"Not to me and the Lineage personally, but to your identification with us."*

Without warning, the matrix shattered, and golden light engulfed me. My awareness expanded out to the edge of existence. My teacher and the Lineage and all of the other beings became one small portion of my Universal Self.

Then the Song of the Spheres coalesced into words, and the universe proclaimed:

"There has never been anything outside of you. Nothing at all."

For more information:

Visit www.UnplugFromThePatriarchy.com

Connect with Lucia René on Facebook

Follow her on Twitter

ENDNOTES

1   *Wikipedia Encyclopedia*, http://en.wikipedia.org/wiki/Carnegie_ Endowment_for_International_Peace, (July 2, 2007)

2   Norman Dodd, interview with G. Edward Griffin, (1982), http:// www.realityzone.com/hiddenagenda2.html, (July 2, 2007)

3   *Wikipedia Encyclopedia*, http://en.wikipedia.org/wiki/Collectivism, (July 2, 2007)

4   G. Edward Griffin, "The Chasm: Two Ethics that Divide the Western World", http://www.scribd.com/doc/3318703/The-Chasm-Collectivism-vs-Individualism-Edward-Griffin, (June 23, 2008)

5   Norman Dodd, interview with G. Edward Griffin, (1982), http:// www.realityzone.com/hiddenagenda2.html, (July 2, 2007)

6   Norman Dodd interview with G. Edward Griffin, 1982, http://www. realityzone.com/hiddenagenda2.html, (July 2, 2007)

7   G. Edward Griffin, *The Creature from Jekyll Island*, (American Media, Westlake Village CA, 1998), 151-2

8   G. Edward Griffin, *The Creature from Jekyll Island*, 165

9   G. Edward Griffin, *The Creature from Jekyll Island*, 158

10 Patrick Chkoreff, "FDR, Thief of America's Gold", www.strike-the-root.com/columns/Chkoreff/chkoreff1.html, (July 5, 2007) and Lyndon H LaRouche, Jr., "How FDR Reversed the 1933 Banking Crisis", *Executive Intelligence Review*, http://www.larouchepub.com/other/2007/3409fdr_banks_33.html, (July 5, 2007)

11 J. Krim Bohren and James Kraft-Lorenz, "Presidential Executive Orders, Mandates For Peace Or War?", http://www.banned-books.com/truth-seeker/1994archive/121_5/ts215a.html, (July 5, 2007)

12 *Wikipedia Encyclopedia*, http://en.wikipedia.org/wiki/Bretton_ Woods_system, (July 5, 2007)

13 Ron Paul, "The End of Dollar Hegemony", (February 15, 2006) http://www.house.gov/paul/congrec/congrec2006/cr021506.htm, (July 5, 2007)

14 Ron Paul, "The End of Dollar Hegemony", (February 15, 2006) http://www.house.gov/paul/congrec/congrec2006/cr021506.htm, (July 5, 2007)

15 Ron Paul, "The End of Dollar Hegemony", (February 15, 2006), http://www.house.gov/paul/congrec/congrec2006/cr021506.htm, (July 5, 2007)

16   Douglas V. Gnazzo, "The Federal Reserve: Fractional Reserve
        Lending", (November 29, 2005) http://www.safehaven.com/article-
        4182.htm, (July 5, 2007)

17   Douglas V. Gnazzo, "The Federal Reserve: Fractional Reserve
        Lending", (November 29, 2005) http://www.safehaven.com/article-
        4182.htm, (July 5, 2007)

18   Dr. Carroll Quigley, *Tragedy and Hope: A History of the World in
        Our Time*, (MacMillan Company, New York, 1966), 52

19   James Perloff, *The Shadows of Power, The Council on Foreign
        Relations And The American Decline*, (Western Islands Publishers,
        Appleton, WI, 2000), 19

20   James Perloff, *The Shadows of Power, The Council on Foreign
        Relations And The American Decline*, 19

21   G. Edward Griffin, *The Creature from Jekyll Island*, 217-233

22   Meyer Nathaniel Rothschild, speech to gathering of world bankers,
        (February 12, 1912), http://www.prisonplanet.com/articles/
        september2007/250907NWOquotes.htm, (July 5, 2007)

23   Gary Allen and Larry Abraham, *None Dare Call It a Conspiracy*,
        (Buccaneer Books, Cutchogue, NY, 1976), 46

24   G. Edward Griffin, *The Creature from Jekyll Island*, 217-8 and Dr.
        Carroll Quigley, *Tragedy and Hope: A History of the World in Our
        Time*, 324-7

25   http://news.bbc.co.uk/1/hi/magazine/3773019.stm, (February 15,
        2007)

26   *Wikipedia Encyclopedia*, http://en.wikipedia.org/wiki/Bilderberg_
        Group, (February 15, 2007)

27   *Wikipedia Encyclopedia*, http://www.bilderberg.org/bernhard.htm,
        (February 15, 2007)

28   *Wikipedia Encyclopedia*, http://en.wikipedia.org/wiki/Bilderberg_
        Group, (February 15, 2007)

29   *Wikipedia Encyclopedia*, http://en.wikipedia.org/wiki/Bilderberg_
        Group, (February 15, 2007)

30   http://www.bilderberg.org, (February 15, 2007)

31   *Wikipedia Encyclopedia*, http://en.wikipedia.org/wiki/Bilderberg_
        Group, (February 15, 2007)

32   BBC, http://news.bbc.co.uk/1/hi/magazine/3773019.stm, (February
        15, 2007)

33 C. Gordon Tether, "Censored Financial Times", Lombard Column, written May 3, 1976, published in *Verdict*, November 1976

34 Abraham Lincoln, "The Gettysburg Address", http://showcase. netins.net/web/creative/lincoln/speeches/gettysburg.htm, (July 9, 2007)

35 http://www.allshookdown.com/newhistory/CH01.htm, (July 8, 2007)

36 *Wikipedia Encyclopedia*, http://en.wikipedia.org/wiki/Corporation (July 8, 2007)

37 Noam Chomsky, http://zena.secureforum.com/Znet/zmag/articles/ chomskyjune98.htm, (July 8, 2007)

38 Noreena Hertz, *The Silent Takeover, Global Capitalism and the Death of Democracy*, (The Free Press, a Division of Simon & Schuster, Inc., New York, NY, 2001), 7

39 Janet Lowe, *The Secret Empire, How 25 Multinationals Rule the World*, (Business One Irwin, Homewood, IL, 1992), 25

40 Noreena Hertz, *The Silent Takeover, Global Capitalism and the Death of Democracy*, 7

41 Noreena Hertz, *The Silent Takeover, Global Capitalism and the Death of Democracy*, 7-8

42 *Wikipedia Encyclopedia*, http://en.wikipedia.org/wiki/ Multinational_corporation, (July 23, 2007)

43 Robert W. McChesney, *Profit Over People*, Introduction, 11

44 Lori Wallach and Michelle Sforza, *Whose Trade Organization? Corporate Globalization and the Erosion of Democracy*, (Public Citizen, Washington, D.C., 1999), 7

45 http://www.wto.org/english/thewto_e/whatis_e/tif_e/fact1_e.htm, (August 17, 2007)

46 Ralph Nadar, *Whose Trade Organization? Corporate Globalization and the Erosion of Democracy*, Preface, ix-xii

47 Jim Marrs, *Rule by Secrecy*, (Perennial, An Imprint of HarperCollins Publishers, New York, NY, 2001), 33

48 Jim Marrs, *Rule by Secrecy*, 32

49 Miguel A. Faria Jr., M.D., "Cuba and the Council on Foreign Relations", http://www.newsmax.com/archives/ articles/2001/2/15/224945.shtml, (July 9, 2007)

50 Jim Marrs, *Rule by Secrecy*, 35

51   Jim Marrs, *Rule by Secrecy*, 35

52   Jim Marrs, *Rule by Secrecy*, 24

53   Jim Marrs, *Rule by Secrecy*, 28

54   *Wikipedia Encyclopedia*, http://en.wikipedia.org/wiki/Zbigniew_
      Brzezinski

55   Zbigniew Brzezinski, *Between Two Ages: America's Role in the
      Technotronic Era*, (The Viking Press, New York, 1970)

56   Robert O'Harrow, Jr., *No Place to Hide*, (Free Press, a division of
      Simon & Schuster, Inc., New York, NY, 2005), 103

57   David R. Hawkins, M.D., Ph.D., *Power Vs. Force, The Hidden
      Determinants of Human Behavior*, (Hay House, Inc., Carlsbad, CA,
      2002)

58   World Bank, http://web.worldbank.org/, (October 5, 2002)

59   50 Years Is Enough Network, http://www.50years.org/, (October 1,
      2002)

60   Corpwatch, http://www.corpwatch.org/, (October 1, 2002)

61   Gary Allen and Larry Abraham, *None Dare Call It a Conspiracy*,
      48-9

62   Jeff Rense, "The Grand Deception, A Second Look at the War
      on Terror", http://www.smilenow.de/from_www/jeff_rense/
      jr2002_101112/jr021111.txt, (July 14, 2007)

63   Eustace Mullins, http://publiccentralbank.com/, (July 14, 2007)

64   Leslie Temple Thurston with Brad Laughlin, *The Marriage of Spirit,
      Enlightened Living in Today's World*, (Corelight Publishing, Santa Fe,
      NM, 2000) and http://www.corelight.org

65   http://www.gangaji.org

66   http://www.pamelasatsang.org

67   http://www.financial-inspiration.com/JP-Morgan-biography.html,
      (July 20, 2007)

68   http://www.biography.com/search/article.do?id=9414735, (July 20,
      2007)

69   G. Edward Griffin, *The Creature from Jekyll Island*, 449

70   G. Edward Griffin, *The Creature from Jekyll Island*, 11

71   http://www.themoneymasters.com/how.htm, March 6, 2007:

      "If the American people ever allow private banks to control the issue
      of their currency, first by inflation, then by deflation, the banks...

will deprive the people of all property until their children wake-up homeless on the continent their fathers conquered.... The issuing power should be taken from the banks and restored to the people, to whom it properly belongs." Thomas Jefferson

"I sincerely believe...that banking establishments are more dangerous than standing armies, and that the principle of spending money to be paid by posterity under the name of funding is but swindling futurity on a large scale." Thomas Jefferson

"History records that the money changers have used every form of abuse, intrigue, deceit, and violent means possible to maintain their control over governments by controlling money and its issuance." James Madison

"If congress has the right under the Constitution to issue paper money, it was given them to use themselves, not to be delegated to individuals or corporations." Andrew Jackson

"The Government should create, issue, and circulate all the currency and credits needed to satisfy the spending power of the Government and the buying power of consumers. By the adoption of these principles, the taxpayers will be saved immense sums of interest. Money will cease to be master and become the servant of humanity." Abraham Lincoln

72 Woodrow Wilson, *The New Freedom: A Call for the Emancipation of the Generous Energies of a People*, (Doubleday, Page & Company, New York and Garden City, 1913)

"A great industrial nation is controlled by its system of credit. Our system of credit is privately concentrated. The growth of the nation, therefore, and all our activities are in the hands of a few men....[W]e have come to be one of the worst ruled, one of the most completely controlled and dominated governments in the civilized world—no longer a government by free opinion, no longer a government by conviction and the vote of the majority, but a government by the opinion and the duress of small groups of dominant men."

73 G. Edward Griffin, *The Creature from Jekyll Island*, 5

74 G. Edward Griffin, *The Creature from Jekyll Island*, 6

75 G. Edward Griffin, *The Creature from Jekyll Island*, 6

76 G. Edward Griffin, *The Creature from Jekyll Island*, 11-16

77 Mark Walter Evans, Public Central Bank, "On Reclaiming Our Central Bank and Monetary Policy", http://publiccentralbank. com/, (July 14, 2007)

78 Public Central Bank, http://publiccentralbank.com/, (July 14, 2007)

79   Ron Paul, "The End of Dollar Hegemony", (February 15, 2006) http://www.house.gov/paul/congrec/congrec2006/cr021506.htm, (March 12, 2007)

80   http://www.themoneymasters.com/how.htm, (March 12, 2007)

81   Dr. Carroll Quigley, *Tragedy and Hope: A History of the World in Our Time*, 324

82   Dr. Carroll Quigley, *Tragedy and Hope: A History of the World in Our Time*, 326-7

83   Noam Chomsky, *Profit Over People*, (Seven Stories Press, New York, NY, 1999), 44

84   Garth S. Jowett and Victoria O'Donnell, *Propaganda And Persuasion*, (Sage Publications, Inc., Thousand Oaks, CA, 1999), 1

85   *Wikipedia Encyclopedia*, http://en.wikipedia.org/wiki/Propaganda

86   Noam Chomsky, http://www.quotes2u.com/histdocs/propaganda. htm, (July 27, 2007)

87   Noam Chomsky, http://www.quotes2u.com/histdocs/propaganda. htm, (July 27, 2007)

88   Noam Chomsky, *Profit Over People*, 53

89   Noam Chomsky, http://www.quotes2u.com/histdocs/propaganda. htm, (July 27, 2007)

90   http://www.geninv.net/women-s-health/entrepreneur-strives-to-change-perceptions-about-smoking-3.html (May 20, 2008)

91   Noam Chomsky, http://www.zmag.org/chomsky/interviews/9201-propaganda.html, July 27, 2007

92   Noam Chomsky, "Propaganda & Control of the Public Mind", Cambridge, MA, (February 7, 1997)

93   Project for a New American Century, http://www.newamericancentury.org/

94   *Wikipedia Encyclopedia*, http://en.wikipedia.org/wiki/Propaganda, (July 30, 2007)

95   http://www.globalresearch.ca/articles/CHO409D.html, (July 30, 2007)

96   http://www.masternewmedia.org/information-access/propaganda/the-war-on-terror-and-victory-of-spin-20070414.htm, (July 30, 2007)

97   *Wikipedia Encyclopedia*, http://en.wikipedia.org/wiki/Propaganda, (July 30, 2007)

98   Noam Chomsky, http://www.zmag.org/chomsky/talks/9103-media-
        control.html, (July 27, 2007)

99   Noam Chomsky, "Propaganda & Control of the Public Mind",
        Cambridge, MA, (February 7, 1997)

100   *Wikipedia Encyclopedia*, http://en.wikipedia.org/wiki/A.J._Liebling,
        (July 28, 2007)

101   Jim Marrs, *Rule by Secrecy*, 235-236

102   Jim Marrs, *Rule by Secrecy*, 239

103   Jim Marrs, *Rule by Secrecy*, 239

104   Woodrow Wilson, *The New Freedom*, 1913

105   John F. Hylan, 1922

106   Edward Bernays, *Propaganda*, 1928

107   Franklin D. Roosevelt, letter written to Colonel E. Mandell House,
        Nov. 21, 1933

108   Joseph Kennedy, *New York Times*, July 26, 1936

109   James Paul Warburg, testimony before the United States Senate
        Foreign Relations Committee, February 17, 1950

110   John Swinton, speaking before the New York Press Club, 1953

111   Edith Kermit Roosevelt, "News, Elite Clique Holds Power in US",
        December, 1961

112   Nelson Rockefeller, speaking at Harvard University, 1962

113   General Douglas MacArthur, speaking before the Texas Legislature
        in Austin, Texas, June, 1951

114   Dr. Carroll Quigley, *Tragedy and Hope: A History of the World in
        Our Time*

115   Curtis Dall, *FDR: My Exploited Father-in-Law*, (Legion for the
        Survival of Freedom, Torrance, CA, 1983)

116   Baron Edmund de Rothschild, 1970

117   John Rarick, 1971

118   Richard M. Nixon, Meeting between President Nixon and Premier
        Chou En-lai, February 23, 1972, US Department of State, Foreign
        Relations, 1969-1976, Volume I, Foundations of Foreign Policy

119   Richard N. Gardner, *Foreign Affairs*, 'The Hard Road to World
        Order.' April, 1974, 558

120   Larry P. McDonald, 1976

121   Mikhail Gorbachev, *Washington Post*, February 25, 1990

122   George Bush, 1991

123   Dr. Henry Kissinger, Bilderberger Conference, Evians, France, 1991

124   David Rockefeller, address to The Trilateral Commission, June, 1991

125   David Rockefeller, United Nations Ambassadors' dinner, Sept. 23, 1994

126   Government of Morocco, *New York Times*, April 15, 1994

127   Walter Cronkite, *A Reporter's Life*, 1996

128   Bill Clinton, *New York Times*, November 25, 1997

129   Project for a New American Century, http://www. newamericancentury.org/

130   Gary Hart, speaking before a televised meeting organized by the CFR in Washington, D.C., Sept 14, 2001

131   David Rockefeller, *Memoirs*, (Random House, New York, NY, 2000), 405

132   Joan Veon, *Prince Charles, the Sustainable Prince*, (Hearthstone Publishing, Ltd, Oklahoma City, OK, 1998)

133   *Wikipedia Encyclopedia*, http://en.wikipedia.org/wiki/British_ Empire, (August 2, 2007)

134   Jim Marrs, *Rule by Secrecy*, 86

135   Jim Marrs, *Rule by Secrecy*, 87

136   Jim Marrs, *Rule by Secrecy*, 85-89

137   Jim Marrs, *Rule by Secrecy*, 88

138   Carlos Castaneda, *Journey to Ixtlan, the Lessons of Don Juan*, (Washington Square Press, published by Pocket Books, a division of Simon & Schuster Inc., New York, 1972)

139   Carlos Castaneda, *Journey to Ixtlan, the Lessons of Don Juan*, 59

140   Dennis Birch, http://www.publiccentralbank.com/, (August 25, 2007)

141   Gordon Michael Scallion, http://www.crawford2000.co.uk/begin. htm, (August 25, 2009)

142   Zecharia Sitchin, The Earth Chronicles, Books I through VI, (Avon Books, an Imprint of HarperCollinsPublishers, New York, 1976)

Notes

Notes

CPSIA information can be obtained at www.ICGtesting.com
Printed in the USA
LVOW091629140212

268677LV00009B/154/P